The Psychology of Religious Belief

The Psychology of Religious Belief

L. B. Brown

Department of Psychology
University of New South Wales
New South Wales 2033
Australia

1987

Academic Press
Harcourt Brace Jovanovich, Publishers
London · Orlando · San Diego · New York · Austin
Boston · Sydney · Tokyo · Toronto

ACADEMIC PRESS INC. (LONDON) LTD
24/28 Oval Road, London NW1 7DX

United States Edition Published by
ACADEMIC PRESS INC.
Orlando, Florida 32887

British Library Cataloguing in Publication Data

Brown, L. B.
   The psychology of religious belief
   1. Psychology, Religious
   I. Title
   200'.1'9   BL53

   ISBN 0–12–136355–4
   ISBN 0–12–136356–2 (Pbk)

Typeset by Colset Pte Limited, Singapore
and printed in Great Britain by
T. J. Press (Padstow) Ltd, Padstow, Cornwall

Preface

This book is concerned with empirical studies of religious belief, and the contexts within which they are to be understood. The first part examines what "religion" connotes, the theories or explanations that have been tested, and the methods that are used to make those tests. It begins with a brief look at the history of psychological studies of religion and at the distinction between a religious psychology and a psychology of religion.

The directions and biases in modern work on the psychology of religion are then examined in relation to the way religions become integrated into the lives of individuals, and expressed. Belief and practice are not equivalent religious variables. The tension between theory and research is emphasized throughout, and resolved by showing the extent to which one informs the other and the extent to which they come together in the measurement of religion, which uses all the procedures to which social and personality psychologists have access. The second part of the book examines the conclusions that can be drawn about the nature and the effects of the institutional and psychological structures of religion, as they are identified through adherence to a doctrinal system, by following prescribed practices and in the less obvious experiences and religious feelings. Concepts of God and other religious beliefs, and their relationships with personality-based processes show that while religion is a uni-dimensional phenomenon at one level, it also appears to be multi-dimensional. Which solution emerges depends on the characteristics of the groups that are studied and the variables assessed. A multi-axial or perignostic view is proposed which acknowledges that separate doctrinal, ritual and experiential components of religions interact, for which separate social scientific perspectives have been developed to describe and account for them. To understand religion as a form of code readily allows contrasts between belief and disbelief, but questions the usefulness of the concept of a special readiness for religion, despite the recognition that it is possible to be religiously immature.

Religious beliefs have been variously seen as self-generated, involving training and conformity to religious "texts", or as an implicit response to an "idea of the holy" (Otto, 1926) or the "sense of God". As Bowker (1973) suggests, general analyses of our sense of God have been so influenced by psychological as well as by theological arguments that we now live in a "psychological society" which has produced an "internal shift in man's psyche" (Gross, 1978, p. 3) and a preoccupation with the self that makes psychology "an art, science, therapy, religion, moral code, life style, philosophy and cult" (ibid.). Gross also asserts that psychology has moved swiftly to fill the power vacuums in such declining professions as the ministry where Freud's "atheistic ideas" have been used "to bulwark the dwindling belief in an anthropomorphic God. Ministers, priests and rabbis now flock to courses in pastoral counselling, making many members of the cloth seem more Freudian than Christian" (p. 11).

While the strength of psychology and its dependence on Freud's ideas can be overstated, its influence is hard to deny, although the work of a few people, including André Godin, Gordon Allport, James E. Dittes, Richard Gorsuch, Newton Malony and Bernard Spilka, is relied on very heavily. Some, like Vitz in his *Psychology as Religion* (1977) have found its destructive role a form of secular humanism, since "the hostility of most psychologists to Christianity is very real" (p. 12). Vitz attacks their "prevailing beliefs" that personality tests can measure religion, that those holding traditional religious views are fascist-authoritarian types and that social psychologists are interested in religion for its "exotic belief systems" (p. 11).

Yet Ragan *et al.* (1980), who drew a two per cent random sample of the American Psychological Association's membership in 1975 to ask them about their personal religion, type of work, and scholarly values and attitudes, found that "Psychologists in areas which study religion were no more, nor less religious than those in areas which do not study religion", while those "who considered religious phenomena in the course of their professional activity were more likely to be religious than those who did not. ... [Nevertheless] The overall level of religiosity among psychologists was much lower than that of the general population and academics in general, which confirmed previous findings." They noted that the "truce" between religion and natural science has not extended to the relationship between religion and social science, and argued for a "scholarly distance hypothesis" in which "those who were the least likely to study religion (e.g. natural scientists) were more religious than those most likely to study religion (e.g. social scientists)".

It is clear that psychology itself and the contexts within which religions operate are different now from what they were when the early psychologists assumed that religion entailed specific psychological responses and that there might even be a religious "instinct". We now recognize that religions themselves have a central place in defining and limiting "religious responses", and usually accept that psychological perspectives can be applied to study religious beliefs and attitudes, experience, action, group processes and the consequences of a religious position.

The inherent uncertainty about religious action and meaning involves more than the problems Dittes (1969) identified when he asked if religion is "explicit and differentiated" or "subjective and diffused", and how it is linked with psychological development, personality processes, and social attitudes. Other problems can be found in the oscillation between social or cultural and internal or personality-based explanations since, to modify the Prayer Book's catechism, religious behaviour involves an "outward and visible sign of an inward and spiritual" process.

A critic remarked of one of Charles Williams's novels that from it "one doesn't get much religion, but one gets an enormous, instant idea of God". While psychologists have tried to clarify the nature of religion, very few expect it to reflect on God as well. That is another of its ambiguities, and Homans (1968), in *The Ambiguity of Religion*, wrote of an uncertainty about whether man is basically secular or religious. There is a similar ambiguity about the positive or negative effects of any religion on its adherents, about the concreteness or intangibility of religious claims or meanings and the appropriateness of religious over scientific or even existential analyses. Commenting on the ambiguity of religious signs, Godin (1964) noted the special problems involved in discerning a valid religious experience, and he contrasted deceptive signs, or "emotions called religious but which are entirely human ... [and] ... set up by a religious pretext or atmosphere" (p. 73), against superficial signs, and against the parallel signs in which religious experiences "coexist with other experiences". For Godin, an important role for any psychological analysis of religion is, therefore, "to purify our religious images". Because of that we should not hope for simple solutions when looking for assumed needs or motives that underpin the mature forms of religion (if they can be confidently identified).

An effective psychology of religion must recognize the variety of religious forms, and the variety of orientations that can fit religion into the lives of those who carry it. Like any other focus of belief and action, religion bores some, rescues others from boredom, and governs the lives of a few. These responses are not evenly distributed, and the claims to their truth or falsity themselves become data for further psychological analyses which can rely on psychoanalysis (cf. Homans, 1967, 1970), phenomenology (Royce, 1964; Strunk, 1970), behaviorism (Skinner, 1953), social psychology (Argyle and Beit-Hallahmi, 1975), personality theory (Allport, 1950), and biology (Hardy, 1978; Reynolds and Tanner, 1983). We can also find eclectic models, like that of Pruyser (1968) who observed that "psychoanalysis said more forcefully what James had said earlier, namely that people use their God" (p. 117), practical models for pastoral psychology (Boisen, 1936) and the psychological measurement paradigm which Gorsuch (1984) argues is the one approach now most widely agreed. The approach that I have adopted is empirically based, and while it is eclectic it is within a social psychological perspective, with some points that keep recurring in different contexts.

The focus here is on religious belief as the primary component of religion and *Religious Behaviour* (cf. Argyle, 1958). Despite an apparent decrease in religious attendance, religious beliefs are still widely accepted, and my primary aim is to show how scientific or empirical approaches have been used to understand that apparently pervasive aspect of behaviour, which has been taken to satisfy psychological and social needs, especially by those who argue that we have made God in our own image or that the masks of God ensure the stability of individuals and of society. Only recently have assertions or beliefs like this been tested empirically (e.g. Vergote and Tamayo, 1980) rather than being asserted in principle. While doubters and disbelievers as well as reformers have disputed the claims of religion and of religious traditions, others have interpreted or translated their meaning to guarantee their continued relevance; and some have explained them away as projections, compensations, or forms of social control. These interpretations have not yet destroyed our religions.

It is now usual for psychologists not to be explicitly evaluative as they explore the effects or consequences of religion, the patterns of religious belief and knowledge, the nature of religious experience, and the place of social membership and group identities in developing and maintaining a religious perspective. Homans (1970) found moral commentaries that are designed to destroy religion (or, we must add, to support it) more common in the sociology than in the psychology of religion. While there may still be a close connection between the concerns of religion and some approaches to psychology, there is not the functional equivalence that Beit-Hallahmi (1977) noted among those who would replace religion with psychology, religify their psychology, or psychologize their religion.

This book has been a long time in the making. It reflects the guidance of many people, not all of whom are either conventionally, or even intrinsically religious. A large number of people have helped by acting as the subjects in many experiments and enquiries. Others (particularly the late Dr Robert Thouless) have conversed or argued about the psychological and other grounds on which religious responses are set. Although it is impossible to mention by name every one who has helped, I will dedicate the book to those who would rather it had not been written.

Sydney   L. B. Brown

Contents

1   Introduction

William James published his Gifford Lectures on the *Varieties of Religious Experience* in 1902. These lectures are still in print and an important starting point for any scientific study of religious phenomena. Their continued appeal may, however, depend more on James's philosophy and prestige than on any systematic work he stimulated; furthermore, his belief that one could not be expected to be original "in a field like this" (p. 510) probably still holds. Dittes's (1976) assessment of James's contribution contrasts his pragmatism and pluralism against the preoccupation with empiricism and objectivity that typifies any modern psychology of religion. Yet James was not immune to data. He drew on Starbuck's (1897) questionnaire study of conversion, and on a wide range of autobiographical material, which has always been an important source of information about the meaning that people find in their religion.

Religious experience, especially in conversion, was a key issue for early psychologists, many of whom had grown up in the Protestant traditions where it was emphasized (cf. Hall, 1904–1905; Leuba, 1896, 1902). Those who did not have that interest turned towards other phenomena, but especially to prayer which many still believe is the crux of religion. Francis Galton (1883) used the statistical methods he developed to test the efficacy of petitionary prayer, and found that although royalty was often prayed for, their longevity was less than that of groups who were not mentioned in religious ceremonies. In a later study of *Hereditary Genius*, Galton (1887) extended his observations to the clergy as a prayerful group that makes petitions for protection against perils and dangers and for recovery from sickness and found they did not survive longer than either lawyers or doctors. Although Galton then concluded that petitionary prayer appeared futile, he recognized that it also has a subjective or confirmatory value.

Deeply religious people usually dispute the validity of such specific tests of the efficacy of prayer, on the ground that it involves communication with God and is not a device to test either God's support or existence: furthermore, the apparent failure of petitionary prayer can itself be interpreted as a

1

positive sign from God (Thouless and Brown, 1964). It has been hard to bring these beliefs under psychological study because of a reticence to expose what is deeply held, because of the fear that they may be misunderstood or would disappear into some psychological reductionism (but cf. Godin, 1967). Those with faith seldom question their prayers, although those who are not religious believe that prayer is a form of arrogant egocentricity (Brown, 1968). Those who do pray are aware that not every one agrees with their "faith", which they support by reference to a body of doctrine or by having received or developed this "gift". (The Collect for the Tenth Sunday after Trinity asks that we may "ask such things as shall please thee").

The moral education of children (Coe, 1900; Hall, 1904, 1917), religious psychopathology (Freud, 1928a, b, 1939), and the development of religious institutions and beliefs, as in Wundt's (1916) "folk psychology" were among other concerns of early psychologists. Wundt's perspective has had its continuing influence through the sociology of religion, which is still dominated by Durkheim's functionalism that emphasizes the social meanings of religion for individuals (cf. Deutscher, 1984), and by the structural views of Weber (1903) for whom religion guaranteed the stability of society.

Religious psychology

The dominance of Watson's (1925) Behaviorism precluded introspective data and drew the attention of psychology away from subjective processes to what was explicitly observable, as in Allport's (1934) work on the ways religious and other behaviour conforms to social rules. Homans (1970), however, argued that a psychology of religion was kept alive in the 1930s by the growth then of the pastoral psychology movement in the work of Anton Boisen (1936) and of Seward Hiltner (1943). As a result, religious psychology and pastoral counselling are still taught in many theological colleges to develop the clinical skills of those who will work for the Church and to interpret and clarify Christian perspectives with psychological insights, even if they are not always supported by actual data. Recent forms of this perspective can be found in the papers in Sadler's (1970) book, *Personality and Religion: The Role of Religion in Personality Development*, and in Fleck and Carter's (1981) "integrative" readings on *Psychology and Christianity* (which are mostly from the *Journal of Psychology and Theology*). Fleck and Carter stress that this *religious psychology* "is in its infancy" (p. 24) and that religious assumptions predominate in it (Oates, 1973; Pruyser, 1968). One also finds theological and philosophical analyses of broad psychological questions, including the validity and meaning of faith and belief, and the nature of sin (Wiles, 1976).

Religion is also approached in our own time from the detached, scientific (or social scientific) stance that displaced theology as queen of the science. Boring (1929, p. 340), however, observed that "At any one time a science is simply what its researches yield, and ... researches can be nothing more than those problems for which effective methods have been found". To illustrate this he contrasted "intelligence" as a scientific term against "will", which was a major issue for William James in his *Principles of Psychology* (1890). Although "will" did not have an operational definition James believed that petitionary prayer had therapeutic effects in illness because it activated the will to recover, while it could have no effect on the weather since human will would not have any direct effects on the natural world or on divine providence. Another view was that the apparent effectiveness of prayer depended on suggestion or auto-suggestion, which were fashionable concepts at that time (Thouless, 1924, p. 17 f.). While that may be a reasonable theory, empirical techniques should test the conjectures, hypotheses, or interpretations that form this or any scientific approach to religion. The effects of suggestion in religion were accepted but inadequately assessed, perhaps because it is hard to maintain a neutral attitude when the data, and conclusions from them, touch fundamental values.

Psychology and religion still converge whenever their phenomena correspond, as for example when Maslow (1956) argued that sin is the lesser of two evils, the other being guilt, or when the validity of glossolalia is questioned by non-religious people as a form of automatic behaviour, depersonalization, or is described in linguistic (Samarin, 1972) or social terms (Malony and Lovekin, 1985). We therefore have religious phenomena and their interpretations on one hand, and social scientific or empirical approaches to these phenomena on the other, which include anthropology and sociology as well as psychology. The methods and the epistemology of science can either confront or be assimilated into the religious domain, which has been seen as dominated by endogenous or exogenous factors and as homogeneous and coherent or heterogeneous.

Interpreting Religious phenomena

To understand religion in social or psychological terms during the nineteenth century involved a search for the facts of primitive life, adopting an evolutionary perspective and a developing awareness of cultural differences, that were contrasted against their own industrial, economic and political situation. Evans-Pritchard (1965), who identified the influence of the thought of Hobbes, Locke and Rousseau, Spencer, Durkheim and Bergson, Darwin, Marx and Engels, Freud, Frazer and "perhaps" Comte in that process, distinguished sociological from psychological theories, which he subdivided into "intellectualist and emotionalist". We might now say that these theories emphasize either the content or the processes that underlie religion. While missionaries in the newly established colonies were converting the natives to Christianity, and the search for the origins of religion was pursued there, at home the origins of religion were looked for in the religions of childhood and among the emotionally disturbed. After Tylor (1873) had identified religious thinking as a form of animism, Freud (1928a) saw it as a projection of infantile wishes, while Malinowski (1925) placed it between magic and science. Such characterizations of religion appear too ideologically consistent to us now. Although they were hard to test independently these theories allowed plausible interpretations of religious phenomena in secular rather than theological terms. The wider range of psychological and other theories that is now being applied are still bound into interpretations that make reference to some religious content.

The effort to find independent or specific explanations of religion in psychological terms that continued into the 1930s was linked with a search for the techniques and methods, as well as theories, that could expose the various aspects of religion. This search allowed Dittes to assert that not only were many procedures applied to religion as soon as they were developed, but "their development was, in fact, prompted in no small part by the search for ways to study religion" (1969, p. 602). He specifically identified questionnaires (Starbuck, 1897), attitude scaling methods (Thurstone and Chave, 1929), case study procedures (James, 1902), and factor analysis (Thurstone, 1934). To those methods, which are still being used, we can add the semantic differential (Osgood, 1952), multidimensional scaling procedures and multivariate data analyses. Attempts to explain religion as a psychological process, in terms of oedipal theories (Freud, 1933) or religious sentiments (and instincts), including gratitude, adoration, forgiveness and "a desire for union", have been replaced by accepting analogies to religious responding in delayed gratification (Fairchild, 1971), frustration (Reiff, 1966), trust (Erikson, 1958), cognitive development (Elkind, 1970) and altruism (Batson and Ventis, 1982). In a similar way confession (Hoffman, 1971, pp. 228–229), sin (Maslow, 1958), prayer (Capps, 1974), conversion (Hall, 1904) and the symbols of the Mass (Jung, 1958) are religious phenomena that have been readily interpreted psychologically. Locus of control (Rotter, 1966), the just world hypothesis (Lerner, 1980) and attribution theory (Spilka *et al.*, 1985a) are secular processes that have recently been used to understand religious phenomena (Deconchy, 1985). The specific indices of religion still, however, involve membership and a religious identity, practice, attitudes, beliefs and religious experiences (cf. Argyle and Beit-Hallahmi, 1975, Ch. 2), or religious belief, practice, experience and their effects (Glock, 1959).

Sociologists of religion have looked for traditional, and for non-doctrinal or universal forms of religion through "civil religion" and in "ultimate" or other systems of meaning that can solve problems of human existence (Yinger, 1977, p. 33), while "secularization" and "orthodoxy", with their specific religious meanings, are now commonly used as general interpretations of social processes.

Research strategies

Beyond the various theories and increasingly sophisticated techniques of data collection that characterize the early steps to a scientific study of religion, analyses of religious beliefs relied on a research strategy that looked at correlations between religion (however it was measured) and age, sex, family background, group membership, or personality traits like suggestibility and aggression. The implicit preoccupation behind this strategy was to explain religion as a dependent variable that was caused by, or at least associated with stable psychological factors so that to accept religious influences and their doctrinal, ideological or ritual content assumed a psychologically prepared ground in which religion took root. This approach neglected the effects of religion itself on that grounding. Religion has more recently been taken to be an independent variable with direct effects on actual behaviour, moral judgement, religious knowledge, prejudice, and coping styles that then influence individual and social integration (Argyle and Beit-Hallahmi, 1975, pp. 201–206).

Baston (1977) stressed that experimental control, "extremely useful (for testing theories) in other areas of psychology, has been used only rarely in the psychology of religion ... because of ethical and practical restrictions". He said in 1977 that he had found only two truly experimental studies (Pahnke, 1966 and Dittes, 1961). With the debate that ensued there has been an increasing realization that experimental designs *can* be used, especially to study the effects of religion on, for example, altruism (Daniel, 1978; Baston and Ventis, 1982), the effect of anonymity (Ungar, 1980) or peer pressure on stated religious attitudes (Carey, 1971), and the effect of clerical dress on conformity with instructions (Long and Long, 1976; Augustin *et al.*, 1979) and as a direct source of bias (Francis, 1979). Deconchy (1985) has summarized this material, identifying quasi-experiments and studies which have two independent variables, one of which is measured and the other manipulated (p. 98). He concluded that despite the protection and the privileges religion is given (Yeatts and Asher, 1979) the lack of a clear theory or paradigm has been a more important reason for the prejudice against experimental studies of religion than any ethical considerations, while the greater implicit plausibility of descriptive over correlational methods of enquiry may depend on the inadequate understanding among theologians and their students of findings that are based on experimental procedures, because, he argues, they have been immunized against evidence that is formally irreconcilable with religious beliefs and with their implicit knowledge (Deconchy, 1981). Clark (1958, p. 39) had earlier observed that "Prejudices and attitudes about religion being what they are, the religious psychologist needs to be either a great diplomat or a courageous investigator if he is to risk the criticism that may fall to his lot if, in cold blood, he uses religious stimuli for experimental purposes".

Systematic correlational and experimental studies both imply a detailed, observer-based (or emic) approach, behind which there are subjective or personal perspectives on religion that can be expressed in terms of a personal commitment to Christ or that are referred to social influences, as when a person says, "my family was religious". While those explanations or attributions (Proudfoot and Shaver, 1975) are built on inferences and on *some* factual information, there is always a tension between the demand for objectivity and an immediate conviction that comes from experience or through the beliefs that can support the "truth". This contrast produces the outside and inside perspectives on religion that Dittes (1969) has identified, each depending on its own kinds and sources of detached or involved knowledge and understanding. Because of that, as Dittes has put it, religion has been seen as "explicit and differentiated" or as "subjective and diffused", a distinction that was drawn by "the Old Testament prophets who distinguished between solemn assemblies and righteousness (Amos 5, 21–24), between sacrifices and steadfast love, between burnt offerings and knowledge of God (Hosea, 6, 6)" (ibid., p. 618).

Religious dimensions

Religion involves other dimensions of response which have been conceptually rather than empirically distinguished. Capps *et al.* (1976a) recognized myth (which they extend to include knowledge and belief), ritual or behaviour, and experience, as well as dispositions, social or institutional processes, and the directional or consequential effects of religion (although I have simplified their actual terms). While that analysis slights different styles of response and orientations to the available forms of religious adherence, it is fuller than the familiar categories that involve belief, practice, feelings or experience, knowledge and the effects of religion. Clayton and Gladden (1974) questioned those categories in a paper that asked if religion is "5D or 1?" (cf. Hilty and Morgan, 1985). But as we shall see later, evidence can be found which supports religion as a unitary variable *and* as a nest of independent factors. Each of these solutions depends on the measures that are used, the subjects' characteristics and the methods of data analysis. Furthermore, non-religious factors like situational and social demands, the compulsiveness or conformity of the subjects and social desirability can all "moderate" and suppress other responses, thereby confounding any relationships between trait predictors, performance and any other psychometric criteria (Wiggins, 1973, p. 51f.). Yet religiousness is directly expressed in only *some* contexts and by *some* individuals because of situational, personal, and perhaps conventional as well as doctrinal demands, so that any hoped for effects are distorted by the effects of the religious traditions or ideologies that lie behind and prescribe specific religious forms. Despite that, religions continue to impinge on our conduct at many points.

Nineteenth century "laws"

To show that religious practices have been differently interpreted, consider the *Lectures on Revivals* that Charles Grandison Finney published in 1834, which were based on an analysis of "laws of the mind" that he said were as soundly scientific as "any laws of physics or engineering". Therefore, "the connection between the right use of means for a revival and a revival itself is as philosophically sure as between the right use of means to raise grain and a crop of wheat. I believe, in fact, it is more certain and that there are fewer instances of failure." Finney's analysis tried to refute Jonathan Edwards's view that revivals were miracles, which men "had no more agency in producing than they had in producing thunder or a storm or hail or an earthquake" (quoted by McLoughlin, 1959, p. 85). Despite Finney's belief that the "laws of the mind" could produce conversions, he asserted that "these means will not produce a revival, we all know, without the blessing of God".

In a similar vein Billy Sunday, another American evangelist, said that "theory has got to go into the scrap heap when it comes to experience" (1915, p. 3). Machiavellianism might be detected there, and as McLoughlin (1959) concluded:

> The significant fact for the history of modern revivalism was not that Finney's psychological theories were crude but that both he and his followers believed it to be the legitimate function of a revivalist to utilize the laws of mind in order to engineer individuals and crowds into making a choice which was ostensibly based upon free will.

Psychologists now have little confidence that they can identify "laws of the mind", and arguments among them about free will have disappeared. We realize that religious belief and behaviour are influenced by theological and historical factors and by the conventional demands that support parties or points of reference in Christianity which can be "mainline", independent, evangelical, fundamentalist, radical-critical and so on, or simply Protestant or Catholic, Eastern or Western, and now Northern or Southern. Academic psychologists have little interest in trying to establish the truth or falsity of religions, although they might criticize particular doctrines or practices when finding how to "read" or understand them, depending on their own beliefs, training and experience. Whether reasoning and logic, intuition and experience, revelation or authority, rather than systematic observation is claimed as a basis for beliefs, they and their supporting data can be questioned. Yet religious beliefs are not simply mental or philosophically idealistic phenomena, since they have shaped our material and institutional environments, and their expression is still occasionally tested against the criteria that those charged or threatened with heresy must face (Geering, 1968). Neither theological *nor* psychological analyses can disregard either the content or the contexts of religion.

Simple enumerations and other interpretations

The simplest observations have counted people or their defined and relevant responses, and several religious censuses are described in the Old Testament (for example, Numbers, 1 and 2 Samuel, 24, 2). Contemporary variants of this procedure are in Church and other statistics (Harris, 1982) and opinion polls and social surveys (Mol, 1985; Abrams *et al.*, 1985). Such quantitative assessments can be set against evidence about and interpretations of the lives and thought of legendary individuals, like Moses (Freud, 1939), Christ (Schweitzer, 1948), Luther (Erikson, 1958), George Fox (Flower, 1927) and St Augustine, whose *Confessions* were assessed by several authors in the *Journal for the Scientific Study of Religion* (1966 and again in 1986). While Jaynes (1976, p. 2) noted "how the metaphors of mind are the world it perceives" (p. 2), psychobiographies emphasize the conflict between accepting the religious claims and insights of influential people and following the social trends that obscure the contributions of individuals. At least in principle, psychology spans these levels of analysis, although each has its own assumptions about what is acceptable evidence. But what is to be explained? Is belief or unbelief the more "natural" state (Rumke, 1952)? Are love and hate or debt and desire the decisively religious motives (Vergote, 1978)?

The fascination with psychological explanations of religion can be found most clearly in Freud's theories of its origins and power to overwhelm reason and science (Freud, 1939, p. 123). But it now seems too easy to follow Freud and characterize religion as a defensive mechanism or neurosis and then identify the personal and social fantasies it feeds, neglecting the role of the other potent processes that modern psychology has identified which include dissonance resolution, mindless conformity and the decision rules for solving problems. Although the popularity of Freud's dynamic or psychopathological explanations may have contributed to a neglect of the explicit effects of religion on behaviour, his views have not always been taken as antagonistic to religion itself, as Lee's *Freud and Christianity* (1948) and Freud's own correspondence with the Lutheran pastor, Pfister (1948), show.

No psychological analysis has to be reductionistic. Although our motives for an enquiry may be mixed, the normative and agreed structures of religious beliefs and institutions must form one of the criteria against which any religious data are assessed, even if the conclusions are not convincing to those who have provided those data.

Church people *are* sensitive about the psychological analyses of religion that too often seem to disregard the content they believe in and hold to. Religious responses are nevertheless interpreted as genuine, or delusional and contrived even when they are supported by a consensus that disguises disagreement or when they might be over-ridden by another authority, such as "science" or medicine. Believers and disbelievers can all be immune to and resist even cautious interpretations about the origins or the meaning of their beliefs. With little confidence that single explanations can account for all forms of religion we must accept the ambiguity and uncertainty of psychological findings about religion, and the ambiguity of religion itself.

Summary

The psychology of religion has used the methods, concepts and theories of psychology to understand the ways religion is fitted into the lives of those who accept or believe in it. Although a fundamental aim of such studies is to make good predictions about these effects, they require clear conceptualizations and methods, and must be firmly based on interpretive theories. These theories have tended to make the psychology of religion appear reductionistic, and to make a "religious psychology" seem apologetic. While the early psychologists like William James naturally turned to religion, not simply because of its dominant social role, there is more caution now about how religion might best be interpreted, and whether religious beliefs and attitudes, experience, action and the consequences of any religious position are better interpreted as a single or as a multi-dimensional process, although those who have adopted an observer's stance recognize religion as a unitary phenomenon.

2   Beyond the classics

... from the middle of the nineteenth century through the first decades of the twentieth a large number of highly gifted social scientists made contributions, now considered classics, to our understanding of the phenomena of religion. It is enough to mention Marx, Freud, Durkheim, Weber, James, Niebuhr, and Malinowski to indicate how remarkably productive the period was. (Glock and Hammond, 1973, p. ix)

Early theories of religion were founded, not on well-controlled data, but on the less formal conjectures about society and social life that were developed during the nineteenth century (cf. Allport, 1968). By the beginning of the twentieth century, religion was as important a field for psychological study as studies of sex and gender are now, although in 1963, Farberow had included religion, sex and politics in his set of psychology's taboo topics. In a study of privacy (Brown 1977) it was found that both married and single people rated their religious beliefs and religious affiliation among the most private aspects of themselves, both when giving information about themselves and when receiving disclosures from others. Religion was as private as information about their family's medical history and income, but it was to be protected even more than their fantasies. To want to protect one's religion could reflect the readiness with which traditional differences have been assumed to involve psychological characteristics or disapproved practices that might lead to the discrimination or prejudice that recent anti-discrimination legislation and complaints procedures have been designed to control. The importance of religious prejudice is shown by the list of 62 studies linking religion and prejudice in Capps *et al.*'s bibliography (1976, p. 174–180), with Allport's work (cf. 1966) the most influential (cf. Gorsuch and Aleshire, 1974).

Many religious differences have seemed easy to interpret psychologically even if in a rather prejudiced way. So Clark (1958) distinguished subjective from objective worship by whether the aim (to him) was to influence the worshipper or the deity. On that basis Clark judged the worship of Protestants to be subjective and that of Catholics objective, and he disregarded the worshipper's own perspective. In a similar way, to argue that the concept of

God the Father as a specifically parental projection or image neglects Christian traditions, myths and religious metaphors about the nature of God, as well as the social recognition that is given to those doctrines, and the doubt or disbelief that can be found in reactions to these concepts among some who are deeply involved with Christianity (Hick, 1977). The empirical work of Godin and Hallez (1964) and Vergote and Tamayo (1980) has shown that the connotative meanings behind our concepts of God do not correspond with any such superficial identification, and O'Connor's (1983) extensive analysis among Roman Catholics of the constituent meaning of self (actual, ideal and so on), parents, and the persons of the Trinity shows that "more subjects saw themselves as closer to Jesus Christ (44 per cent) than to God the Father (28 per cent) or to the Holy Spirit (20 per cent)" (p. 380) and that "the relation of the 'Ideal Mother' to each of the God Figures was more varied among subjects of both sexes than between the Ideal Father and any of the God Figures" (p. 381). What one says is not necessarily what is intended.

Western biases

The new ecumenism among Christian Churches and their liturgical reforms have helped to reduce apparently firm sectarian prejudices. There is also less interest in giving deep psychological explanations of the appeal of others' religions, and an increased interest in the phenomenology of religion beyond the confines of Christianity (Smart, 1969, 1983). The multi-culturalism produced by immigration in Europe and in Australasia, for example, has also forced greater respect and tolerance for other religions. The "Minority group support service" in the Coventry Education Authority has therefore produced pamphlets for schools on "How a Hindu (and a Moslem and a Sikh) prays", and Hassall (1981) argues that "religious education has an important part to play in the multi-racial school" (p. 46).

Despite such changes in our social context, the psychology of religion is still almost entirely confined to work within the broadly Judeo-Christian traditions. Apart from the essays on, for example, *Muslim Society* (Gellner, 1981), and a limited number of cross-cultural replications of essentially Western studies (e.g. Vergote and Tamayo, 1980), we have primarily Western analyses of, for example, Buddhist or Islamic psychology (Harré and Lamb, 1984; Jung, 1958), although Murphy and Murphy (1968) emphasized the importance of cultural (and religious) factors in fixing boundaries between body or mind and between life and death. When Thouless (1940) discussed the different religious contexts for psychological development provided by Buddhist and Christian traditions he noted especially the place of the teaching of their founders, the importance given to concepts of the person of God, and the religious involvement with other aspects of these cultures. This field has, however, been of more concern to anthropologists and sociologists than to psychologists, although as Heelas (1985) has shown, even their interpretations and theories rely on Western rather than indigenous psychologies. While many young people have now made pilgrimages to the East for enlightenment, or to study ascetic and meditational techniques, it is unfortunate that we have almost no systematic information about how those experiences have influenced their beliefs and their outlook, except among members of the "new religions" (Richardson, 1985).

Working at a macro-level, Swanson (1960), following Durkheim, used the Yale Human Relations Area Files (Murdock, 1961) to explore the way specific experiences in a society might form the basis for its concepts of supernature and of the deities that exist behind the natural or cultural order. He found across the 50 societies he examined that monotheism is associated with social hierarchies of three or more "sovereign" groups, giving a negative correlation between the number of deities and of superior social groups. This analysis rested on a broad phenomenology of both religion and other cultural traditions. Conventional arguments also support our taken-for-granted modes of religious thought. William James's (1912) comment (in his essay on the *Will to Believe*) on Pascal's wager that the benefits of religious belief outweigh the costs of disbelief should those beliefs be found to be true, was that "Certainly no Turk ever took to masses and holy water on its account; and even to us Protestants those means of salvation seem such foregone impossibilities that Pascal's logic, invoked for them specifically, leaves us unmoved" (p. 6). Similarly Renan, the nineteenth-century French historian who applied his methods to the biblical narratives, when asked if, having abandoned Catholicism, he would become a Protestant, is said to have replied, "It was my faith that I lost, not my reason." To clarify the plausibility of established religious arguments I asked Australian students to write comments on Pascal's wager. None of them found it a plausible reason for their own belief in God, and although its religious implications were recognized many did not readily follow the game-theoretical logic.

Schaub (1926), who noted that the twentieth century brought a new approach to the study of religion through "Psychological investigations along strictly empirical and scientific lines", echoed Starbuck's (1899) statement in his book, the first to be concerned exclusively with the psychology of religion, that "Science has conquered one field after another, until it is now entering the most complex, the most inaccessible and, of all, the most sacred domain — that of religion" (p. 1).

Religion within psychology

Beit-Hallahmi's (1974) study of the rise and fall of the "Psychology of religion" as a psychological movement, between 1880 and 1930, identifies its early leaders as Hall and James, Leuba and Starbuck, Pratt and Conklin. The movement itself was centred at Clark University where G. S. Hall had founded the "Clark School of religious psychology" and the *American Journal of Religious Psychology and Education* that ran from 1894 until 1911, when it changed its name to the *Journal of Religious Psychology including its Anthropological and Sociological Aspects*, and then ceased publication in 1915. Their influence, however, continued into the 1930s: the *Psychological Bulletin* had begun regular reviews of the the field in 1909 with Coe's paper on "Psychological aspects of religious education" followed in 1914 with a paper by Ellsworth Faris on "Psychology of Religion (Practical)" and further papers by Coe and by Leuba in 1915. Cronbach's (1933) paper, which referred mainly to German and French sources, was its last. Douglas (1963) and Strunk (1957) both explain the failure of this movement in the 1930s with reference to the dominance of Behaviorism over American psychology and to changed views about religion itself. Beit-Hallahmi, however, tends to agree with Glock and Hammond (1973) that any serious attempt to study religion must be a threat to it, which was resolved then by pushing this field of psychological study toward religion itself. Homans (1970), however, attributes that change in attitudes to religion to the beginnings of theological existentialism, a shift in cultural modes of self-understanding (p. 99) and the development of pastoral psychology which prepared the current religious interest in counselling and psychotherapy.

Whatever their reasons, psychologists themselves began to favour more scientifically respectable preoccupations in the 1930s, although they retained an interest in religious attitudes if not in religion itself. Hunsberger (1979) therefore argues that the "psychology of religion" is still in disfavour, despite the specialized journals that began to be published around 1960. As well as the *Journal for the Scientific Study of Religion* and the *Review of Religious Research* there is now the *Journal of Psychology and Theology* (1972, Vol. 1) and the *Journal of Psychology and Christianity* (1981, Vol. 1), as well as the *Archives de Sciences Sociales des Religions* and quite specialist journals like *Omega, Journal of Death and Dying*.

But a psychology of religion did not actually die out in the 1930s, since it was kept alive in social psychology and personality study, especially through the work on social attitudes and religious development which G. W. Allport in particular nourished with his work on religious attitudes, religion and prejudice and individual differences in religious orientations and personality, producing *The Individual and His Religion* in 1950 (cf. Beit-Hallahmi,

1985). Allport's work contributed to a recognition of the effects and the nature of a religious outlook on life (Allport *et al.*, 1948), changing the early emphasis on general psychological processes as the roots of religion (e.g. Thouless, 1923, 1971) to a concern with the ground on which religion grows, and from attention to specifically religious phenomena like sacrifice, prayer, or conversion (Ames, 1910), and interpretations of religion from such single perspectives as that given by psychoanalytic theory (Faber, 1969) to a multi-dimensional view. As Dittes (1969) said, "Religion seems far too complex an arena of human behaviour — as diverse and heterogeneous as human behaviour itself — not to include many different and unrelated types of variables." Hunsberger (1979) emphasized that generality when he examined the references in Argyle and Beit-Hallahmi's *Social Psychology of Religion* (1975), and found that specialized religious journals predominated after 1960, although even then many references (39 per cent in the 1970s) were to general academic journals. Valentine's (1962) *"Experimental Psychology of Beauty"* is an example in another domain of the empiricism that developed once a theoretically committed psychology of religion, with its various schools (Woodworth, 1940), died out.

Scientific studies of religion

The Society for the Scientific Study of Religion began the publication of its *Journal* in 1961. That, and the *Review of Religious Research* (1959, Vol. 1) mark a new period of growth, with an emphasis on cooperation between "all the intellectual disciplines concerned with the dynamics of modern culture" (Kallen and Pemberton, 1961), and the promise of "the use of scientific disciplines in the study of religion everywhere". The Editors' "introductory word" in the first number of the *Journal for the Scientific Study of Religion* asserts that "Studies and appraisals of religious experience, mystical and other, of religious beliefs, practices, organizations, and purposes from the points of view and by the methods of the psychological and economic sciences, each year increase in number, diversity and fruitfulness". *Religious Education, Sociological Analysis*, several European journals, as well as the *Journal of Social Psychology* and the *Journal of Personality and Social Psychology* continue to publish empirical work on the psychology of religion which largely depends on procedures or scales that measure religious attitudes (sometimes called "religionism" or "religiosity"). Robinson and Shaver (1973) presented 17 and Shaw and Wright (1967) seven such scales each of which is evaluated for its reliability and, if available validity. These scales derive from the measurement theory and procedures that Thurstone and Chave (1929) first used to measure attitudes to the Church, and from the later, but equally reliable summated rating scale method that was developed by Likert (1932). Gorsuch (1984), in the first paper on the psychology of religion to be published in the *American Psychologist*, argues that these models of measurement offer *the* paradigm for studies of religion.

The publication trends from 1950 to 1974 that were examined by Gapps *et al.* (1976) show the dominating concern for "religious beliefs, attitudes and values", which they classify under a dispositional dimension, and for work on the relation of religion to personal growth classified in their directional dimension. But as Fishbein and Ajzen (1975) show, religious research also provides many examples in general analyses of the operation and development of attitudes and beliefs, since religion is a widespread phenomenon, used, for example, to handle anxiety (Parker and Brown, 1979) and maintain self-referential and other personality processes. No longer can it be said that the psychology of religion is aligned with religion rather than with psychology, or that it is biased or partisan. Increased agreement on definitional problems and measured variables has made it possible to plan studies that circumvent disagreements about the underlying models of man (Chapman and Jones, 1980), whether they are mechanistic or behavioural, humanistic (Strunk, 1970), or essentially social.

But we should not disregard the importance of what Godin described as the "eagerness for and resistance to the scientific psychology of religion" (1962), nor can we assume that all the problems about theory, measurement, and the data have been solved. While some would focus on religious experience and others exphasize behaviour, belief necessarily links those perspectives together. The establishment of Division 36 within the American Psychological Association, for "psychologists interested in religious issues", has fostered the discussion that will help to produce greater coherence. Empiricism certainly provides a tolerant stance from which to observe those who are strongly committed to religious beliefs, which Strunk (1970, quoting Royce) thinks deal "with the subjective meaning of life", but about which he and many others would probably not accept an entirely secular perspective.

What is religion?

Few now doubt that the assurance of twentieth-century secular movements about the decline of powers beyond man has produced "vague abstractions or pale shadows of the objects of historic religion, and in effect led to a concentration on the human subject" (Marty *et al.*, 1968). But "the death of God did not mean the end of religious observance, whether as despair or as celebration" (ibid). Marty *et al.* therefore argue that most psychologists and other social scientists:

find religion to be pervasive but undergoing transformation. They share with nineteenth century social thinkers the view of the social character of religions. They share the twentieth century theological thinkers' view of the radical change which the psyche is undergoing, or which social groups are experiencing in the industrialized and pluralist West.

But what is this "religion", beyond the wide ranging beliefs and prescriptions of Christianity and other world religions that we recognize?

Although the Shorter Oxford English Dictionary holds the etymology of "religion" to be obscure, its definitions refer to the Church, to a unitive response through activities like prayer, metaphysical meanings, and group dependence. Webster's Dictionary (1934), however, offers two derivations, one from the Latin *religio*, properly "taboo, restraint", and the other from *religare*, "to hold back, bind fast", although Ducasse (1953, p. 94) noted that "Cicero traced the word 'religion' to *religere*, meaning 'to read over again, rehearse' ". While Webster identified nine uses of "religion" it also notes that "religion is used rather narrowly, and even prescriptively". So when Mr. Thwackum, in Fielding's *Tom Jones* (Book III, Ch. 3), mentioned religion he said he meant the Christian religion; and not only the Christian religion, but the Protestant religion; and not only the Protestant religion, but the Church of England. That Leuba (1912) could collect 48 definitions of religion, to which Ducasse (1953) later added more, with their typical "kinds of bias" (p. 97), implies that definitions are formed to emphasize whatever suits a particular purpose. So Leuba remarked that the chief service of the word "infinite" in a definition of religion is to "betray man's ineradicable megalomania" (1912, p. 341), and Ducasse said that terms like "truth", "power", "unknowable" and "ultimate reality" are "symptoms of the user's craving to revere ... and invitations to the reader to stop trying to think" (1953, p. 98).

The High Court of Australia's ruling on 27 October 1983, after considering social science and theological views on religion, looked to "inherently formal views embedded in legal judgements" and found that not only does the law protect and define religion, but that while minority religions stand in need of especial protection, that protection may apply to the adherents more than to the religions themselves. It is because of the freedom of individuals to "adhere to any religion of his choosing or to none", that "the variety of religious beliefs which are within the area of legal immunity is not restricted" (p. 5). Since, as they said, "religious institutions must also be given freedom, in the sense of being allowed to function", they therefore decided that Scientology warrants legal protection as a "religion".

The search for definitions of religion can proceed almost indefinitely, but some sense of otherness and transcendence seems essential simply because of religion's concern with "the last things". Thouless defined religion as a "felt practical relationship with what is believed in as a super-human being or beings" (1924, p. 4), which might however raise questions about satanic beings. Bowker (1973) therefore suggested a felt practical relationship with what is believed to be *transcendental* (and is implicitly positive). Flower was more specific, and identified religion as an "attitude determined by the discrimination of an element of 'utterly-beyondness', brought about by a mental development which is able to appreciate the existence of more in the world than that to which existing endowment effects adequate adjustment" (1927, p. 30). William James argued that "religion cannot stand for any single principle or essence, but is rather a collective name" (1902), and Thouless later modified his definition to make religion "a particular kind of attitude (which includes characteristic ways of behaving, feeling and believing) towards the world as a whole" (1971, p. 11). Max Weber was more cautious and asserted that any definition of religion could come only at the end of an analysis.

Berger (1973, pp. 177–180) surveyed sociological definitions of religion and remarked on the limited spheres within which religion was classified in the nineteenth century, citing Max Mueller's conception of religion as a disease of language as well as Tylor's view of religion being based on animism, which made primitive man a kind of philosopher (with which Piaget (1932) would have agreed). More recently Luckmann, following Durkheim's recognition of religion as a social fact, equated religion with "symbolic self-transcendence". For Berger himself "religion is the human enterprise by which a sacred cosmos is established" (p. 34).

These definitions all recognize the sacred quality of some mysterious and awesome power that is beyond man yet related to him and carries potent social implications. This is picked up in Argyle and Beit-Hallahmi's (1975) definition of religion as "a system of *beliefs* in a divine or superhuman power, and *practices* of worship or other rituals directed to that power" (p. 2 with emphasis added). That definition leaves open the question of religion as a state of mind, and of the ways it is tied to the doctrinal and institutional concerns that themselves shape or direct the ways we express our beliefs and control the doctrines that can properly be held.

To identify someone as "religious" implies detecting a stance or attitude that finds order and meaning in social and personal life: to use religious beliefs or practices instrumentally implies an external referent that supports them, or a power that is carried by them. So Allport defined a mature religious sentiment as a "disposition ... to respond favourably ... to objects or principles that the individual regards as of ultimate importance in his own life, and as having to do with what he regards as permanent or central in the nature of things" (1950, p. 56). That is similar to William James's view of religion as "the feelings, acts, and experiences of individual men in their solitude, so far as they apprehend themselves to stand in relation to whatever they may consider the divine" (1902, pp. 31–32); he said that was an arbitrary definition, leaving out philosophical problems about the object or religion and its "institutional branch", while recognizing the "reality of the unseen".

The meanings of "religion"

The definitions of religion have also been approached empirically. Clark (1958), for example, sent a questionnaire to members of the Society for the Scientific Study of Religion that asked them to define religion. From the 68 replies, he found that the most frequent response advanced supernatural concepts relating to the ultimate. In descending order, other answers referred to social groups, institutional or credal specifications, or had a theological emphasis. This material led Clark to conclude that "religion has many meanings and facets". In a study of the opinions of religious Teachers' College students in New Zealand about what religion is, I found that a majority made conventional references to a way of life, that "gives everlasting life", "the most wonderful thing in life", "beyond our reach and understanding", or as "a personal relationship with God".

Common usage also gives religion both specific and more spread out meanings which identify it with "ultimate truth", superstition, or simply enjoying money and football, with little sense of the numinous. Campbell (1960, p. 235) writes of the "considerable disservice to the English language to use "religion" in the flattened-out sense of an all-absorbing devotion to X, irrespective of what X may be". In that sense, it is also a disservice to the phenomenology of religion to assume that all religions are theistic. While some have found God there others lose him in theism, and in the consequences of demands of a religious system. That is why Bonhoeffer (1953) advocated "religionless Christianity". David Hume (1757) wrote of two people reading the same novel. Although one took it to be true and the other as fictional they could make sense of what they read because it is possible in varying degrees to enter another's "world-view", if not their "reality".

Yinger, who said that "Many studies of religion stumble over the first hurdle; the problem of definition" (1970, p. 3) having earlier decided that "any definition of religion is likely to be satisfactory only to its author" (1967, p. 18), proposed an operational definition of non-doctrinal religion that focussed on an "awareness of, and interest in the continuing, recurrent, permanent problems of human existence" (1970, p. 33). Nelsen *et al.* (1976) found that the seven items which Yinger used to operationalize that concept formed separate factors covering "acceptance of belief and order" and the "value of suffering", while Roof *et al*. (1977) found factors that involved the "value of religious efforts", "difficult experience" and "belief in order and pattern", each being related to measures of traditional religion, including self-rated religiosity (cf. Brown, 1981).

That political ideologies like nationalism, capitalism, or communism (as in Koestler and Crossman's *God That Failed*, 1950), have been aligned with religion shows the ubiquitous usefulness of religion as an analytic model. It is, however, enough for us to recognize that a wide range of behaviour, belief and feelings have been recognized as "religious", and whether particular manifestations are judged irreligious, sacrilegious or extreme in other ways depends on implicit criteria about what is normal and acceptable, or accords with recognized doctrines or rituals. Extreme religious manifestations are hard to deal with, not least because of their ambiguity. When McCready administered the sacrament in 1799 "many fell to the ground, and lay power-less, groaning and praying and crying for mercy ... a woman screamed 'I have no religion; I am going to hell' " (Weisberger, 1958, p. 24). Such enthusiasm (Knox, 1950) can hardly be compared with the liturgical restraint of a College Chapel or religious community. On the basis of therapy with an ordinand, Bragon (1977) argued that the gains and losses to personal rela-tedness following a religious conversion may always need "to be followed by a therapeutic experience".

Another kind of definition establishes religion as a "value", which Scott (1965) saw as "any individual's conception of an ideal relationship between people — a state of affairs that he considers ultimately, absolutely and uni-versally good". Religiousness is one of Scott's 12 values, together with intellectualism, kindness, social skills, creativity, independence, self-control and so on. He assessed the religious value from ratings of the degree of liking for statements like "Being devout in one's religious faith", "Always living one's religion in his daily life", "Always attending religious services regu-larly and faithfully", "Avoiding the physical pleasures that are prohibited in the Bible" and "Encouraging others to attend services and lead religious lives". Those items could be a microcosm of the religious virtues. The Allport, Vernon, Lindzey (1960) *Study of Values*, first developed in 1931 and based on Spranger's (1928) *Types of Men* with its six values, theoretical, economic, aesthetic, social, political and religious, is the best known of the value-oriented measures, despite its ipsative scoring.

These and the other measures that will be looked at in Chapter Four hardly tap the felt practical relationship that William James identified with religion, or the conceptions of its involvement with a supernatural order that perfo-rates this one. Nearly all the measures focus on accepting or rejecting an ethical or doctrinal system that specifies what is to be believed and what religious people should do (cf. Fullerton and Hunsberger, 1982). Even then, the lowest common denominator is taken by asking, for example, "How often do you go to church?" rather than "How often do you take communion?" to overcome the many specific or conventional differences between religious traditions and what they prescribe. One way to escape from that level of generality is to look for the idiosyncratic connotations or constructions of religious concepts that are tapped by the semantic differential (Snyder and Osgood, 1969) or by the Repertory Grid (Fransella and Bannister, 1977). The focus there is on secondary meanings, and not on the "doxemes" (Deconchy, 1980) that are found in statements from the Creeds, with the doctrinal meanings that they carry. These secondary meanings have been investigated less often than has the degree of acceptance of the truth of doctrinal statements, which neglects the ways we make sense of our beliefs and experiences. Case study and free response procedures, which offer another escape from closed response categories and grouped data, are more useful heuristically than as tests of theories.

Multi-dimensional analyses

The work that Eleanor Rosch has stimulated on "the structure of real world categories" (Rosch and Lloyd, 1978, p. 5) has not yet been systematically applied to religions, although Brown and Forgas (1980), having identified 33 commonly accepted elements of "religion" in concepts like faith, scriptures, peace of mind, Church authority, miracles, revelation, salvation, and so on, found with an INDSCAL analysis that they formed three dimensions which contrasted institutional against individual orientations, positive against negative evaluations and what is tangible or familiar against what is intangible in religion. A comparable study by Muthen *et al.* (1977) yielded factors covering tradition, evaluation, familiarity and activity in religion. These factors are very different from King and Hunt's (1975) 11 religious dimensions of credal assent, personal religious experience, church attendance, organizational activities, Church work with friends, talking and reading about religion, financial support, religious knowledge, orientations to religious growth and striving, religious security and dogmatism, and an extrinsic orientation. Robinson and Shaver (1973, pp. 656–662), however, emphasize that King and Hunt's actual scales of measurement "tap church-related religious beliefs and activities ... (and) ... the social rather than the more private aspects of religiosity" (p. 658), which Hilty *et al.*'s (1984) reanalyses have reduced to faith, knowledge, purpose, involvement, "orthodoxy", social conscience, and fundamentalism (although not with these names).

Dittes (1969, p. 643), on the other hand, identified nine psychological variables underlying religious belief, in a 3 × 3 matrix of dependent variables (intensity of belief, content of belief and protection of belief) and independent variables (reinforcement from objective reality, social reinforcement, and intrapsychic reinforcement) that integrate social, psychological and religious perspectives and content. He also contrasted content-free against the content-based characteristics of belief, and the psychological differences between acquiring a belief and then protecting it. Dittes conjectured one other independent variable as vulnerability to challenge or dissonance, which he believed could itself be motivating, and he emphasized that social norms and other influence processes "are an obvious source of religious beliefs", with objective reality providing "a major source of protective rationalization" for them (p. 644). This analysis directly aligns religious with psychological and social processes, and identifies how each of these facets can control some of the variance in religious responding. Spilka *et al.* (1985b, pp. 9–11) emphasize the variety of names that have been given to the different ways in which it is possible for people to be or to show their religiousness, beyond Clark's (1958) primary, secondary and tertiary religions which depend on whether one's religion is sanctioned by experience, habit or a social authority.

Beyond the meanings and the structures behind received or traditional beliefs, emphasis can be given, following Elkind (1971), to supernatural or transcendental perspectives, to the personal needs that a religion may satisfy, whether in security, consolation or social recognition, and to its shaping by cultural, historical or social processes, its expression in Church-based or in secular activities, and the sanctions that it gives to other activities and intentions. Since serving coffee or giving a party seems to some people an activity that is as religious as going to church, we must expect to find highly diverse forms and responses.

In the semantic atlas (Snyder and Osgood, 1969, p. 265.), familiar religious (mostly Christian) concepts draw high evaluation and potency scores. The list of concepts in Table 1 suggests the importance of a knowledge of religious forms when making these ratings, since "Buddhists" and "Moslems" were rated neutrally.

Religion and the self

In looking for consistent religious responses, psychologists have tended to disregard the extent to which each religious tradition fixes its own meanings, and makes specific roles available to those who are aligned with it. Religions are discovered or offered and they are not invented by their adherents, who must extract or impose meaning on what they find because few can alter or influence the traditions they belong to, although they can select and emphasize their own beliefs. These emphases give the orientations to religion that have been a productive focus for recent research (Batson and Ventis, 1982). The attractions or consolations of a religion do not necessarily result from any deliberate search, nor can they inevitably resolve personal or social problems through the specific appeal of the particular beliefs and other aspects of any system. At least initially, most people accept a set of religious beliefs as a package, later differentiating what is obligatory from the beliefs that are optional or appealing.

Table 1   *Composite semantic differential factor scores for 12 religious words (from Snyder and Osgood, 1969, p. 626f.)*

	Evaluation	Potency	Activity
Atheists	—0.925	—0.525	—0.119
Buddhists	—0.362	0.440	—0.656
Christians	2.106	1.900	0.344
Clergyman	1.519	1.050	0.312
God	0.425	2.426	0.431
Heaven	2.550	2.469	—0.644
Hell	—2.089	1.925	—0.912
Missionary	1.925	1.344	0.031
Moslems	—0.131	0.469	—0.350
Non-believers	—1.006	—0.694	—0.094
Prayer	2.394	2.212	—0.381
Resurrection	1.494	1.637	—2.231

A recent study at the University of New South Wales asked 60 psychology students to "list as many issues as you can, of both a general and specific kind that religion or religious people have been concerned with". In all, 560 issues were given that identify areas of recognized religious activity in Australia. The most frequent issues had a primary focus on God, heaven and hell, conversion and evangelism, spirituality, sin, love, charity, life, and death, in that order. Next were social issues involving sex, marriage, the family, divorce, abortion and contraception, and alcohol, with education, politics, welfare, freedom and social control (especially through censorship), and peace and war being less often mentioned. Abortion, education, marriage, life, morality, and war were each given by at least one third of the sample, suggesting that they show the most noticeable and expected involvements of religion with social life. In a parallel study, another sample of students was asked to explain what being or not being "religious" means. Those who said they were aligned with religion mentioned holding Christian beliefs or practising one's beliefs, and those who were not religious most often mentioned not going to church. (A parallel question that asked what being "sexy" means was consistently answered in terms of physical appearance or behaviour.)

Identifying oneself as "religious" is an important form of definition that has been studied through answers to the simple question, "Who are you?", which has been used to assess self-concepts. Mulford and Salisbury (1964) in a US study, found that 24 per cent of men and 35 per cent of women offered either a specific denomination or similar religious identity as one of 20 separate answers to the question "Who am I?". Only occupation (65 per cent) and marital status (34 per cent) were given more frequently. Their broad religious answers included, "I am religious", "I believe in God", and "I try to live by the Ten Commandments". Kuhn and McPartland (1954) had earlier related the use of religious self-concepts to religious affiliation, on the hypothesis that members of "majority groups would use a religious identification more readily and so earlier in their answers than would the members of minority groups that set their members at odds with the norms of the larger society". They found that the "mean salience of religious references" ranged from 7.40 for Roman Catholics to 7.04 for "small sects", 3.22 for Methodists and 1.82 for "Christian", and they concluded that "Religious affiliation references are significantly more salient among the self attitudes of members of 'differentistic' religious groups than among members of 'majority or conventional religious groups'."

In research in Sydney, only 23 per cent of a student sample gave a religious identifier in a modified "Who are you?" task, which suggests that religion sits lightly on Australians (cf. Hunsberger and Brown, 1984). In a more recent study of self-identity among psychology students at the University of New South Wales, 15 categories (family, age, social class, occupation, religion, and so on) were rated on each of six scales for how well each "identifies you as a person". The results in Table 2, which shows the judgements of eight categories including "religion", "family" and "friends", stress the comparative unimportance of social disapproval, and yet the relevance of religion as a defining characteristic of the "self".

In another facet of that study, the students were asked to give free descriptions of themselves under the same headings. These answers show that religious self descriptions are readily elaborated and also constrained. One person wrote "Catholic — still practising but not accepting all of the roles that go with it", and others said "I don't know whether I believe in God", "Yes I am religious but I don't have a set religion — does religion relate only to God?", "No conventional one but 'Christian' ethics are important", "Church of England agnostic", "Greek Orthodox — not religious but christened in Orthodox Church", "No religious aspirations", "Agnostic to theistic, pluralistic with respect to other religions", "I don't believe I have one. I question religion so much, and read about it. But I constantly find too many loopholes. I guess I believe in something strong and steadfast but I'm unsure whether it is the traditional God. I was christened Presbyterian and brought up within a Church background", and "Am supposedly Catholic but believe in a God and that's about all. I don't enjoy being pressured into attending church — too hypocritical. Conversely I enjoy time to think about God".

Of the 80 subjects in this study, 8.8 per cent wrote "none" or "nil" to describe their religion, 62.5 per cent briefly identified a specific position (including "atheist") and 28.7 per cent gave elaborated answers in the forms exemplified above. These data show that religious identifications *are* readily accepted while the detail disclosed depends on the method that is used to assess it and the person's attitude. Those who reject simplified descriptions of their religion will still focus on beliefs that refer to processes and institutions, creeds and activities that support, manage or control the supernatural, Terms like theism, atheism, agnosticism, scepticism, naturalism, deism, monotheism, polytheism, henotheism, and pantheism were not mentioned, nor was the universalism which argues that all religions lead to the same goal, whether it is the satori or shiatsu of Japanese Zen (Sato, 1972), maksha in Hinduism, enlightenment, cosmic consciousness or salvation in the West.

Table 2 *The mean ratings of selected bases for the identity of Australian students with high scores defined by the description given*

	Defines Poorly	Unimportant	Socially Disapproved	Private	Irrelevant	Concealing
Religion	3.81	3.58	3.56	4.02	2.00	3.17
Nationality	3.73	3.58	2.50	2.67	3.08	3.08
Family	2.92	2.00	2.50	4.19	1.98	2.67
Occupation	3.17	2.85	2.69	2.65	2.60	2.88
Age	3.94	3.73	2.73	3.06	3.29	3.13
Friends	2.48	2.02	2.31	3.77	1.96	3.94
Social class	3.63	3.88	2.85	3.13	3.00	3.48
Sex	2.50	2.42	2.52	2.38	2.21	3.81

Parametric data

It is perhaps unfortunate that psychologists of religion have disregarded parametric questions, and that we must look to sociology, and the work of survey centres, especially in the United States, to identify these broad social trends (cf. the contributions of Andrew M. Greeley (McNamara, 1974), Charles T. Glock and Merton P. Strommen). In evaluating that work, however, we must remember that the context in which survey questionnaires are presented has been shown to have direct effects on the answers that are given in the sense that a Church-sanctioned religious survey draws more variability in the responses of people than do the same questions presented from a secular source (Deconchy, 1980). Despite that, the high level of formal agreement that has been found in public opinion surveys of religious attitudes and beliefs shows at least nominal support for religious institutions. A report on church and State in Britain, for example, concluded that the Church of England was nominally supported "by at least half and probably nearer two-thirds of the adult population" (1970, pp. 117–118). That it can be asserted that church attendance is declining in the West (Wilson, 1983), except in conservative Churches (Kelley, 1972, 1979), sects, and other cohesive groups raises questions about what religion means, and how it can be recognized. Currie *et al*. (1977) in *Churches and Churchgoers: Patterns of Church Growth in the British Isles since 1700*, relied largely on parish records and drew attention to the problems they faced with the time series analysis that they attempted, as well as the unknown effects of the changes that occurred within the religious systems themselves, and as a result of the exogenous influences on them (p. 38). They concluded that Church growth "appears to display a largely cyclical pattern" (p. 39), and that short-term conclusions are misleading (cf. Boyd, 1980).

Census data, when they are available, give information about baseline response rates to religion, and show, for example, that the number who exercise their statutory right to "object" to stating "their religious profession" in the regular population censuses in Australia and in New Zealand has increased. In New Zealand, those who objected to stating their religious preference rose from 4.8 per cent in 1936, to 8 per cent in 1956, and 14 per cent in 1976, the last year for which figures are available. As well as that, in 1976 3.2 per cent returned "no religion" (1.2 per cent in 1966), 1 per cent returned "atheist" or "agnostic" and 2.8 per cent returned "Christian" or "Protestant". The New Zealand Report on the 1976 Census (May 1980) shows that 72 per cent of the population was spread across seven religious groups, the largest being Anglican or Church of England (29.2 per cent), Presbyterian (18.1. per cent), Roman Catholic (15.3 per cent), and then Methodist (5.5 per cent), Baptist (1.6 per cent), Mormon (1.2 per cent), with Ratana, a Maori sect (cf. Henderson, 1972), drawing 1.1 per cent. Since that census question is quite open, a range of small groups and implicit definitions of religion can be found among the other 72 headings that are set out. The smallest of those groups were the 100 members of the New Apostolic Church, 104 in the Full Gospel Fellowship, 254 Pantheists, 291 Theosophists, 309 Scientologists, 559 Rationalists and 1060 Humanists.

The comparable question in the Australian census says, "State the full name of the religious denomination. (There is no penalty for failure to answer this question.)''. In 1966, 88.35 per cent were classified as Christians, 9.86 per cent gave no reply, 0.81 per cent gave "no religion" and 0.31 per cent were "indefinite" (Census Bulletin, 1966, Number 8.1, p. 16). While the number who claimed no religious affiliation rose by 2.5 per cent between 1976 and 1981, to 10.18 per cent, the vast majority of Australians (77.8 per cent) claim religious membership, and 76.4 per cent identified themselves with a Christian tradition. The major non-Christian religions in Australia are Islam (0.5 per cent), Judaism (0.4 per cent) and Buddhism (0.2 per cent). The Church of England, which was the largest group in 1966 (33.57 per cent) dropped to 26.1 per cent in 1981, while the Roman Catholics increased to 26 per cent in 1981 from 25.7 per cent in 1976 (cf. Price, 1981; Harris, 1982).

These results, which are of more interest to Church administrators, demographers and sociologists than to psychologists who feel uneasy with data from a whole population, show that religion is still accepted by large numbers of people, despite claims about the effects of secularization in Western societies. That a religious identification may be held loosely is shown in the 1981 Australian census, where 490,767 (3.4 per cent) gave their religion as "Methodist", although the Methodist Church there had disappeared into the Uniting Church in 1975. That is also stressed by Hynd's (1982) analysis of Australian Gallup poll data on actual church attendance. He found that only 42 per cent of the number expected from the poll data actually attend, and although regular church-going may be claimed because it is thought to be socially approved, many go to church irregularly, or they go only for marriages or funerals. That, however, is also changing. The proportion of marriages performed in Australia by religious celebrants dropped from 89.4 per cent in 1968 to 71.1 per cent in 1976, although in England in 1972 only 54.5 per cent of marriages were in religious contexts, the rest being in Registry offices. In Australia a profession of "civil marriage celebrant" was created in 1975, and by 1981 the proportion of marriages performed by religious celebrants had dropped to 64.2 per cent. Yet it is most unusual for funerals not to be presided over by a clergyman: of 29 scheduled cremations at one of Sydney's crematoria on May 25 1985 only one did not have a clegyman presiding.

Church-going and religious belief

Kotre's (1971) study of lapsed Catholics found that the religious attitudes of regular attenders were similar to those of a matched group that had lapsed, and he suggested that church attendance by itself is not a critical identifier of one's religiousness. It depends on what is actually available and the other contextual constraints. An Anglican report in Australia (A.C.C., 1976) showed a net decline from 1963 to 1974 of 59 per cent in Sunday School attendance, 20 per cent in infant Baptisms and 41 per cent in confirmations. During the same period, Baptists in Western Australia and Victoria showed a net gain in Sunday School attendance. More sensitive information is needed if we are to tease out the interaction between a group's sanctions and traditions and the reactions of those who are linked to it. Religious groups certainly differ in their stringency or in the latitude they will tolerate from those who would retain a formal but inactive membership, and in the techniques they use to maintain contact with, and continuing support from their casual members, although every religious group is an essentially voluntary association.

To claim a religious membership or identity can convey an attitude that does not entail explicitly religious behaviour or any commitment, and many say they worship God without going to church, although even that claim is influenced by the country in which one lives. Webb and Wybrow (1982) show national differences in religious attendance, with 87 per cent in Ireland who said they go to religious service at least once a week, and 32 per cent in Italy, 12 per cent in France and five per cent in Denmark. Mol (1985) argues that one's church-going depends directly on the orientation of the Church so that "the more our religious organisations move towards the exclusive end of the continuum the higher their attendance rate and the more they go in the opposite direction the more tenuous, apparently, is the hold on their membership" (p. 63).

It is obvious that many people who do not go to church regularly continue to hold specifically religious beliefs. The 1981 Gallup Report (Webb and Wybrow, 1982) shows that, in Britain, 73 per cent of their regular omnibus survey for April 1981 said they believe in God, 53 per cent believe in heaven, 28 per cent in reincarnation, 21 per cent in the Devil and 21 per cent in hell: while 36 per cent believe in a personal God and 37 per cent believe in "some kind of spirit or life force" (p. 152). Australian Gallup data which breaks down these beliefs by denomination are shown in Table 3.

Table 3 *Percentage of believers in five Christian concepts in the major denominations in Australia*

Percentage of respondents believing in:	Anglican	Catholic	Methodist	Presbyterian
God	88	94	90	91
Heaven	60	82	70	60
Life after death	40	65	46	40
Hell	26	64	28	17
The devil	23	59	26	21

Source: Gallup poll, 1969.

Such data themselves reinforce the wide acceptance of transcendental beliefs, although only 15 per cent said they went to religious services at least once a week, with 38 per cent going several times a year and 46 per cent "less often or never" (p. 155). Closed alternatives may be easy to answer and to analyse, but they do not capture the "depth" of religious beliefs or practice. When Webb and Wybrow asked "Which of these comes nearest to expressing your views about the Old Testament?" (pp. 152–153), their conventional and telegraphic alternatives (with the percentages by which they were chosen) were:

> It is of divine authority and its commands should be followed without question. (14 per cent)
> It is mostly of divine authority but some of it needs interpretation. (34 per cent)
> It is mostly a collection of stories and fables. (42 per cent, and with 34 per cent accepting that alternative for the New Testament)

None of this material captures the power or the strength of the religious identities that focus current political confrontations in Northern Ireland, the Middle East or Central America, where party lines appear to transcend the benign religious orientations that social surveys explore, and on which very little hangs. Wuthnow (1981), however, argues that "A response to a survey item, such as 'I believe in God' should be treated as an objective utterance, or symbol, rather than a mere indicator of an internal but unobservable orientation" (p. 30). Even if they are symbols or concepts they draw on historical, institutional and social as well as psychological processes to give meaning to any language of belief, although their theological implications may be recognized by only a few of those who are their believers.

The nature of belief

Any examination of the meaning of "belief" inevitably turns us to religion itself: the Oxford Dictionary traces "belief" from trust or confidence in a person, as "*fides*", although "faith" has superseded belief in that sense. As a verb, belief "gives" credence, or shows faith, which Biblically is "the substance of things hoped for, the evidence of things not seen". Belief in a modern sense involves assent to a proposition, statement (even when it implies a certain knowledge), or fact, and is established on the basis of authority or perhaps because of inadequate evidence. "Opinion" involves a "judgement or belief based on grounds short of proof" or a "view held as probable", so that an opinionated believer is "obstinate in opinion, dogmatic, self-willed" and a strict believer adheres to a specified religion. Belief also refers to what is believed, which may be found in religious creeds, with some propositions judged "unworthy of belief". That Christ was born is a fact, although who he was draws on our belief. Many different statements of belief can therefore be identified and they differ in the confidence they draw (Thouless, 1935). More caution is expressed about unusual facts than about traditional religious beliefs, as Table 4 shows. The linguistic cline "I think", "I believe", "I know" emphasizes that judgements about beliefs have been readily identified with different states of mind. Values, on the other hand, are identified through their judged worth or desirability. All these procedures involve judgements or states of mind. While religions are defined by their beliefs and creeds, other belief systems, like those referred to as "scientific", are deemed to be closer to facts that are checked by systematic observation rather than by argument, authority or a simple consensus. Yet science itself demands many assumptions, and preferences or fashions dictate the problems that are thought to be tractable, while doubt and uncertainty, or confidence and conviction are found in both science and religion. Comparisons between the political and religious connotations of a prophet who foretells, propagandists who persuade or aim for conversion, and the loyalty of those who are authoritarian could enlarge our understanding of the peculiar characteristics of religious believers.

Although the truth of religious beliefs is guaranteed by a tradition and supported by philosophical or theological argument, dogmatic theology and the history of the Church both show that sharp changes in religious systems took place at the time of the Reformation and again recently, following the Second Vatican Council. Industrial and scientific revolutions forced an accommodation, or at least a reaction from religion, by confronting the plausibility of some received positions and doctrines that may still be affecting the beliefs Church people profess. Scientific theories and findings, especially about evolution, have changed what many once took to be true and have forced new interpretations of traditional beliefs onto others, leaving only the adherents to fundamentalist positions holding concretely to the truths of traditional religion. While the unchanging nature of religious faith is still asserted by some, others positively enjoy the dialectic between the Bible (and its own evolution) and the social or ideological contexts within which it is now interpreted. This, together with dilemmas about the focus of religion on individuals or society, on myth or reality, emotion or intellect, piety or pragmatism, or on faith and works must be resolved if a coherent system is to develop with an immediacy that ensures its own validity. In that sense God might be less an object of our knowledge than a cause of our wonder.

Religious beliefs and personality

William James (1889), who identified an hypothesis as "anything proposed to our belief", classified hypotheses as "alive" or "dead", as likely to be true

Table 4 The mean certainty of different statements (after Thouless, 1935) and percentages in each denominational group in an Australian replication, with "a complete certainty that the belief is true" or, for items followed by -3, false

Group[a]	Item	Mean certainty		Complete certainty				
		Thouless	Brown	Nothing	Others	Methodist	C of E	RC
A	1 God	2.25	2.44	26	76	84	45	83
	2 Christ	2.27	2.43	15	76	87	52	96
	3 Spirit is real	2.40	2.22	30	59	55	50	79
	4 Created world	2.19	2.33	11	76	76	45	92
	5 Devil	2.19	1.98	11	47	24	17	50
	7 God is powerful	2.32	2.44	21	76	84	52	96
	8 God is good	2.38	2.42	23	79	84	52	98
	9 Angels	1.67	1.86	2	38	20	10	79
	10 Jonah	2.01	1.74	2	32	13	10	25
	14 Spirit survives death	2.07	2.24	13	59	67	40	88
	18 Sunday Church	1.82	1.73	0	24	33	21	58
	20 Christianity is better than Buddhism	1.80	1.70	6	50	44	19	63
	21 Bible literal	2.44	2.25	0	24	2	2	17
	22 Man responsible	2.62	2.63	64	65	73	62	83
	23 Hell	2.35	2.10	6	47	16	10	92
B	6 Matter is sole reality (-3)	2.25	2.06	23	44	62	50	83
	16 There is no God (-3)	2.34	2.55	34	79	95	74	92

Table 4 *continued*

Group[a]	Item	Mean certainty			Complete certainty			
		Thouless	Brown	Nothing	Others	Methodist	C of E	RC
C	11 Man evolved	2.23	2.11	30	29	44	52	8
	12 God is impersonal (-3)	1.89	1.91	21	56	60	29	58
	13 Evil a reality	2.32	2.21	19	65	62	5–	75
	19 Moses wrote the Pentateuch (-3)	1.30	1.24	17	12	31	19	13
	24 Spirits commune (-3)	1.66	1.61	15	38	33	13	25
	26 Evolution and religion compatible	2.17	2.11	26	41	62	50	50
D	28 Mary, Queen of Scots	1.22	0.67	6	3	7	10	4
	30 Tigers in China	1.23	1.20	6	3	16	2	4
	31 Hornets live in nests (-3)	1.21	1.60	19	26	35	33	21
	33 Light speed (-3)	2.01	1.94	47	29	38	33	29
	35 Green a primary colour	2.33	2.32	21	35	27	31	29
	40 National debt	1.82	0.51	6	6	5	5	4
	17 Expanding universe (-3)	0.95	1.14	11	12	15	19	17
	34 Bacon wrote Shakespeare (-3)	1.83	1.84	26	32	42	40	25
E	37 Leisured class (-3)	1.99	1.23	2	9	11	5	21
	38 Tariffs improve trade(-3)	1.72	0.98	4	3	7	4	
	39 India	1.78	1.34	12	12	20	7	4
F	15 Religion is like opium (-3)	2.07	1.81	13	32	49	12	54
	25 Right triumphs	2.01	1.80	13	50	60	24	79

Table 4 *continued*

Group[a]	Item	Mean certainty		Complete certainty				
		Thouless	Brown	Nothing	Others	Methodist	C of E	RC
G	27 Hardship strengthens	1.77	1.55	6	18	18	14	0
	29 Relativity	1.87	1.39	21	6	13	10	25
	32 Sex evil (-3)	2.48	2.68	74	82	87	71	88
	36 Sunlight good for health	2.83	2.59	68	76	76	67	54

[a]The grouping is that made by Thouless (1935). He called the groups **A** and **B**, religious beliefs; **C**, unorthodox religious beliefs; **D**, affectively indifferent non-religious beliefs; **E**, political beliefs; **F**, religious "tabloids"; **G**, non-religious "tabloids". The actual items are to be found in Brown (1962)

or not. Certainly, some hypotheses and beliefs are, for many people, as dead as E.S.P. (which is now being referred to by some of its proponents as "extended sensory perception") or astrology, because of the conflict between them and other beliefs or assumptions about, for example, the material world (Marks and Kammann, 1980). Others accept their potency. William James also distinguished forced or avoidable from momentous or trivial beliefs. To know or predict what makes Christianity, or any other religious system, a live or a dead option for somebody might resolve the fundamental problem of the psychology of religion but fail to explain why *particular* statements of belief, like "The world is rational", "There is a personal God", "The mind only knows its own ideas", "There is an endless chain of causes", carry conviction (James, 1912, p. 16) — unless the circularity of faith and factual belief itself helps to turn them into facts (ibid., p. 25). Psychologists now, however, approach such questions indirectly, despite the ways a person's beliefs are directly used to assess sanity or madness, through their certainty about the veridicality of what most others consider unbelievable or questionable. A few patients ask if the devil is winning in their head, whether their dreams are true or if the immaculate conception applies to them. The clearest phenomenology of religious abnormality is to be found among the paranoid delusions of reference, where egocentricity is beyond control and primitive beliefs (Rokeach, 1960) have been defined too broadly (or narrowly).

Rokeach assumed that personality traits lie behind the nature and structure of belief systems, and he distinguished between the ideological content and the structure of these systems in his search for content-free measures of Dogmatism and Opinionation (1960, p. 125). That analysis was derived from the authoritarian ideological structure that Adorno *et al.* (1950) identified. It has become commonplace for psychologists (and others) to assume that the beliefs or the information we hold, and the sources of that information become confused, especially when beliefs seem to resolve or compensate for our basic anxiety or alienation (Sullivan and Adelson, 1954). Agreed measurements are, however, essential to test the validity of such assertions, although Argyle and Beit-Hallahmi (1975) argued that "Since large proportions of the population are involved in religious behaviour and beliefs, we should not expect to find very large differences in personality between different groups" (p. 80), or (we might add) between those who hold different traditional beliefs.

Belief in a transcendental world is made plausible by the acceptance of those doctrines by the wider society that maintains them, and perhaps by individual experience rather than by any personality characteristics. Attempts by reformers who would modify existing systems of belief are resisted when they are in conflict, at least initially, with the received structures, as Luther, Galileo, Darwin, Freud and many others have found. More recent examples can be seen in the reactions to Pentecostalism and the charismatic movements, and in the reactions of religious and psychiatric establishments to "the new religious movements" (Richardson, 1985). Those developments have been distanced by describing their members as emotionally disturbed, although the actors themselves believe that they have discovered signs of divine intervention, a revelation, or a proper life-style for themselves. The religious variable has carried this ambiguity, for those who believe in de-programming as much as for those who on the day of Pentecost mocked, saying "these men are full of new wine" (Acts 2, 13).

Summary

Religion has been easy to interpret in psychological terms, usually to the detriment of the credibility of religion itself. Those criticisms may be changing because of a greater tolerance of religious differences, new perspectives on the analysis of religion and an increased realization that any religion is set within a socio-cultural context. While the psychology of religion has essentially been carried out within a Judeo-Christian framework, an increasingly empirical orientation to it has helped to reduce the prejudiced interpretations that were made largely in principle by the early psychologists of religion, for whom religion was a natural field in which to apply psychology itself. Only in the 1960s was religion fully aligned with the contemporary scientific study of psychology, with the canons of measurement being well satisfied and the conclusions not appearing to be partisan.

A clear recognition of what the psychology of religion might achieve was developed once distinctions were drawn between its basis in cognition or belief, experience and practice, and the effects or implications it has for other activities or functions. The extent to which religion is learned or taught lies behind, and influences the specific forms of any of those components, as does their integration into the concepts of self in such a way that religious belief does not simply suggest religious observance and accepting some traditional formulations. Our psychological formulations and findings may, however, be too tame to account for the political uses of religion to support divisions within and between countries. Religious believers (and their beliefs or personalities) have such evaluative strength and potency that we should probably consider using procedures and methods of assessment that are more directly observational than the verbally-based methods of self-report that have become standard in the psychology of religion.

3   Identifying the religious variable

> For at the moment when religion becomes conscious of religion, when it becomes a psychologically and historically conceivable magnitude in the world, it falls away from its inner character, from its truth to idols. (Karl Barth, 1957, p. 68)

Research begins by identifying or describing some phenomenon. To do that we need concepts, measurement techniques and a theoretical model of what is involved. Unless the data for a psychological account of religion are to be derived from the direct or unaided observation of religious behaviour, or from quite anecdotal evidence, special techniques are needed to capture them. Nevertheless, Schleiermacher among others suggested that religion is more involved with intuition and feeling than with thinking, action (or behaviour), and social processes. Despite Behaviorism's efforts to deny the relevance of self-reports, for most studies of religion, people themselves must be consulted. The fluctuations in their religious faith, is however, a mystery they do not explain any more easily than they can explain falling in love, except directly in terms of God's action or as their own fault.

The psychological methods developed since the time of Wundt, which allow subjective data about conscious processes and reactions to be reliably quantified, have been constructively applied in studies of religious and other responses. That such data can validly reflect internal states and processes is shown in recent work on the manipulation of mental images, which give data that are as potent as any behavioural reaction, through which of course they are mediated (Shepard, 1971).

Systematically collected evidence must, however, be interpreted in terms of a theory or model. Psychological theories are tested by their empirical and theoretical coherence, and whenever it is possible, against predictions. For most theories about religion, however, predictive tests may still be an ideal that is hard to satisfy. Behind any systematic theories there are numerous common-sense explanations of religious and other events that rest on prejudiced generalizations from a few instances, self-fulfilling interpretations of experience, or generalizations about the actions of people (cf. Scott and Lyman, 1970).

Reviews of the literature on the psychology of religion show that it has been especially vulnerable to these casual or unsubstantiated explanations (Godin, 1962; Klausner, 1964, 1970; Dittes, 1969; Flakoll, 1977; Capps *et al.*, 1976a) and that only about one-third of the papers published since 1950 report systematically empirical data. This may depend partly on the fact that religion itself carries many of its own explanations, since Christianity, for example, concerns the activities and the beliefs that flow from the revelation that God is able to do things and change people. The evidence that supports those beliefs is apprehended directly, or referred to tradition, reason, the examples of others, and by detecting consistent patterns in history or in one's own experience.

Empirical approaches

There is no shortage of empirical methods that have been used to study religion. Flakoll (1977) listed 20 separate approaches ranging from questionnaires through interviews, to biographies, content analysis, projective methods, observation rating scales, experiments, and a few specific procedures, like "reconstruction" (Stolz, 1973) that are no longer important. It is easy to criticize the methods that have been used, as when Warren (1977) gave special attention to the "paucity of experimental studies", the prevalence of correlational procedures, poorly designed studies and the extent to which the samples studied involved students or volunteers, the lack of control over extraneous variables, an over-generalization of findings and the absence of programmatic research. Other criticisms that have been made include the crudely worded questions or items, the artificiality of responding to them with a simple "agree" or "disagree", and the common failure even to try to establish the ecological or external validity of the scores or findings that are derived from them. Some limitations on any conclusions must, however, be recognized: as Vergote said, "everyone agrees that the psychology of religion sets aside the fact of the effective existence of God to whom religious rites and attitudes refer" (1969, p. 2), so that except in the apologetic uses of psychology, "the truth of the transcendent reality escapes the psychology of observation" (Godin, 1964a, p. 53). It might be possible, however, to make some assessment of the believed authenticity of a person's religious beliefs and of the experiences that bear on them.

Early studies in the psychology of religion had to find a way to move beyond the anecdotal and phenomenological approaches that were in common use in the late nineteenth century, as in G. Stanley Hall's (1904) study of conversion which focussed on individual constructions of reality, and in such enumerative surveys as the 1851 religious census in Britain (Inglis,

1960). The data that we need have to be both informative and replicable.

A counterpoint between description and theory soon developed in the psychology of religion. William James's cautiously descriptive analysis of *The Varieties of Religious Experience* (1902) contrasts against Sigmund Freud's theoretical reduction of religious practices to obsessional acts (1907), and the character of God as Father to projected parental images. Dittes (1972) interpreted this difference in approach to the investigators' sympathies with religion, James being predisposed towards it. Such an interpretation may be an oversimplification, since description should precede any scientific theorizing, which does not have to reduce or destroy the phenomena that are to be exposed or accounted for. McClelland and Atkinson (1953) noted that "the scientific mode of apprehending reality is only one possible mode" (p. 15), and he argued that "many problems can be solved only in terms of other approaches to reality, through aesthetics or religion, for instance" (pp. 15–16). Despite that, scientific results are able to alter convictions about the origins or the credibility of religious beliefs.

A search for the pure, mature forms of religion has driven many movements for religious reform, and led others to strip away "unwanted value judgements" in hoping to find an essential core (Dittes, 1971b). Dittes argued that it is this which lies behind the dichotomous orientations or perspectives on religion, in which one pole is pure religion and the other contaminated in some way. He cited Troeltsch's church-sect classification and Allport's intrinsic-extrinsic typology as specific examples, both of which show "a mistrust of established, acculturated religion and the celebration of primitive purity (which) is the classic prophetic posture" (ibid.). He also contrasted a "priestly" perspective on the path to a coherent analysis against the mystical approach which transcends but does not have to oppose religious institutions, since it relies on open or unstructured procedures. While it is not necessary to align any of these distinctions with specifically religious concepts, it is quite easy to do that because religious terms provide a ready model for describing ideological positions, and can point up one way in which extraneous attitudes influence decisions about what is worth investigating, which influence decisions about how to proceed.

There is still some prejudice against measurement in studies of religion, because it could destroy the mystery. This objection goes beyond the ethical constraints and practical difficulties that must be overcome before any study is possible. It is also important to understand how religious and scientific explanations interact, and to separate these domains epistemologically. Deconchy (1985) has begun that task in theoretical terms, and empirically (1982) with a study of the acceptability of experimental and observational evidence among religious subjects who were asked questions about the best ways to find how the natural world operates, by asking how one might establish how birds learn to sing. It is clear that religious dogma has protected religion itself as well as biology from strict experimental procedures.

Despite what Batson calls "an avalanche of descriptive and correlational data", there are still only a few experimental studies in the literature on religion, although psychologists are agreed that they provide the soundest basis from which to draw conclusions. While a few still argue that experiments are not possible within religion, because it entails an organismic variable and cannot become a treatment variable, an increasing number of experiments is being reported, since cause and effect cannot be disentangled by using simple correlational analyses. Path analysis and multivariate procedures allow some progress to be made, and while it may always be hard to validate all the different theories about religion, it should be possible to find some empirical support for any theoretical model.

Implicit theories

While it is thought to be unethical to expose religious people to different religious conditions in the name of science, it is quite usual to "try out" new approaches to evangelism or the liturgy and to make other changes in principle and in the name of religion itself. The basic problems and even the need and the ease with which the acceptability and effectiveness of change might be evaluated by experimental or quasi-experimental procedures are seldom considered.

When Dittes (1977) asked why there are more studies of various religious types than criticisms or attacks on typological constructs, he found an answer in our implicit theories about religion, and, we might add, in theories about personality and the philosophy of science. So Mancias and Secord (1983) argue that new heuristics are forcing the acceptance of a "realist theory of science" (Bhaskar, 1978) that rejects a covering law model of scientific explanation and its "attending instrumentalist idea that explanation and prediction are symmetrical". One feature of this approach is the integration of "subjective" and "objective", which has profound implications for understanding behavioural and other responses that are socially or ideologically based. Since social structures as well as language, and religious or other beliefs "pre-exist" each individual, they must be reproduced and transformed when anybody accepts or enacts them. While these structures can support meaningful and intentional action they are also "coercive and limit the ways we can act". A similar ambiguity can be found in religion, and in other domains like politics or health care, with their established traditions and structures that allow and perhaps encourage different attitudes, intentions, and consequences for apparently similar beliefs, whether they concern the prerequisites for a healthy life-style, or the nature of salvation, "man" and prayer. While Godin (1968) identified conservative, purifying and symbolist attitudes to prayer, Allport (1966) showed that religion can both make and unmake prejudice. These ambiguities can be resolved categorically and authoritatively, or they can be regarded as steps in an open-ended process of understanding. Godin (1971) therefore identified the developmental tasks behind religion as producing an historical consciousness, identifying relationships between material signs and spiritual meanings, transforming a magical or superstitious mentality into a life of faith, reducing moralism, and purifying the Christian beliefs that are based on ambiguous parental images (pp. 141 ff.). To achieve any of these transformations requires a willingness to do so and presupposes that society or a particular tradition gives permission for change, even if the tradition might itself change in the process, as happened during Vatican II (Curran, 1963).

While someone may assume that a religious experience is unique, it must have been prepared for in psychological or social terms, if it is to be plausible. Identifying how that is possible, deciding where to focus an understanding and how that can be captured are important problems. While systematic study might clarify the meaning of religious experience or belief, at least to those who are directly involved (Berger, 1971), there is a variety of perspectives on how that might be done best.

Theoretical perspectives

Sociology distinguishes the structural and functional perspectives (another typology) that are found classically in the work of Weber, who looked for the meanings of religion, and Durkheim who stressed the roles of ritual in group identity. The early psychologists of religion (Hall, Coe, Leuba, and Ames) were also in a functionalist tradition in the sense that they were concerned with the place of religion in adaptation, and adopted an implicity individual model to describe what "being religious" means. That approach later embraced the broadly psychoanalytic and psychiatric perspectives that Strunk (1962, p. 108) thought led away from an empirical basis for the psychology of religion to the direct interpretations of observed phenomena and a neglect of the importance of the social contexts or situations in which religion becomes most relevant.

Methodologists now distinguish emic from etic approaches, or they refer to actors' and observers', or insiders' and outsiders' views. Dittes (1969, p. 619 f.) aligned those contrasts in the study of religion with an emphasis on the spiritual life or on the public, formal and explicit nature of religion. Each perspective yields different conclusions so that the outsiders' view is identified with a unitary religious variable while the data from insiders throw up several independent religious factors, which will be considered in Ch. 5 (cf. Dittes, 1969, p. 609). Each of those patterns depends on the degree of homogeneity of the subjects, the content of the questions they are asked, and the methods that are used to find or impose structure on the data. Behind those effects lies the subjects' assumptions and experience of what "religion" is about and the meaning of religious concepts, like God's "responsibility". The social position of the subjects is also important: religious leaders or people closely involved with religion will have different conceptions of it from those on the periphery (cf. Fichter, 1954). Asch (1952) and Doise (1978) are among those who recognized the effects of the source or the authority behind a questionnaire on the replies that are given to it, while Deconchy (1980) showed that implicit social controls shape the information that can be elicited from the insiders to any "orthodox" system or context.

Although some of our interest must be in the differences between religious and non-religious people we can expect the responses of both groups to be patterned in part by their social alignments, and in the ways their responses are categorized. Those categorizations may be quite formal: Rauff (1979, p. 6) writes that "A Cathoic who has been baptised in the Church is considered a member, even though he or she might not have attended Church for several years. ... Baptism is the authentic entrance and the indelible incorporation into the Church." Such a fixed definition does not allow those who have been baptized to lapse even if they become unbelieving. A less formal criterion of membership can be found by relying on "God's activity, moving one to faith, and on the individual's applying the Spirit's invitation to himself or herself and accepting it" (ibid., p. 8). The subjects' own identification has also been accepted, in terms of whether they call themselves Methodists, Catholics or "None", how they describe their practices, beliefs or inner state (cf. Hood, 1975) and other characteristics.

These self-reports must form the primary data for any psychology of religion, whether the material is offered spontaneously and however its collection is aided or controlled. Exceptions are found when theological or ecclesiastical systems are directly interpreted in psychological terms, as in Jung's (1958) "psychological approach to the dogma of the Trinity" or in his analysis of the "Transformation symbolism in the Mass". The effects of editing any data pervades the processes by which it is gathered. Summarizing the data begins with an investigator's decision about what and whom to study, while the subjects make their own decisions about the relevant or appropriate answers they should give, and whether they will cooperate at all. The final encoding and reduction of the data is only one stage in this process. The importance of the setting, the investigators' characteristics (Hunsberger and Ennis, 1982) and probably their theoretical perspectives on the religious ideas that are expressed or detected cannot be overemphasized (Capps, 1980). Every enquiry imposes its own demands, and Deconchy (1980) has clearly shown that an explicitly approved or disapproved source for any study determines whether the group members will respond to it in a divergent or convergent manner. Any report of the findings must blend the voices of individuals.

The positivism of psychology, which stresses numbers (in which the Churches are also interested), has largely eliminated the possibility of capturing what Alvarez (1984) calls "the hesitant, double-tracked, qualified answers which emerge from a conversation between two consenting adults", except when researchers themselves, in their efforts after meaning suspend their demands or hope for reliable, reproducible and, hopefully, valid data, and continue to ask questions that do not entirely disregard spontaneously expressed ideas in favour of the reproducibility of rated responses. Both of these group and individual perspectives should somehow be preserved. Thurstone (1954) recognized that problem when he said that a person should really be asked for his attitudes privately when he is free to speak his mind and is not likely to be quoted. It is simply for convenience that we take the opinions that can be elicited anonymously to be more honest, true or real. In that connection Alvarez (1984, p. 16) quoted Freud, who said of neuroses, "All cases are unique and similar": they are "similar to the observer, unique to the participants".

To take religious membership or identity as a socio-demographic category or independent variable also disguises the extent to which it, unlike age and sex, embodies both informal and confused as well as quite formal definitions. Grassby (1984) reported on a 19 year old who told him that:

> I only discovered two years ago what my religion is. I had to enter hospital and they required me to state my religion on the form of admittance. I recalled that as a child I had attended Sunday School at St. Stephen's on the corner and I made enquiries and found it was Presbyterian, so I put down Presbyterian. Because I was under 18 my mother also completed a hospital form and she put down my religion as Methodist, because she had been a Methodist originally. This confused the hospital who rang home and spoke to my father. He told them I had been baptised in the Church of England of which he was a member. I have not yet been to a Church of England.

Religious behaviour

In 1963, Douglas (p. 81) offered the uncritical use of data collection methods as one reason why the psychology of religion failed to develop after about 1925, adding to that explanation a change of interest towards positivistic world views and away from a humanistic understanding, and the lack of a general psychological theory that could embrace the psychology of religion. Those problems were tied to the subjectivity of religion and a disregard for the content and structure of religious beliefs themselves. The early interest in religion was eclipsed by a developing concern for psychological processes that were amenable to behavioural analyses. Until quite recently, the interest in learning, perception, social influence, and even suggestion, drew attention away from the actual material that was to be learnt and from the differential effects of social contexts (see Argyle *et al.*, 1981) to the processes themselves. But verbal learning, for example, is now preoccupied with natural language and not with learning lists of "nonsense syllables".

While some still believe that what people say about their feelings is less important than what they will do, direct observation of religious behaviour has discovered little about its psychological meaning or significance, beyond its apparent coherence or consistency (F. H. Allport, 1934). Because most public religious actions conform to prescribed "orders of service", it is quite hard to find religious behaviour outside those contexts. Even then its intentionality can be ambiguous, as when votive candles are being lit (Godin, 1964). Indeed it was the repetitiveness of religious behaviour that enabled Freud (1907) to over-interpret religion as a universal obsessional neurosis, without recourse to any intentionality. (Against Freud's analysis is the traditional Christian view that since we would forget we must continue to "Do this in remembrance of me ...".)

The recent interest in non-verbal cues to meaning has not yet been systematically applied to religion, although Marketa Luskacova's photographs of pilgrims travelling between Prague and Slovakia give an eloquent account of one traditional form of religious piety and devotion (Fuller, 1984). Psychologists have not, however, turned their attention to the possible uses of such data.

To find the attitudes, or the behavioural intentions that lie behind any action, and to decide whether the Mass, for example, is an obsession or a deeply symbolic expression of worship (and whether it might be both), we must identify the meanings that it carries for the priest and for his congregation. These attitudes can only be elicited through direct enquiries among those who participate (or communicate). As Malony put it, "religion is that which an individual says he does in relation to the divine" (1977, p. 359). While the validity of that may be left open or deliberately distorted, it is evaluated and assessed by those who decide who will be accepted for ordination, and even for other religious offices, as much as it is judged by those who must decide that a person's religious behaviour is pathological, psychotic, immature or faked up. Hartshorne and May (1928), however, showed very clearly from their tests of cheating and other forms of dishonesty, and from measures of moral knowledge and social background that were administered to several thousand children aged from eight to 16, that the intercorrelations among their tests were low. They concluded that "The mere urging of honest behaviour by teachers or the discussion of standards and ideals of honesty, no matter how much such general ideas may be 'emotionalized' has no necessary relation to the control of conduct" (p. 412).

Judgements about religious practice and belief will always have practical and political as well as moral implications, but uncertainty about the meaning of religious behaviour is typically resolved by appeals to psychological arguments that make reference to an internal state (even if it is dissimulated). So Paul, when accused of madness by Festus said, "I am not mad, most noble Festus; I but speak forth the words of truth and soberness" (Acts 26, 25). This is a further instance of the ambiguity of any religious statement or experience.

When unusual phenomena are to be investigated (as in Samarin's study of glossolalia, 1972) or the investigator cannot enlist the support of a group for some detailed study, non-reactive methods (Webb *et al.*, 1966) and even participant observation offer other approaches to the analysis of what can be said or done in particular situations. These have become the classical methods for anthropologists, and although they may be time-consuming they stay close to the context of what is to be studied. Heelas (1985) has shown that anthropologists' interpretations of such data from traditional societies usually rely on untestable psychological interpretations that are too readily generalized from formal psychological theories. Sociologists have also used these methods to study groups that are involved with spiritualism or Pentecostalism and at revival meetings (Stolz, 1937), although there are traps, as when one observer who was using a Bible as a cover for his note-taking was assumed to be so strongly influenced that he was invited to lead the next meeting. Some modification of these procedures might, however, allow psychologists to develop or establish the ecological validity of their hypotheses, and of the specific measures they use to test them.

Summary

It is neither easy nor straightforward to identify religious variables, except at the level of social prejudice or when we complain about another's religiousness. Yet the "religious variables" must be able to capture and carry empirical analyses of religion which acquire their meaning within some other religious, psychological or social context. Operationalizations of religion have, however, been made directly with reference to the frequency of church-going or through variables that combine the answers to separate questions, whether empirically or *a priori*. Scientific procedures are not the only way to catch hold of reality, since insight and experience are religiously recognized sources of inspiration. The priestly perspective of one who *knows* contrasts against the strength of a prophetic criticism that rests only on the person's own authority. Another important perspective is that of the observer who, as a detached outsider, lacks the privileged knowledge of any insider. Those separate perspectives differentially recognize the religion found in self-reports, theory-dominated measures, controlled observations, socially-defined actions and hidden intentions. The practical, moral and political implications of any perspective should not be neglected since they give their own meaning to what can be discovered.

4   The measurement of religion

Many years ago Dr. Starbuck tried to enlist my sympathies in his statistical enquiry into the religious ideas and experiences of the circumambient population. I fear that to his mind I rather damned the whole project with my words of faint praise. The question-circular method of collecting information had already, in America, reached the proportion of an incipient nuisance ... So few minds have the least spark of originality that answers to questions scattered broadcast would be likely to show a purely conventional content. The writer's ideas ... would be ... historically and not psychologically based ..." (William James in the preface to E. D. Starbuck's *The Psychology of Religion*. London: Walter Scott, 1901, p. xii).

The basic methods of data collection for any psychology of religion (Flakoll, 1977) depend on observing relevant behaviour or evoking reactions to religious materials by self-reports, interpretations of partially structured stimuli or scaled ratings (cf. Kidder, 1981). The oldest approach simply counts the numbers of people in defined groups (e.g. Numbers 13, 25–31), or those at church, their time of arrival and what they do there (Allport, 1934). Such data could give some index of piety or simply show conformity with the local rules and customs. These observational methods contrast with individuals' reports of the reasons for action, or about their beliefs, attitudes, feelings and experiences (Hay, 1982).

Each of these approaches has a long history, and statistical data in particular have been used to assess the continued support of one or another religion. So Argyle and Beit-Hallahmi (1975, p. 88) documented the declining levels of religious activity in Britain with reference to Church membership, Sunday School attendance and Bible reading. Other measures of religious activity include professed belief, the frequency of prayer, size of donations and the numbers of published articles that are favourable to religion. Since observations and reports of behaviour and attitudes readily intertwine, they give the correlations that are an important criterion for the validity of any single measure.

Religious observance

Although religious observance might be declining in Britain, the *Psychological Abstracts* show that studies of religion continue to increase. Klausner's (1964) count of the methods of data collection in studies of the psychology and sociology of religion published in the United States between 1950 and 1960 found that self-administered questionnaires (44 per cent) and individual interviews (26 per cent) were the most common techniques, followed by statistical records (19 per cent), content analyses (ten per cent) and field observations (nine per cent). "Laboratory experimental methods" accounted for only two per cent of the total, and across all these papers measures of personality factors formed the most common dependent variables (47 per cent). Since that time experimental procedures have established themselves in the psychology of religion (Deconchy, 1985), although attitude-type scales or questionnaires with closed alternative answers are still the method of choice. Bassett *et al.* (1981) summarized the characteristics of the 107 scales that "potentially discriminate Christians from non-Christians" they found in their survey of 95 separate papers since Thurstone and Chave (1929) developed their scaled measure of attitude to the Church. Bassett shows that less than half of them had been evaluated for their reliability and validity, a point that is also made by Robinson and Shaver (1973) about the 17 religious scales they reviewed, which cover religious commitment and orientations, beliefs, attitudes and values.

While the data from these procedures have been used descriptively, as in opinion polls (Abrams *et al.*, 1985), or to test hypotheses about, for example, altruism (Batson and Ventis, 1982), none of them is theologically or religiously neutral. Thus Elizabeth Isichei (1970) argued that when the Quakers acknowledged a place for historical studies they had given up their directly eschatological orientation, having recognized that secular, political and institutional involvements were necessary. Furthermore, the results of psychological measures of religion might not be conclusive because they are unable to tap directly into the belief states and intentions that are central to religious understanding itself. That problem might, however, be resolved if methods analogous to those developed by Shepard (1971; Cooper and Shepard, 1973) to study mental imagery could adequately externalize a religious perspective or its operation. Until then the best procedure is to improve the tests of psychological theories about religion and to identify the specific social and personal contexts within which it functions.

The numbers of people going to church, how much money they give and the time they spend there, the numbers of children or adults baptized, and the "acts of communion" (cf. Bouma, 1983, pp. 22–23) help to define those contexts, and perhaps improve the "marketing" of religion and monitor its support and material achievements. Such data from parish and other records have, however, hardly been touched by psychologists, who have been little interested in social or economic behaviour at that level. Yet Currie *et al.*'s (1977) analysis of Church growth in Britain since 1700 stresses the paradox that this growth depends on adherents who at the very least believe they have some independence of action, and "can perceive the utility (sic) of church membership", with its "cultic function relating to the performance of religious rites deemed to be valid and efficacious" and to the "non-cultic aspects of the church's existence as an organisation" (p. 7).

Beyond those explicit and reactive methods a continuing search for valid non-reactive or disguised procedures (Webb *et al.*, 1966) has proved of little value to psychologists of religion who still depend on direct methods and descriptive or theoretical starting points that have adopted either outside or inside perspectives on religion. Their theories about religion have been produced *a priori* or developed empirically (Dittes, 1969) but the progress has been so slow that Malony (1976) called for new approaches to theory, to the subjects who are studied and the techniques and dependent measures that are used, to bring the psychology of religion as close to the rest of psychology as it was in the early part of the century.

Church people seem to be suspicious of controlled studies, preferring direct questions with an obvious purpose or aim. That is not a new problem, and Deconchy (1981) stressed the functional censorship that appears when studies impinge on confessional interests, while Clark (1958, p. 39) noted the protectedness of religion. Despite that, quantitative research has increased our understanding beyond any findings that qualitative procedures can establish, whether religion is being taken as an independent or as a dependent variable.

Ploch (1974) notes that the use of religion as an independent variable has centred on differences between religious groups and on the effects of religiosity (or rather religious orthodoxy). Major studies include Lenski's *The Religious Factor* (1961), and Glock and Stark's (1965) work. Ploch criticized these studies for exaggerating the differences between religious groups and neglecting the within-group variance, and for accumulating separate indices without attempting the causal modelling and path analysis that sociologists now rely on. He also stressed that "continuing to center on matters of verbalized doctrine and belief is to focus on matters of public rhetoric which may bear a different relation to social reality than nonverbalized beliefs" (p. 282). As a sociologist Ploch might have implicity expected too much from the non-verbal research procedures.

Verbal measures

Gorsuch (1984) argues that "carefully chosen single item questions (like, 'How often do you go to church?') can be as effective as long, extensive questionnaires", while Fishbein and Ajzen (1975) showed that a "single-item self report measure shows approximately the same median correlation – 0.76 – with the other scales as do those full-length scales with each other" (Gorsuch, *loc. cit.*). Gorsuch believes that this occurs because religion is a widely discussed phenomenon, but it could also be that the details and facts of our religious denomination, frequency of church-going or prayer, and the time or money spent on Church-related activities are categorical and readily disclosed. Such easily encoded information neglects the orientations to religion, and the meanings or limitations on the beliefs that those involved with it might want to express. Perhaps it was because of the stereotyped nature of those formal responses that some people have rejected them in favour of spontaneous expressions of opinion, although questionnaires have become intrinsic to the empirical study of religion (Gorsuch, 1984). These measures are shared with sociologists, and allow direct comparisons of the responses of individuals and groups, although the sociologists seem to prefer extensive (rather than intensive) investigations and use *a priori* scales of measurement to develop theories at a macroscopic level. Psychologists have preferred empirical scaling procedures based on formal psychometric models and they are acutely aware of the difficulties of independently validating what is said (beyond its internal consistency) and the bias that is introduced by any questioning procedure. While it is better to ask, "Is religion important to you?" than "Are you interested in religion?", investigators assume a naive, and even passive subject who will faithfully answer whatever questions are asked, despite the response biases from acquiescence and social desirability that were found by Hartshorne and May (1928) in the responses of Sunday School children, who said they would not cheat on an arithmetic test, although they did so. A religious training seems to make children especially sensitive to the "correct" answers and they act as if they think they can avoid detection.

A firm empirical tradition in the psychological study of religion was consolidated by Thurstone's use of psychophysics as a model for attitude measurement, which had begun with Starbuck's (1897) questionnaire-based studies of conversion, at that time an important Protestant phenomenon. (Incidently, it is not clear why the French "questionnaire", which dates from 1908 and is defined in the Shorter Oxford Dictionary as a "formal list of questions (especially in an official enquiry)" has come to be preferred over the English "questionary" that was in use from 1653. Nor is it obvious why an empirical research tradition did not develop within Catholicism until the

1950's, although an answer may be found in the central control of Catholic theology and epistemology.)

In 1896, Leuba published a "Questionnaire for a study of conversion" that was sent "to persons who were thought to have 'experienced religion', to mission leaders and pastors, and through them to a large class which we could not have reached directly". From it he identified "typical and striking cases". Starbuck, on the other hand, was more systematic. He said that, "In order to get together a number of typical cases of sudden awakenings, to compare them, to discover what life forces are at work and to see where they belong from the standpoint of modern psychology, ... [a] ... list of ... [eleven] ... questions was sent out promiscuously" (1897). The answers were carefully summarized, and Elmer T. Clark (1929) repeated that study to establish the changes over 30 years. In 1906 J. B. Pratt published the results of a questionnaire study of the nature and meaning of religious beliefs, and William James's (1926) answers to it are published with his *Letters*. A summary of Pratt's results are published in the second number of G. Stanley Hall's *American Journal of Religious Psychology and Education* (1906–1907).

Leuba (1896) also used interviews, a method that is, of course, closely aligned with questionnaires, but, as Johnson (1957, p. 21) put it, which have the advantage of "sharpening issues in face to face conversation". Both questionnaires and interviews are more systematic methods than relying simply on what is recorded in diaries or autobiographies, which William James (1902) used as his source of vivid data to exemplify experience and belief. Such writing usually involves unusual, even legendary figures, although the growing interest in oral history could be giving a voice to those who do not write freely, or who are not well-known. That is not, however, a psychological method, although such direct statements of attitude and belief are an essential source for the items in sophisticated measurement scales.

Flakoll (1977, p. 83) refers to the resolution passed by a meeting of experimental psychologists at the University of Pennsylvania in 1926 which deplored "the increasing practice of collecting administrative or supposedly scientific data by way of questionnaires". While tension and disagreements over appropriate methods for the study of religion have continued (e.g. Batson, 1976), guiding principles are readily available for framing questions, sampling subjects, analyzing and reporting results (cf. Lemon, 1973). Although formal attitude scales show better reliability than either questionnaires or interviews, guided interview schedules are not necessarily unreliable, as the "present state examination" for psychiatric diagnosis shows (Wing, 1974), and they are an essential pilot stage in any enquiry. Gorsuch (1984) argues that better progress will be made by refining a few agreed scales than by continuing to diversify the measures and approaches to what are essentially the same few religious variables.

Survey methods

Survey methods are not a recent invention (cf. 2 Samuel 24, 1–17), although they are now widely used to establish and describe characteristics of defined groups. Argyle and Beit-Hallahmi (1975), for example, used the reported differences between men and women to test psychological theories about the role of guilt, projection, socialization and social influence in religion (pp. 71–79). The reports of Charles Y. Glock's survey-based Research Program in Religion and Society from the Survey Research Center at the University of California, Berkeley, have been reviewed by Hargrove *et al.* (1973), and Andrew M. Greeley's studies from the Center for the Study of American Pluralism and the National Opinion Research Center of the University of Chicago include *The Denominational Society* (1972), *Ecstacy: A Way of Knowing* (1974), *Catholic Schools in a Declining Church* (1976), and more since then.

The direct effects on Church members of the recent liturgical changes, and the effectiveness of Church-based educational programmes might have been monitored by survey methods, although the Churches, which are sensitive to their members' opinions because of being essentially voluntary organizations, seem to prefer less formal methods of evaluation. Changes to liturgies, for example, have been introduced on an "experimental" basis, which assumes further modification without clearly identifying what is needed before any action will be taken. Liturgical change is probably thought to involve an evolutionary process that is immune to disconfirmation (cf. Dix, 1960). Other surveys have established the social differentiations that are part of the Church's social structure, and have been used to build social maps for a geograpy of religion (Gay, 1971) or to improve the Church's mission (Berger, 1967). The tradition of Gallup polling that began in the 1930s has assumed an important role in documenting gross social and attitudinal changes, including responses to religion (cf. Mol, 1985).

The success of any survey rests initially on the quality of the questions and on the sample that is drawn. Some of their inherent limitations may be overcome by supplementing formal surveys with panel methods in which the same participants are repeatedly interviewed for detailed and continuing study (cf. Kidder, 1981).

Typical instructions for survey-type studies ask for "your first response", deliberately trying to avoid careful reflection but giving defined categories for the responses. It could be, however, that religious people differ on this very dimension of reflectiveness, and that the differences between our first response and what is said later might well be aligned with a search for meaning and a tolerance of new information. What is said also depends on the attitude to the survey itself. Whatever approach is adopted, surveys usually rest on the responses of a large number of subjects, and explore the various aspects of social involvement, and how class or cultural context influence and limit religious expressions.

Theoretical models of measurement

The first phase in developing systematic measures of religion followed an *intuitive model* that was directed by a common sense knowledge of religion, tested against the reactions of those who could be persuaded to cooperate in various studies.

A development of this procedure framed alternative answers that embodied the common or theoretically important replies, and subjects were told to choose the alternative closest to their own position, or to use yes or no categories to give their answer to each alternative. This *public opinion model* of measurement is still widely used, and not only by sociologists. For example, Benson (1981), an historian, in a paper on "The Polls: a rebirth of religion?" refers to data from the Princeton Research Center which, he says, "has become perhaps the most prestigious institution dealing with public attitudes to religion", to argue that there has been little change in religious responding, using George Gallup Jr.'s seven indicators of religion. These indicators cover confidence in organized religion, religious identification, Church or Synagogue membership and attendance, the importance of religion in personal life, perceptions of the influence of religion on society, and the salience of religion in society. Each of these components was reported as a separate variable, and no attempt has been made to integrate them, although they seem to be coherent. Not only have they been used continuously since the 1940s, they are easily administered, and the answers have been tabulated against religious preference, age, education, race and other sociodemographic variables.

George Gallup pioneered scientific polling techniques as a method of assessing public opinion by means of sample surveys, and beginning in 1935 he sponsored weekly reports on the state of public opinion on national issues in the USA that continue to appear in newspapers: one of his most important contributions was to show that comparatively small but representative samples can provide both reliable and valid data about replies from the whole population.

An escape from intuitive analyses and interpretation based on answers to direct questions about beliefs or experiences was achieved by the development of attitude scaling models. Bogardus (1927) was among the first to apply the concept of a "scale" to attitude measurement, and his social distance scale is the classic technique to assess attitudes toward ethnic groups. It consists of cumulative but *a priori* steps that define degrees of social acceptability. These steps were defined as answers to questions about admitting members of specific national or other groups "To close kinship by marriage", "To my club", "As neighbours", or "Would exclude them from my country".

A refined method of cumulative scoring was developed by Guttman (1950) on the assumption that an appropriate set of items measuring a single dimension or trait can be ordered along a continuum of magnitude, with a subject's position on the scale defined by the most favourable item that would be accepted. On a perfect Guttman scale an individual necessarily endorses all items below the most favourable one that is agreed to, so that knowing the number of items checked should identify the specific items that have been checked. Since this method also tests whether a unitary dimension can be formed for a domain, the first task is to establish if subjects respond to a set of items in accordance with a "scale type" assumption of unidimensionality. The method therefore rests on the items that have been selected forming a cumulative scale. The Guttman procedure has only occasionally been used for religious data, perhaps because of the difficulties in conceptualizing a single scale from the expected diversity of religious responses. Yinger cited Golden *et al.*'s (1960) scale as an example, the steps being, "Need for religious faith", "I believe in a divine God", "Church or religion 'has its own personality' (something over and above individual members)", and "Religion is expected to be a major source of satisfaction in life." The less arduous method of factor analysis is now the most commonly used procedure to identify the implicit structure of any scale.

Yet it was the access to directly quantifiable data that broke the reliance of social scientists on introspection and self-report as the primary data for studies of religion and other important social domains. This was made possible by the application of the psychophysical methods to psychological or subjective judgements.

Thurstone's scaling procedure

Thurstone and Chave (1929, p. 2) note that, "Cattell seems to have been the first to have extended the psychophysical methods to stimuli other than simple sensory values" by applying it to "the estimated degrees of eminence of scientific men". Using the law of comparative judgement and the method of equal-appearing intervals they developed a "univocal measure" of attitudes to the Church and showed by it that attitudes can be scaled and "values measured". Not only was their method widely accepted, it aligned measures of religion with the main body of psychology. In 1939 Chave published a manual of 52 separate measures of different facets of religion.

Thurstone also developed the centroid method of factor analysis which allowed an identification of the structure of primary social attitudes. Ferguson (1939) and later Kirkpatrick (1949) and Sanai (1952) used that factor analytic method to identify a "religionism" factor which contrasted religiously related against non-religious and political items in the same questionnaire.

Thurstone's actual scaling procedure has, however, been largely disregarded now in favour of simpler, more direct Likert-type measures which still assume that attitude dimensions are latent variables indicated by action or by verbally stated opinions. Thurstone said that because opinions are multi-dimensional, "they cannot all be represented in a linear continuum" (1931) so that "All that we can do with an attitude scale is to measure the attitude actually expressed with the full realization that the subject may be consciously hiding his true attitude or that social pressure of the situation has made him really believe what he expresses" (ibid.). This formulation seems to have been forgotten by those searching for behavioural evidence for the attitudes that are held, as was Thurstone's statement that "It is, of course, not to be expected that every person will find only one single opinion on the whole scale that he is willing to endorse and that he will reject all the others" (p. 15).

Thurstone's scaling procedure is time-consuming and entails collecting a large number of items relating to the object to be assessed and having them judged for their relative favourableness, either by a paired comparison procedure if there are only a few items, or by assigning them to nine or eleven ordered categories. Items with known values are then selected to form a scale, and the respondents are asked to identify the items they accept or agree with. Their attitude score is the median scale value of the items they have selected.

Because Thurstone's scales give scores that correlate highly with those obtained from the simpler Likert-type scales, they have been almost completely replaced by summated scales (Likert, 1932). Nevertheless, one can not only identify an individual's score and group means from a Thurstone scale, but the range that is tolerated, the popularity of each statement for designated groups and the homogeneity of attitudes within a group can also be deduced from the scale values of the items that are accepted.

Thurstone (1954) said that a person's expressed opinion does not "thereby imply that he will necessarily act in accordance with the opinions he has endorsed" and that "we shall assume that it is of interest to know what people *say* that they believe even if their conduct turns out to be inconsistent with their professed opinions". This necessary limitation on attitude measurement and theory was also forgotten and a great deal of unproductive effort went into checking the validity of attitude and other measures against actual behaviour (cf. Lalljee *et al.*, 1984). Social constraints influence when, and what attitudes or beliefs can be expressed, and in that sense, attitude measures are simply a microcosm of social action, since they are used in conversation and social interaction to establish a position and foster an argument.

Edwards and Kenney (1946) compared scores on Thurstone and Chave's original attitude toward the Church scale with Likert's summated rating scale method of measurement. They found that a 25 item Likert scale had a slightly higher reliability (0.94 compared with 0.88), and that the Likert scores correlated 0.74 and 0.92 with two parallel forms of the Thurstone scale. Green (1954, p. 365), however, criticized such direct comparisons for failing to recognize that the item-operating characteristics required by the two methods are not strictly comparable since Thurstone-type items are non-monotonic and Likert items are monotonic.

Likert's scaling method

In Likert's (1932) technique of attitude assessment, subjects respond to a set of items by indicating the strength of their agreement or disagreement, usually on a five — or seven — point rating scale, from strongly disagree (-3) through neutral (0) to strongly agree ($+3$). It is assumed that "each item is a linear (or at least monotonic) function of the same attribute ... [and that] ... the relation of any item to the (presumably) common attribute is ordinarily established by correlational procedures" (Scott, 1968, p. 219). Items showing the best correlations with the total score are then included in the final scale. Scott warns that the results will be deceptive if the initial scale is made up from independent clusters of roughly equal portions of the total: "whether that is so can be established by examining the inter-correlations of the items, or by a factor analysis. Continued refinement of these scales is needed, and it is a process in which judgement, theory and the data from independent samples of subjects are important." Scott (p. 220) refers to:

> This cyclic process of writing items, intercorrelating responses, and reconceptualizing the construct ... [which] may continue for quite some time before a satisfactory cluster of mutually intercorrelated items results. A common reason to show convergence is the researcher's stubborn clinging to a preconception of what constitutes the relevant attitudinal domain.

Packaged computer programs have made it easy to factor analyse items, and so identify those that belong together, generating weighted scores from the factors or from arithmetic weights assigned to a factor's items. An advantage, or hazard of Likert scaling is the way heterogeneous items can now be readily assembled into *a priori* scales, with the latent variables identified by factor analysis. Scales produced in this way require little forethought beyond collecting items that are assumed to bear on the variable. Yet a strength of Likert's response procedures is their suitability for assessing attitudes and beliefs as well as factual knowledge, and the ease with which separate sets of items can be written to cover a range of variables and targets or issues. The breadth of these measures is well-illustrated by Bassett *et al.*'s (1981) list of 93 references to scaled measures of religious belief, behaviour, knowledge, affiliation, validity, religiosity (defined by them as the importance of religion in a person's life), attitudes, orientations, and experience.

Dittes notes that questions about religion are more readily answered if they refer to buildings, money, staff and church attendance than to the sense of religion in life among those who are strongly involved or committed to a Church, or to the ultimate and intimate aspects of life (1971b, p. 11). He also notes that some studies commissioned by Churches have been carried out in a way which leaves the research subjects "much as mediaeval people were 'subjects' of a king" (ibid.), by having preconceived categories imposed on them. The recent denominational studies by Johnson (1983) and Chiffister and Marty (1983) retain that emphasis.

Strommen *et al.*'s (1972) "portrait or mirror" of Lutherans in the United States was a study financially supported by the Lutheran church, based on 740 questionnaire items, answered in 1970 by a representative sample of 4,475 adults aged from 15 to 65. That questionnaire information was supplemented by interviews with at least three people in each of the 316 congregations that were visited. Strommen *et al.* identified 78 separate dimensions that formed 64 basic scales and 14 sub-scales, which yielded 14 factors "relating to what Lutherans believe, value, aspire to, and do". They noted the diversity of the responses, although the majority of subjects were found to hold a transcendental world view, with a vision of a dependable, controllable world and the desire for a life of detachment from the world, and only a minority viewing religion as a means of "self-development" (see their Ch. 8). Their account of these findings covers values, beliefs (and misbeliefs), opinions, and attitudes towards institutional loyalty, mission and ministry, self and others, and to life styles and self-reported behaviour. This massive collection of scales that were applied to a single denomination matches King and Hunt's work (King, 1967) which was based on Methodism in the United States, and which Dittes described in 1969 as "the most thorough mapping yet of religious space" (p. 611).

Using 121 carefully formulated items, King identified 11 factors in the responses of a large sample of Southern Methodists. As Dittes (1969, p. 611) described them:

> The first three (credal assent and personal commitment, participation in con-
> gregational activities, and personal religious experience) correspond remark-
> ably closely to the first three of Glock's proposed dimensions (which involved
> religious beliefs, practice, and feeling, as well as knowledge, and the effects of
> religion). Most of the other factors correspond to categories that have been
> identified in previous theoretical or empirical work, including personal ties in
> the congregation (Lenski's "communal involvement"), openness to religious
> growth, dogmatism, extrinsicness, financial behaviour and attitudes, and a
> final factor that indicates the salience or importance of religion.

These factors all seem to describe "how to be a Church member", and identify "religion" with a specified institutional affiliation. Their coherence reflects the way religion is traditionally structured in both normative and ideological terms. No scale has yet captured the orientation of the theologies of Barth, Bonhoeffer, Brunner and Bultmann who would rescue Christianity from the traditional forms of religion. But it is obviously much harder to do that than to identify the obvious and institutionally defined characteristics of religion.

Robinson and Shaver's (1973) section on religious measures collected and assessed six multi-dimensional scales, six direct measures of orthodoxy or fundamentalism, as well as measures of extrinsic and intrinsic orientations, and attitudes to the Church, the Bible, and conceptions of God. Each of these scales is carefully evaluated, and they stress that the authors of six of the 17 scales did not assess its reliability and that four were not validated at all, with only a construct validation available for five, concurrent validation against known groups for another five, and a simple face validity for two.

Bassett *et al.* (1981) have reported a scale that was designed to differentiate Christians from non-Christians, based on the assumption that the Bible, particularly the New Testament, has been under-utilized as a resource for attitude or belief items. They called it the "Shepherd Scale" because it seemed "to separate the sheep from the goats", and each item can be specifically referred back to a biblical text. These items refer to beliefs, for example, "I believe I can have the personal presence of God in my life" (John 14, 16) and "Because of my personal commitment to Jesus Christ, I have eternal life" (John 3, 13–15, 31–35; Romans 5, 17–21) and behaviour as in "I enjoy spending time with Christians" (Acts 2, 24–27, John 1, 7) and "I am concerned that my behaviour and speech reflect the teachings of Christ" (Matthew 5, 13–14; Colossians 4, 6). The whole scale has a test reliability of 0.82, a split half reliability of 0.9, and alpha is 0.86.

Limitations on questionnaire findings

Any examination of these methods of measuring religious variables impresses by their achievements. Their inadequacies are also striking. Godin (1967) refers to deficient items, and Dittes (1969) complained of a lack of agreement about the measures, subjects and statistical procedures, while Gorsuch (1984) adds the "importance of measurement issues themselves" and Deconchy (1985) writes of the "formal ambiguity of this type of research". Using only degrees of agreement with "found" items inevitably emphasizes a conventional perspective on the belief content, at the cost of more subtle reactions to them. Items derived from statements in the Church's traditional creeds (as in Fullerton and Hunsberger, 1982) may be personally irrelevant, while other scales may form a "hodge-podge of beliefs, values and reports of behaviour" (Gorsuch, 1984). While individual differences in emphasis are essential for psychological analyses, measures that are normative or prescriptive do not tap how religion or religious beliefs are used in practice. When the questions for either free response or closed procedures are drawn *a priori* from an assumed corpus of beliefs, the inter-relationships and structures that are discovered must reflect formal traditions. Although some items might be unanswerable, no one has reported that their subjects said they could not complete their questionnaire or belief scale, which further emphasizes the inherent conformity to an experimenter's demands. Asking the subjects to gloss or justify their answers, or to suggest how the items might be modified to make them more acceptable have not yet been well enough explored as ways to clarify what lies behind the formal responses.

The results that are obtained depend not only on the actual items, and the way they are combined into scales, but on the subjects' social and other characteristics (which may be religiously irrelevant), their cooperativeness and sophistication about the religious domain itself. Our methods can be criticized on technical grounds for their inadequate scale formation, for the actual task they impose on the subjects, and the procedures that are used to analyse the data. They have also been criticized for what they assume about the nature of religion, and for their conceptual and operational or empirical definitions (cf. Lenski, 1961).

Open questionnaire methods try to reproduce, in a controlled way how religion is typically expressed in conversation. Although Mandler and Kessen (1964, pp. 33–34) wrote of "introspection and the data of consciousness as something to be observed", and of a content analysis as a "description of responses in another language, the system language of psychology", translations from one register to another are not only features of any psychological theory or interpretation, they can also be found in any religious person's account of their beliefs.

Two steps away from the free response methods in which the subjects themselves control the answers they give, and to some extent the questions they are asked, one finds the investigator controlling both the questions and the allowable answers. Allport *et al.* (1984) used that procedure, which avoids the problems of analysing or encoding free responses, by specifying the complex alternative answers from which to choose one's responses. Their item 14 is typical, and shows the difficulty of making a sensible answer:

The Deity (check the one statement which most nearly expresses your belief)
1. There is an infinitely wise, omnipotent Creator of the universe and of natural laws, whose protection and favor may be supplicated through worship and prayer. God is a personal God.
2. There is an infinitely intelligent and friendly Being, working according to natural laws through which He expresses His power and goodness. There is the possibility of communication with this Deity in the sense that prayer may at least affect our moral attitude toward nature and toward our own place in the scheme of things.
3. There is a vast, impersonal, spiritual source or principle throughout nature and working in man, incapable of being swayed or communicated with through prayer.
4. Because of our necessary ignorance in this matter, I neither believe nor disbelieve in a God.
5. The only power is natural law. There is neither a personal creator nor an infinite intelligent Being. Nature is wholly indifferent to man. Natural law may be spoken of as "spiritual force," but this in no way adds to or changes its character.
6. The universe is merely a machine. Man and nature are creatures of cause and effect. All notions of a Deity as intelligent Being or as "spiritual force" are fictitious, and prayer is a useless superstition.
7. None of these alternatives sufficiently resembles my views to justify a choice between them.

Glock's questionnaire concerning religious experiences in *Psychology Today* (1973) offered a similarly Procrustean bed that might test the investigator's hypotheses about religion, with alternatives that could not fit every subject. It is not only in religion that scientific data and theories compete with experience. As an example, consider Spilka *et al,*'s (1975) test among Catholics of the Freudian, Adlerian, social learning and self-esteem theories of the origins of God concepts. On the basis of semantic differential ratings of the applicability of carefully chosen adjectives to God, they say that they "failed to come up with definitive answers relative to the theories on which assessment has been attempted", and then wondered if the methods that they employed might not themselves have been too restrictive. After emphasizing the different responses of males and females, they conclude that God images and their correlates may simply be "the points at which cultural stereotypes in both spheres match each other."

It is a truism to remark on the ambiguity of religious facts or symbols, which depend on one's perspective, and can only be resolved by an authoritative orthodoxy that authenticates a particular content and set of interpretations. Another source of ambiguity lies in the fact that one might not be able to explain oneself and what one observes as clearly as one can explain whatever outside things are observed (Wiles, 1976, p. 71). The ambiguity is found classically in the view that "man" has fashioned God in his own image to satisfy his desire for omnipotence. This, like the contrary belief, is empirically untestable and must be held as an act of faith. But since God made man, the way man creates God, because he is already in God's image, will be like God anyway (Wiles, 1976, p. 81). It is hard to keep the logic (and the theology) of such assertions away from whatever psychological evidence there might be about such beliefs or claims.

Any correspondence between the latent structures of parental and divine images or concepts will bear on psychological interpretations of the evidence for such similarities, but not on the truth of any doctrine about what the case might actually be. Psychological interpretations might, however, inform (or purify) *beliefs* about God's characteristics and so perhaps about his believed exsitence or non-existence. Psychological interpretations of the Virgin (as a representation of the feminine aspect of God's love) and the Trinity as exclusively masculine (Jung, 1958, p. 62), have influenced theologians who might reconstruct their understanding of the past but cannot change the history. To recognize the diversity in religious forms and the necessity of a decentred attitude rather than a limited single-minded perspective may be an essential feature of the maturely intellectual or emotional forms of religion. Godin (1971) similarly argues that we must forego moralism, ritualism and animism as forms of religious belief.

In the same sense, religious practices, rituals and doctrines have been interpreted and reinterpreted throughout the history of the Church in theological and liturgical terms, both symbolically and realistically. Bakan's (1974) analysis of the uses of paternity in religion emphasizes the importance of some of those psychological and linguistic similarities.

Responding to closed alternatives has, however, become the paradigmatic method of measurement because of its psychometric advantages, but especially in terms of reliability, despite the inevitable effects of moderator variables like demand characteristics (Orne, 1969) and evaluation apprehension (Rosenthal, 1964), and the difficulties of behavioural validation. That closed alternatives can work at all reflects our basic recognition, if not a personal acceptance, of religion and the widely recognized and social processes that support those who accept (or reject) it. Specific problems centre on the "careless slide" from religious belief to practice (Demerath and Levinson, 1971), assuming the equality of verbal and non-verbal responses, and neglecting the problem of respondents who are only allowed to report a perspective outside the accepted institutional forms by refusing to recognize the investigator's task at all. The standard doctrinal beliefs may be too flat, and response frequencies, correlation coefficients between them, and even attitude measurement itself can be seen as over-simplified analytic procedures. These are old criticisms, and those who still search for the deeper meanings in religion or for a language that can convey the experiences of individuals are aware of the contradiction of religion being inside and yet beyond (in some subjective sense) its institutional forms.

Alternative techniques

Religious experiences and variants of religious doctrines are not confined to Church members or adherents. The attention that has been given to non-traditional beliefs, beyond recognizing that they are held and the groups that sanction them, has been through sociological studies of sects and new religious movements. To operationalize some of these alternative ideologies in Likert scales might show the overlap of modern beliefs and their traditional formulations.

Several specific techniques have been developed to broaden the base of the work. An early departure from asking for the degree of agreement with items was to use Q-sort methods (Stephenson, 1953) to identify the idiosyncratic patterns. Monaghan (1967) applied this procedure to study the attitudes of members of a theologically conservative Church. The first stage in his study involved hour-long focussed interviews, from which a 56 item set of statements was developed. These items were then sorted on an 11-point scale by a matched sample, "according to how well the items described their own feelings about the church". The rankings of these items were intercorrelated and from a factor analysis of that matrix three "hypothetical person" profiles were identified in the authority-seeker, the comfort-seeker and the social participator. Gorlow and Schroeder (1968) also used the Q-sort to analyse the reasons for participating in religious activities. Their 87 items were generated by 125 active Church members in response to an open question about how "feeling, acts or experience . . . (in the religious domain of your life) . . . has been, is, or continues to be of greatest personal significance or meaning to you?" These items were then evaluated by 129 undergraduates who each made a 13 category sort in terms of their "importance-to-me", and an inverse factor analysis of persons (rather than items) was carried out. From that analysis they identified seven types, as the humble servants of God, self-improvers, family guidance seekers, moralists, God-seekers, socially oriented servants of God and "religious eggheads". Each of these religious types was identified with a separate pattern of personal, social and demographic variables. The "humble servants of God", for example, were likely to be Roman Catholic and not Jewish, to rate themselves as having strong religious feelings, and were unlikely to have a high parental income, or to have "parents who have a good deal of formal education, and have frequent and regular participation at religious services".

Brown and Forgas (1980) and Muthen *et al.* (1977) attempted to offset the use of a traditionally biased item content with a derivative of the repertory grid procedures (Fransella and Bannister, 1977) to elicit the commonly recognized "religious" concepts among a sub-set of their subjects. These concepts, when later rated on bipolar semantic scales by another group of subjects, showed that "religious" concepts are well-recognized and organized along dimensions of tradition, tangibility and evaluation, even by those who do not accept them (cf. page 21). That rating procedure derives from Osgood's (1952) semantic differential method which defines the connotative meanings of constructs such as those in Table 1 on page 23 independently of whether they are believed or accepted.

Kelly's (1955) personal construct theory is related to the repertory grid procedures he developed, and which he applied to religion in a paper on "Sin and Psychotherapy". The repertory grid, which aims to describe idiosyncratic or connotative meanings, has been little used to investigate constructions of religion, except in the work of Hass (1974), who modified it to compare conservative and ultra-conservative Lutheran pastors, Todd (1977), who was concerned with the way construct systems were linked to religious experience, and by O'Connor (1983) who built and refined a composite grid of religious meanings from a set of individual case studies. With this procedure she moved beyond the formal and traditional level of religion to explore the unique emphases in each person's religious reality or context. In doing this she escaped from the investigator's implicit theories about what the religious elements should be, to approximate the openness of conversations about religion that the investigator can observe but does not have to control. The approach stresses a contrast between the people (cf. Vergote's, 1969, *Religious Man*) who carry or reject religion and the attitudes or beliefs that are formed around some received content and which depend on the traditions within which any believer has been trained. Religious beliefs can be expected to be somewhat fluid, except among those who are conservative, dogmatic, or unthinking and unreflective about their religion.

The mean number of words in each item in usual attitude scales is about 17, and the meaning of these items will not necessarily be the same for all subjects, despite their apparently similar content. A simpler but even more closed 50 item conservatism scale was therefore developed by Wilson and

Patterson (1968), predicated on accepting or rejecting simple catch-phrases like "Bible truth", "Church authority" and "Divine law", "Horoscopes", "Divorce" and "Evolution theory" that were believed to characterize the "ideal conservative" (Wilson, 1973). This scale produced a factor called "religious-puritanism", on which the concepts that were just listed were loaded. In that conservatism scale there were also factors covering militarism-punitiveness, anti-hedonism, ethnocentrism and out-group hostility (ibid., p. 89).

A possible modification of the closed methods of attitude measurement invites each subject to show how they would change the alternatives that are offered to make them conform more closely to their own "true" position. When I have used this approach I have, however, found that few subjects take advantage of the invitation, which emphasizes that using any method relies on the cooperation of the subjects. The detailed changes they might make depend on their knowledge and their attitudes to religion and to any study of it, which, together with the response bias that is an important moderator variable, implies a rather docile attitude to the task among typical subjects.

Measured aspects of religion

Scale refinement is a continuing process that clarifies the dimensions assessed by a scale's content and the meaning of items. Gorsuch's (1984) argument that measurement itself, rather than any separate schools of thought or disciplines through which findings can be interpreted, now forms the paradigm of the psychology of religion emphasizes that it *is* possible to measure religiousness. Several scaling methods and procedures (Torgerson, 1958; Edwards, 1970) and a large number of specific scales are available, as we have seen.

Because the logic of psychophysical attitude scaling and other scaling models may be counter-intuitive, single questions or Likert's *a priori* summated rating scale model remain the two most widely accepted procedures. That is shown clearly in Robinson and Shaver's (1973) comments on the religious scales that they collected. To establish the coherence and internal structure of any scale is time-consuming, but it is an essential step towards identifying the construct validity of a scale and its empirical characteristics. External validity is harder to establish because beliefs are not necessarily consistent, nor do they always influence actual behaviour and whatever else is assessable about anyone's religion: there is even uncertainty about the criteria that might be used to establish what is "religious". A Church member could appear inactive and seldom go to church, but will experience intensely strong "unitive" feelings and readily gives religious reasons for involvement with secular activities, while a regular church attender might have superficial religious feelings but goes to church because he finds it, like one of Allport's extrinsic people, a good place to sell insurance. Similarly, it is hard to find valid criteria for an effective Church beyond its support, property, political control, historical, or traditional base. The criteria for judging successful pubs or race meetings are not necessarily those applied to a Church, although the behaviour of people in those organizations might follow some of the same social and psychological rules.

One solution to this problem has been to find theological or theoretical, rather than empirical criteria for religiousness. The statements of doctrine that can be taken from traditional creeds and catechisms therefore have formed an important basis for the items in many measures of religious belief.

Fullerton and Hunsberger (1982), for example, aimed to produce a unidimensional scale that covered "acceptance of well-defined, central tenets of the Christian religion" that were derived from the Nicene Creed. They identified ten categories of belief in that Creed (e.g. existence of God, the Trinity of Father, Son and Holy Ghost, and that God created all things), and they added three other categories of beliefs they thought were "universally endorsed by orthodox Christian groups even though they are not mentioned in the Creeds" which covered divine inspiration of the Bible, miracles, and the efficacy of prayer. They wrote 150 items which were reduced after a Likert scaling to 26 items, 13 being in a positive and 13 in a negative direction. These items were then factored, and they produced a single factor that accounted for 52.5 per cent of the variance on which all the items loaded more than 0.60, with an alpha coefficient of 0.96. In an independent replication, with these items embedded in a longer questionnaire, that religious factor accounted for 66.7 per cent of the variance. The scale was further refined and successfully validated against apostates and those who had, or had not switched their religious allegiance. Scores on their Christian Orthodoxy scale, correlated 0.84 with a 5-point item assessing belief in God, and 0.85 with a 5-point item assessing belief in Jesus. Similarly, the scales correlated 0.77 with a 3-point item scale to measure frequency of religious activities and 0.76 with Stark and Glock's 4-item measure of "orthodoxy" (ibid). The coherence of a religionism factor is once again well demonstrated but one wonders what advantages the longer scale has over the single items against which they validated it.

In a similar way Brown and Lowe (1951) produced a scale relating to the inspiration of the Bible, creation, God, life after death, the birth of Jesus, the Trinity, salvation, heaven and hell and the second coming. Martin and Westie (1959) included items about the inspiration of the Bible, heaven, the person of Christ and life after death. Lenski (1961) covered items about God,

Jesus, and life after death, while Putney and Middleton (1961) included references to a divine plan, life after death, hell and the devil, salvation and prayer. Poppleton and Pilkington (1963) included questions about miracles and ethics. These scale items are readily classified, and Brown (1964) showed empirically that judges agreed when sorting a heterogeneous collection of items into categories covering beliefs about God and Christ, orthodox beliefs about the devil, evil and spirits, as well as general religious beliefs about angels, the nature of matter, the Bible as a sacred document and the need for good behaviour (see Table 4, p. 31). Core Christian doctrines can therefore be distinguished from more general religious beliefs about, for example angels, that lack a specific doctrinal base. Thouless (1935) showed that all of these religious beliefs are accepted more confidently than are statements judged to be about matters of fact which are in principle verifiable, probably because of the great differences in the ways they can be tested.

But even when one escapes from the shackles of doctrine by asking open-ended questions about what people will say they believe, to establish their subjective frames of belief, what is said is not self-generated but reflects some conventional religious knowledge, although the emphasis that is given, and its specific elaboration, may be idiosyncratic. Certainly the beliefs that are held by the insider to a system are more highly differentiated and more tenaciously held than outsiders often recognize and they are beyond the constraints of the enquiry itself (Deconchy, 1982) and even outside the traditional formulations. One always hopes to find what supports beliefs, what will be said about them, and how what is available is modified so that it can be accepted and made credible (as was tried by John Robinson's controversial *"Honest to God"*, 1964, and by David Jenkins, the present Bishop of Durham). Establishing how system-based beliefs are construed and justified, or linked and "laddered" (Fransella and Bannister, 1977, p. 16) in psychological rather than theological terms is a neglected question, although some solutions are described in autobiographies (cf. Kenny, 1985). The differences between closed and open research procedures is similar to a difference between the demands of a salesman's questionnaire about one's preference for his product and the clarity required of any philospher's explanations. Direct questions have continued to be used, however, and the answers are tabulated and compared with other opinions. But because opinions are multi-dimensional, "they cannot all be represented in a linear continuum" (Thurstone and Chave, 1929, p. 10): "all that we can do with an attitude scale is to measure the attitude actually expressed with the full realization that the subject may be consciously hiding his true attitude or that social pressure of the 'situation' has made him really believe what he expresses" (ibid.). The clarity of this formulation of Thurstone's was forgotten by those (like La Piere, 1934) searching for some behavioural evidence for the attitudes that are held, as was his statement that, "It is of course not to be expected that every person will find only one single opinion on the whole scale that he is willing to endorse and that he will reject all the others" (p. 15).

It is important to remember that all measures include some error variance that is attributable first to the items or questions themselves, which have probabilistic rather than deterministic values on the target variable, and then to the subjects and their characteristics (which of course are what one wants to assess). No item can draw categorical and unequivocal responses from a whole group because of the individual differences among the group members.

Direct measures of religious knowledge

Stark and Glock (1968, p. 145) found that:

> members of the general American public are less likely to know that Jews and Christians share in the Ten Commandments than are Americans who belong to church congregations. The national data show that 62 per cent of the Roman Catholics knew this, and five per cent of the Protestants did so. Among Protestants, members of the more liberal churches are somewhat more likely to know Jews believe in the Ten Commandments than are the members of the more conservative bodies.

Those conclusions were based on a national survey of 1,976 adult Americans in October, 1964, that had been preceded by "an elaborate questionnaire study of church members in Northern California" (ibid., p. 6). Stark and Glock (ibid., p. 41) acknowledge the coarseness of their survey questions, and remark that their knowledge questions:

> seem extremely obvious and easy. Indeed several theologians who assisted us in fashioning the questionnaire felt that to use these questions to measure religious knowledge is a travesty on the meaning of knowledge ... but if we had used more sophisticated items we would not be able to study variations in religious knowledge among rank-and-file Christians for virtually no one in our sample would have been able to answer them.

The superficiality of religious knowledge is also shown in results from Gallup (1954) (in Stark and Glock, 1968, p. 161) which show that "79 per cent of the Protestants and 86 per cent of the Catholics could not name a *single* Old Testament prophet. More than two thirds of American Christians did not know who preached the Sermon on the Mount. More than a third did not know where Jesus was born" (ibid., pp. 161–162). One question asked, "If you were asked, do you think you could recite the Ten Commandments?" and their alternatives were, "Yes, but not the exact words", "Yes, the exact words", and "I'm not sure that I can remember all ten" (pp. 142–143). They give no information about the validity of the answers on that scale, which would have been easily established by asking even a few people to make a list. But despite its crudeness, that question produced sharp denominational differences (shown in their Table 50, p. 144) which could simply reflect socially desirable replies or an acquaintance or alignment with a liturgical tradition, since those who answered positively ranged from 34 per cent of Roman Catholics to a mean of nine per cent for the Protestants (who varied from one per cent for Congregationalists to 27 per cent of Missouri Lutherans).

Stark and Glock's measure of scriptural knowledge was more subtle. They devised six statements that were to be identified as being "from the Bible or not", and found that "Thou shalt not suffer a witch to live" (Exodus 11, 18) was correctly identified as biblical by 11 per cent of Protestants and three per cent of Catholics, while a deliberately contrived statement, "Blessed are the strong: for they shall be the sword of God" was said to be biblical by 72 per cent of Protestants and 59 per cent of Catholics. Stark and Glock note that this quotation "is akin to items used in the usual measures of authoritarianism", and that its content was agreed to by 25 per cent of the Protestants and by 32 per cent of the Catholics (p. 152). It also shows an inconsistently pro-religious bias, since it is likely that these responses were made to the linguistic register rather than to the content. Welford (1948) showed a similar preference among regular church-goers for the language of the Authorised Version.

The clear interaction here between the content and the language of these statements supports the apparently paradoxical finding that, while religious doctrines usually emphasize love and brotherhood, church-goers are less tolerant or more prejudiced than non-church-goers (Allport, 1960; Rokeach, 1960; Adorno *et al.*, 1950). It was this finding that led Allport to distinguish institutional and individual orientations to religion from his observation that not only are frequent church attenders significantly less prejudiced than infrequent attenders, they are also less prejudiced than non-attenders. Allport and Ross (1967) developed a measure of these differences through the "motives" or orientations of church attenders, in which they identified extrinsic or consensual, and intrinsic or committed, forms of religious response. Batson and Ventis (1982) extended Allport's original model to include a quest orientation, while Allport also found that many were inconsistently pro-religious or anti-religious, in the sense that they seemed to respond only to the tenor of the questions and not to their content, suggesting that many people respond uncritically to religious beliefs or disbeliefs (Thompson, 1974). Donahue (1985) shows that this intrinsic/extrinsic distinction has been an extremely important variable for psychological study.

While some argue that only an active religious participant has the knowledge or sympathy to make a psychological analysis of religion, others assert that only detached observers can achieve that. Sir Alister Hardy's (1966) initial study of religious experience was directly phenomenological and he categorized under about 42 headings the replies of those who accepted his invitation to answer the question, "How much do you think that you owe your early religious ideas or feelings to the influence of your family or to any other individuals who were helpful, whether as models to imitate or just as sympathetic people to talk to?" (cf. Malony, 1981). A less direct approach was adopted by Brown (1964) who related reports of childhood religious influences to scores for the strength of religious belief and found that those accepting religious beliefs were more likely to have been exposed to religion as children. The generality of findings like these might be tested in specifically parametric studies.

Indirect methods

Cook and Selltiz (1964) identified the following indicators that have been used to assess attitudes, and by extension, beliefs.

1. Self reports about beliefs, feelings behaviour and so on.
2. Reactions to or interpretations of partially structured material that relates to some attitude object.
3. Observations of overt behaviour.
4. Performance on objectice tasks where the functioning is influenced by some disposition towards the object.
5. Physiological reactions to the object.

Early psychologists plunged unselfconsciously into direct analyses of the reactions to orthodox religious material. Their subjects could see what the studies were about and probably gave the expected responses. Deconchy (1980) and Brown and Pallant (1962) have, however, shown that expressed attitudes and responses to orthodox religious statements can be manipulated by the instructions and the context of the study, and by whether the investigator is identified as a clergyman or wears a clerical collar (Pallone, 1964, 1966). This emphasizes our convergence in responding to recognized beliefs, and the social processes that support them. Because of this, religious responses cohere (and so do religious people), especially when they are contrasted against non-religious responses and contexts (or groups). An obvious solution to that problem is, of course, to gather data from groups that are religiously homogeneous, in an attempt to break up the homogeneous variance of the single religious variable that necessarily emerges.

Another way to break down expected replies has been to use non-reactive or disguised methods to gather responses about attitudes and beliefs. (Incidentally, we do not yet know the rules for combining public and private responses about religion, although we usually know when to keep quiet about our religious and our other beliefs.) One stimulus to the use of disguised methods can be found in psychoanalytic theory, particularly in the development of projective tests, following the work of Rorschach (1921). While the underlying theory of projection was at the base of Freud's explanation of the origins and nature of religion, projective tests assume that ambiguous stimuli are perceived as, or will have ascribed to them, personal and hidden interests, desires, fears, wishes or expectations.

Projective methods favour completely unstructured stimuli, although Godin and Coupez (1957) used photographs of religious scenes and asked their subject's to build stories about them. Other indirect measures use secondary tasks that are not made an explicit part of the instructions, as when the experimenter simply measures the reaction time needed to give associations to religious words (Strunk, 1966; Malony, 1977), or records the heart rate (King and Funkenstein, 1957) or GSR (Brown, 1965) while a task relevant to religion is being carried out. Although Triandis rejected physiological measures as indicators of attitudes, because of their low reliability, they aim to elicit unguarded disclosures, or to index physiological changes, as when, for example, meditation is understood as a "spiritual technology" (Wallace and Benson, 1972). These indirect measures have, however, fallen out of use in the psychology of religion because of the current preoccupation with conscious or cognitive processes. The last use of indirect measures in the *Journal for the Scientific Study of Religion* was in a paper by Embree in 1973, which used Jung's free-association procedure that has also been used in studies of the images and ideas about God (Deconchy, 1967; Vergote and Tamayo 1980). The well-known Rorschach ink-blot cards had been earlier used in studies of religion (Eisenman *et al.*, 1966; Larsen and Knapp, 1964), as well as Murray's Thematic Apperception Test (1938) which was modified by Godin and Coupez (1957) as a model for a "Religious projective pictures test". Goldman's (1964) use of an open-ended enquiry into the interpretations of bible stories as a developmental test of religious understanding also belongs with these indirect measures.

Although repertory grid methods are unstructured, they are not disguised and may also have helped to displace the strictly projective methods. Flakoll (1977, pp. 387–388) identified several other methods as "projective" that are not usually classed in this way, which Warren, in the same collection of papers, does not mention. He also refers to Cline and Richards's (1965) multi-method–multi-trait approach. They used conventional questionnaires as well as projective procedures, which appeared unusual at that time, despite Campbell and Fiske's (1959) advocacy of such procedures. Warren's (1977) use of the comprehension of a prose passage that involved religious beliefs, although not within a religious context, is potentially fruitful, as are the "Who am I?" and "Twenty Questions" procedures that were developed by sociologists to assess self-images as unstructured measures which can show the potency of religious labels for some people (Kuhn and McPartland, 1954). Stringer and Cairns (1983) report a Northern Ireland study of the judgements of stereotyped Catholic and Protestant faces which align with their group membership.

Miscellaneous procedures

A different unstructured measure of potential usefulness is found in Eiser and Osman's (1978) analysis of the semantic features of language as an index of self-presentation, which has some similarity to Coe's (1900) content analysis of 1,100 hymns to find the "temperamental factors" in religious experience, and with Schneider and Dornbusch's (1958) analysis of hymns and inspirational books which emphasized the context, the ideology, and common beliefs that encircle religious people. (Hymns have, oddly enough, been disregarded as a source of items for scaled measures of religion, although "Jesus loves me this I know" may even now be too familiar to elicit any sensible believe or disbelieve responses.) Galton's use of actuarial statistics about longevity to test the efficacy of prayer falls into a similar category, but it would now be seen as an application of demographic rather than psychological procedures.

Clinical case study methods aim to assess or reconstruct a life history, and to clarify implicit reactions in terms of psychopathological models. They have been applied in studies of those who are strongly committed (including the clergy, by Bowers, 1968) or frankly deviant, to identify idiosyncratic effects that could have some generality, although there are more potent sources of bias here than in the other procedures. The uniqueness of a person's life readily disappears into whatever scheme is used to describe it, and into the tradition which formed it and which give it meaning (Malony, 1978).

Despite that, Stewart's study of *Adolescent Religion* (1967), which reports a series of non-directive depth interviews supplemented by scaled questionnaire data, Godin's "Religious pictures test" and Q-sort data, emphasizes the variability in religious responding (Stewart, 1967, p. 168).

Meta-analysis of published papers has recently emerged as a method that plots trends in the results of a number of related studies to extract their consensus. Batson *et al.* (1985) has used this procedure to show that altruism is an important dependent measure of intrinsic religious orientations, and Bergin (1983) used it to show that religion is more closely linked to good than to bad mental health.

Summary

All the methods that have been developed by social psychologists have been applied in studies of religious belief and knowledge, attitudes and practice, and experience, but not many of them have been well validated. As we have seen, the impetus to develop some of these methods came from a wish to improve the study of religion itself, and the results have been used to describe the characteristics of defined groups, and to establish differences between groups.

There has not yet been enough constructive criticism of the established methods (and theories) within the psychology of religion for radically new procedures to develop. The concepts, methods and even the hypotheses that have been tested have therefore maintained their enduring thematic hold, and have stayed close to intuition and common-sense. The theoretical models have more often been hermeneutic than heuristic. But change may not come essily because of the normative control of both science and religion over studies of the psychological functions of religion, which are themselves socially prescribed. Tradition and convention over-ride the likelihood that psychoanalytic or other clinical theories of religion could ever be found to be generally true, although they probably apply to some people (or perhaps to extreme "cases"). Despite that, reductionists and unbelievers continue to assert that any manifestations of religion are in themselves irrational, pathogenic, or focus prior psychopathological processes. Just as we do not know how many Church members or religious believers have been precipitated into a mental illness by their religion, we do not know how many have been rescued by it. Furthermore, to argue that religion is pathological implies that the creative fantasies that are also found in painting or poetry cannot have a visionary component. Religious and aesthetic experiences are of necessity ambiguous and they can even be contradictory.

Any religion is unified by social and traditional control over its doctrines, ritual and experienced content. Every scientific study of religion is similarly controlled by agreement about the proper methods by which to quantify "religious commitments" and beliefs, whether in organizational or personal and psychological terms, or with reference to some abstract conception of religion or towards specific objects like the Bible, the Church, or God. Our reliance on convergent approaches has forced us to neglect responses to religion that are unconventional or beyond the ordinary demands that are to be met (or rejected) and which religion is allowed to be involved with.

Reliable scales of measurement must be distinguished from the enumerations or counts of whatever can be put into discrete categories, for example, as right or wrong answers to factual questions, or as yea- or nay-sayers and Catholics or Protestants. Careful measurement is at the heart of any scientific study of social phenomena, and we can assume that religious attitudes and beliefs will form one or more continuous, if latent, variables on which people's responses can be arrayed. These dimensions may be specified intuitively or derived from an empirical analysis. Early conceptions of religious responsiveness grouped people on the basis of the attitudes or beliefs they professed, or by their other responses. A basic difficulty with any typological model is the large number of types that are usually identified and which are theoretically arbitrary, "inelegant and intellectually unmanageable" (Scott, 1968, p. 246). Furthermore, an unknown proportion of any subject population may have to be excluded or misclassified to make such models fit the data. But those models were popular, and numerous overlapping, usually bipolar typologies of religious orientation have been proposed, of which one of the most important is the distinction Allport drew between intrinsic and extrinsic orientations from the reasons that were given to explain a Church involvement. Alternative procedures have directly assessed or surveyed religious behaviour and the claims to religious belief itself, or they have indirectly inferred religiousness from adjectival ratings, free word associations and the reconstructive procedures that require telling a story. Every method of measurement rests on a model of the measurement process itself, which the data from religion have contributed to substantially.

The criteria by which any measure or theory is validated must be social, and they show a necessary convergence that obscures what is behind verbal statements. Using the methods developed for attitude measurements has, however, aligned the psychology of religion with the rest of social psychology, even if it has meant pursuing current orthodoxies and adopting a "behavioural" posture. The recent growth of an emperimental psychology of religion (Batson and Ventis, 1982; Deconchy, 1981) and the increased use of multi-variate analyses will allow us to identify non-linear relationships between variables that were obscured by the ubiquitous correlational procedures, and the simple comparisons between known groups that were common until the early 1970s.

5   The structures of religion

We clearly have to consider the possibility that metaphor is not an incidental ornament of Biblical language, but one of its controlling modes of thought. We get into a more rarified area of literary criticism with Jesus' aphorism "the kingdom of the Lord is within you." The New English Bible, which seems particularly unhappy with this remark for some reason, translates it: "For in fact the kingdom of God is among you", and offers as alternates: "For in fact the kingdom of God is within your grasp", and "For suddenly the kingdom of God will be among you". Several critical principles may be dimly discerned in this. First, the translator's own attitude is important for the translation. Those who feel that psychological metaphors express the profoundest truths will prefer "within"; those who want a more social gospel — and these translators clearly have a social conscience — will prefer "among". Second, Jesus may very well have meant, or even said, what is recorded in the Gospel of Thomas: "The kingdom of God is inside and it is outside you", although the Gospel of Thomas was undiscovered until 1945. (Northrop Frye, *The Great Code*, 1982, pp. 54–55)

A continuing argument has centred on the nature or characteristics of religion, and about its elements and the structures behind any items. Glock and Stark (1965) defined the dimensions of religion in terms of belief, practice (especially rites and rituals), experience, knowledge and the consequences of religion or its everyday effects. Ninian Smart (1969) called the same dimensions doctrinal, mythological, ethical, ritual, and experiential, and he added a social dimension, since: "Religions are not just systems of belief: they are also organisations or parts of organisations. They have a communal and social significance" (p. 20).

Clayton and Gladden (1969), who questioned the assertion that religion is multi-dimensional, produced scales to measure five basic dimensions. A factor analysis of the responses to their scales led them to conclude that religionism involves a single dimension. While Glock and Stark had conceded that religious belief is central to a multi-dimensional conception of religion, Clayton and Gladden identified belief with religion itself, because the other aspects are referred to it.

Formal structures

If we accept that religion is predominantly concerned with belief in God or the gods, and that Christianity is one of the major world religions, we find there a hierarchical ordering of vertical (since God is "up there") and horizontal components (because "we are the body of Christ"). (The notion that some religions are "superior" to others has become outmoded, because Christianity always came out on top.) Christianity was bred from Judaism, as was Islam, and any historical perspective on those "structures" is different from the contemporary psychological usage of that term, which is identified by English and English (1958) as "any enduring arrangement, grouping, pattern or articulation of parts (or elements) to form a relatively stable system or whole ... contrasted with function or process (though these may themselves have structure)". While English and English say the expression "personality structure" is redundant, "since personality itself connotes a complex structure", different structures of religion are recognized by those who occupy different relationships with it. First come the religious traditions and within them are their "Orders", which are not necessarily similar, nor are they always recognized by other traditions or denominations. Furthermore bishops, priests and deacons each have their own functions while sharing other functions. Dittes (1969) also distinguished inside and outside perspectives on religion, the first recognizing the diversity in religions, and in Christianity in particular, the other distinguishing religion from non-religion in terms of "favourableness of attitudes towards religions, institutions ... and official doctrine" (p. 610). Rokeach's (1960) "Scaling of religious denominations" which goes from Methodist to Presbyterian, Baptist, Lutheran, Episcopalian and Catholic, and is almost completely independent of the relative positions of husbands and wives on that scale (p. 305), shows that denominations are well structured both in terms of their historical origins and in the responses to them.

Religious doctrines are also structured, as when Davidson (1972a) distinguished "between other-worldly oriented (vertical) beliefs and this-worldly oriented (horizontal) beliefs", and Thouless (1924) distinguished obligatory from optional Christian beliefs. Davidson reports that "on the vertical belief dimensions, congregational affiliation was the most influential variable; denominational affiliation ranked second, and socio-economic status ranked third ... [while] ... on the horizontal belief dimension, denominational affiliation ranked as the most influential variable and congregational affiliation ranked second". Those vertical belief items included belief about:

(1) a life after death; (2) the divinity of Christ; (3) the existence of God; (4) the virgin birth of Christ; (5) Christ's walking on water; and (6) Biblical miracles. The horizontal belief items pertained to (1) the need to love one's neighbour;

(2) the need to help others; (3) the effects of discriminating against others on one's chances for gaining salvation; and (4) importance of helping one's fellow man compared to the importance attached to other types of religious practice.

Psychologically identified structures

Dittes (1969) found that the studies which produce a single religious factor contrast a comparatively few religious items concerning the Church and conventionally theistic or Christocentric statements against other social attitudes, tapping the way religion is generally characterized by those heterogeneous in their religion or religious affiliation. The subjects in these studies are typically late adolescents "for whom issues of autonomy versus institutional loyalty and conventional orthodoxy would seem to be especially keen" (p. 93). While our culture often treats religion in less coherent ways than that (Dittes 1969, p. 610), he noted that the outside approach to religion taps church attendance and the acceptance of broadly theistic beliefs (and, we should add, a general approval of it).

King (1967) tested the alternative view, that religion is multi-dimensional, against the questionnaire responses of 575 Methodists in Dallas. From extensive pilot tests and a literature review, he devised a 121 item questionnaire and identified nine dimensions, including credal assent and commitment, participation in congregational activities, congregational ties, religious experience, commitment to an intellectual search despite doubt (which is similar to Batson and Ventis's (1982) "quest" dimension), openness to religious growth, dependence, and an extrinsic orientation, financial contributions and talking and reading about religion. These factors are similar to the dimensions that others have identified in the literature that is now extensive and will not be reviewed (but see Dittes, 1969; Gorsuch, 1984). Hilty and Morgan (1985) have recently argued that there is a "strong support for seven factors covering personal faith, intolerance of ambiguity, 'orthodoxy' (or a rather conventional Christianity), social conscience, (factual) knowledge of religion, life purpose, and church involvement".

Replications of King's study (King, 1967; King and Hung, 1975) converge at a second order on a contrast of religious feelings, beliefs and a positive orientation to religion, against religious behaviour or involvement. King and Hung themselves drew attention to a telling criticism of their work when they said that, "It emphasises, and is largely confined to congregationally-related aspects of institutional, mainline Protestant Christianity", although they also said they hoped to extend their descriptions to more diverse populations.

Strommen *et al.*'s (1972) massive study of Lutherans in the United States, that was referred to in the previous chapter, concerned a group known to be "religious", and measured 72 religious variables among its members. By including sophisticated statements about religion and reducing the variability in Church participation, they gave an opportunity for subtle differences in reactions to emerge. Maranell (1974) studied eight separate religious groups with eight *a priori* scales, and consistently found two religious factors. The first was defined by scales of fundamentalism and theism, the other by Church orientation and ritualism.

Using a similar approach, but with an interview and a projective test as well as a questionnaire, Cline and Richards (1965) found that "the first factor that emerged for both men and women (and accounted for the lion's share of the variance in both factor solutions) was religious in content". They called it "Religious belief and behaviour" among the women and "Religious behaviour or activity" for the men. The other factors were readily interpretable, although relationships with religious parents and spouse emerged on three factors for women and two for men. In a study among four separate religious groups and religious "non-affiliates" Keene (1967) found a first factor of religious salience and other factors that covered spiritual/ secular, skeptical/approving and orthodox/personal, and conversative or liberal beliefs as well as institutional loyalty. When Keene focussed his analysis on data from Baha'is he found cognitive and experiential (or personal), and administrative or meditative factors. Tapp (1971) administered Keene's questionnaire to a group of Unitarians and found a first "personal belief" factor and smaller factors covering social and ethical values, Church values and participation, psychological development, worship values, religious knowledge, humanism and an emphasis on religious education. This broad convergence demands a search for greater precision.

Francis's (1984) structural analysis of religion was in terms of conservative, liberal or dogmatic belief, with simple "unbelief", uncertainty, and dogmatic rejection as *a priori* categories. His factor analysis used 15 items to assess each of these six positions, and the first factor covered belief uncertainty, the second belief itself and the third and fourth factors referred to dogmatic acceptance and rejection of belief.

That Christianity is being challenged by oriental mysticism, quasi religions like the human potential movement, and the therapeutic sub-culture, Christian groups themselves are challenged by fundamentalism, evangelism, Pentecostalism, and even by some aspects of Catholicism which makes any psychological structures a little unstable. Systematic findings, must however, depend on careful psychometric scales, factor analysis or structural modelling, and not on intuitive judgements and common-sense knowledge. The empirical scales do, however, depend on the assumption that attitudes and beliefs consistently form latent psychological variables. Thurstone and

Chave's (1929) scale to measure attitudes to the Church depended on a single dimension of favourable or unfavourable responses, although Thurstone helped to develop factor analysis as a method by which structural relationships between variables (whether as items or scales) could be identified. Likert, Guttman and Osgood have all contributed to these measurement procedures, which have made it possible to represent "religious phenomena on some reasonably limited set of theoretical dimensions" (Robinson and Shaver, 1973, p. 630). The stimuli or items for these scales are drawn from beliefs and values that are rated for an acceptance of their content, or as adequate descriptions of one's behaviour. They necessarily involve what "being religious" involves in principle and in a culturally approved or empirically observed way, that also reflects in a person's beliefs or behaviour.

Scott has commented on "the impossibility of writing items (and we might add, in defining behaviour) which only represent the intended attribute and have precisely the same location on that dimension for each person" (1968, p. 246). We should therefore be clear about the level at which any analysis is planned, which more often has a group rather than an individual focus. Those two levels of analysis require quite different procedures. A defect of the group analyses lies in the extent to which the items must be "found" for the subjects and therefore do not necessarily correspond with their own formulations, which can be either vague or well differentiated. If the items are taken from the creeds, they define a position with which Church members are expected to be aligned, but which they might wish to reformulate.

Concepts of God

A different approach to psychological structures that allows the subjects a broader range of responses than simply to agree or disagree, believe or disbelieve, is found in Osgood's semantic differential method which extends single response scales to other adjectively defined responses that have been found to load on factors of evaluation (good — bad), potency (strong — weak), and activity (active — passive) (Osgood *et al.*, 1957). Although Osgood's semantic differential procedure was developed to measure the denotative meanings of words and concepts it has been widely applied in the study of religion, but especially to the conceptualizations of God that people have, and it was an advance on the earlier work which asked about those concepts directly. Harms (1944) examined children's concepts of God through the drawings they produced, and he structured those drawings into a sequence of developmental stages from fairy tales to abstract formulations. This method itself implies that God can be concretely represented, and so it is only older children who might have the social skill to refuse that task, or say, when they are asked, that they were being metaphorical or schematic in whatever they produced. But Goldman's (1964) work on religious thinking, which focussed on the interpretation of religious stories, also found a developmental sequence or structure that conformed to Piaget's theory of cognitive development. (A further discussion of this material is in Ch. 9.)

Less direct approaches to unpacking the symbolism of the deity have been reported by Eisenman *et al.* (1960) who asked their subjects to rank Rorschach cards for their similarity to God, while Larsen and Knapp (1969) had unfamiliar ink-blots rated on semantic scales, for the extent to which they "symbolized God". Both of those papers, however, interpret their findings within a context that is defined by the conventional meaning of "God", and they were not concerned with how those concepts were structured or aligned with each other.

Nelson (1971) tested Freud's hypothesis that God is really "the father, clothed in the grandeur in which he once appeared to the small child". With a Q-sort procedure (Stephenson, 1953) he compared descriptive concepts of God, Jesus, mother and father and found that concepts of the mother were more similar to the concept of God than were concepts of the father. Strunk (1959), however, had found a close similarity between the concept of father and the concept of God. Spilka *et al.* (1964) argued that judgements of mother, father, self and God were determined by linear transformations of social desirability values, and therefore collected free responses to the question, "What does God mean to you?". The 64 most common replies were Q-sorted by various groups and the data factor analysed. In a Catholic sample, eight factors were interpreted, the first referring to a "wrathful, avenging and damning God", the second to an unyielding-permissive continuum, and the third to the "omni—" words. In a general sample, the first factor was aligned with social desirability and the second with the negative, or punishing characteristics.

Gorsuch (1968) re-analysed Spilka's separate analyses, and identified God concepts in terms of a stern father, the omni-concept of God, the impersonal God, the kindly father and the supreme ruler. In an extension of that study, he had Spilka's adjectives and 28 of Osgood's semantic scales rated for their applicability to God. The results of first, second and third order factor analyses are shown in Table 5.

Gorsuch concluded that three factors have been firmly established for the concept of God that cover "omni-ness", "deisticness", and "wrathfulness", and that these separate factors provide a firm base for more detailed comparative studies. This analysis also suggests that to align God concepts with parental figures is an over-simplification that neglects the traditional formulations held, for example, by liberal and by fundamentalistic Christian groups.

Table 5 *Organization of the factors involved in the concept of God (from Gorsuch, 1968)*

I.   TRADITIONAL CHRISTIAN[a]
A.   Companionable[b]
1.   Evaluation[c]
2.   Kindness[c]
3.   Relevancy[d]
B.   Benevolent Deity[b]
1.   Lack of deisticness[c]
2.   Eternality[c]
3.   Kindliness[c]
II.   Wrathfulness[d]
III.   Omni-ness[d]
IV.   Potently passive[d]

[a] This concept appeared at the third order in the present study.

[b] This concept appeared at the second order in the present study.

[c] This factor appeared at the first order, primary factor level in the present study.

[d] This factor appeared among the primary factors, but was unrelated to any other primary factor.

Vergote and Tamayo (1980) reached similar conclusions from a slightly different starting point in which they had their subjects make semantic ratings on 18 maternal and 18 paternal items (e.g. "warmth", "tenderness", "strength", and "power"). Each was rated first for its symbolic and remembered relevance to "mother" and "father", and the significant differences originally found in Holland were validated across other Western cultures (in Belgium, France, Italy and the United States). When these words were applied to God as well as to the parents, paternal items that defined God involved power and strength, knowledge and justice, whereas the natural father was associated with action and initiative. The maternal items that represented God "express unconditional love and acceptance rather than those that reflect active concern and solicitude or those that refer to a more immediate affective bond" (p. 59). The broad conclusions were that "the father figure is more strongly maternal than the mother figure is paternal. Likewise, the maternal component is also of more importance in God than the paternal one" (p 67) and produces "smaller distances between the figures than the paternal one" (ibid.) although "in its complexity the father figure is a more adequate symbol for God than the mother figure" (p. 68). So the "representation of God is structured by the paternal items quite independently of the parental figures" (ibid.), with God "viewed as law giver and judge, as representing ethical exigencies and, though powerful and firm, as being patient and loving, as just but not stern" (p. 69).

A study among Hindus that was part of Vergote's cross-cultural extension of this work emphasized the traditional basis for these representations. Parental figures did not mediate the representation of God among the Hindus, and "The divine law that arches over the society does not allow here for mediation by a father who himself is almost completely deprived of this function. Moreover, the absence of an affective bond with God obviously manifests much less dependence on maternal mediation" (p. 214). Vergote concluded that, "From the psychological point of view, the divine name of father is thus indeed a metaphor: its affective recognition is motivated by a complex mode of relations already psychologically constituted. Nevertheless, the transfer to God of the name of father responds to the invocation of religious language" (p. 225), while its signifying power in language supports the established concepts that are held by believers.

The content of religious beliefs

Following Thouless (1935), Brown (1962) identified the content of religious beliefs, in categories that referred to God, Christ and the Church as an institution, orthodox religious beliefs ("evil is a reality"), general religious beliefs ("Christianity is a better religion than Buddhism"), matters of opinion ("hardship strengthens character"), fact ("the universe is expanding") and a collection of miscellaneous statements like "everything is relative". I found that the tendency to certainty was less for statements with a nonreligious than with a religious content (with means of 1.56 and 2.10 respectively) and that the religious items loaded on a single religious factor, unrelated to certainty or confidence itself, which was most closely related to an anxiety factor. (See Table 4, pages 31–33 for these data.)

In another study among university students, Wearing and Brown (1972), used Poppleton and Pilkington's (1963) measure of religious belief, questions about religious behaviour, as well as items that had distinguished the members of theologically conservative and liberal student groups (Brown, 1962) and the Allport-Vernon-Lindzey religious value score. They found a strong religious belief first factor. The second factor involved moral integrity and career determinants and the third was defined by religious denomination and attendance, the fourth factor by the frequency of mother's church attendance and the fifth factor by anxious dogmatism.

It is clear from these studies that the acceptance or rejection of religious beliefs in independent of the modes of affiliation or acceptance of them (and in these results, independent of anxiety), although that only becomes clear when the strength of belief is controlled. A recent analysis of similar data by Hunsberger and Brown (1984) used a questionnaire designed to identify the characteristics of those who drop-out from religion ("collapsed Christians"?), and they found that social variables, like the parents' education, were more important than was belief itself in characterizing those who left the Church.

Approaches to these questions of structure have become quite stereotyped and they continue to support the conclusion that with religiously heterogeneous populations religiosity can be reasonably well summarized with a single score, whether religion is being taken as a dependent or independent variable. From a different ground Fishbein and Ajzen (1975) argue that the frequency of church attendance is as good a general religious measure as any other, although to improve the face validity, investigators usually include general statements of religious belief as well.

But with religiously homogeneous subjects and a diverse item content the general religious factor breaks down to specific factors, especially when the items reflect explicitly different doctrines or carry implicit assumptions about the components of religion that are like those which Glock has assessed with *a priori* scales. When Glock's work was reviewed in the *Journal for the Scientific Study of Religion*, Hargrove (1973) emphasized that a "refusal to abandon logical categories to computer based factors ... keeps the conceptual field more open". Newman (1973, p. 471) similarly said that:

> bland doctrinal belief questions, inventories of parish activities, measures of frequency of church attendance, correlations of religious belief, indexes with questions on social attitudes, critics argue, are too "flat", and simplistic to reveal the deeper meanings of religion within both the personality and the cultural systems of a society.

Yet it is at this level that the structures of religion reveal themselves, and it hardly seems good enough to have to conclude that the structures of religion either recapture or reflect our social knowledge of what religion entails, or that they reflect the content of the way religion is assessed. Beyond these formal structures of belief, behaviour and experience, core religious beliefs are necessarily surrounded by peripheral beliefs and by the meta-assumptions we have about the beliefs themselves.

Multi-dimensional solutions

Coherent attempts to find the structure of the religious concepts in common use have been made by Weima (1965), Muthen *et al.* (1976) and Brown and Forgas (1980) using recent derivatives from factor analysis. Muthen used a three mode factor analysis, while Brown and Forgas set their data up within INDSCAL, a multi-dimensional scaling procedure based on an algorithm that examines the arithmetic distances between judgements of variables (Carroll and Chang, 1970). Each of these studies was within an explicitly Christian context. Muthen's study involved a three mode factor analysis of the ratings made by 120 university students of six religious concepts (altar, the conciliating Christ, love, prayer for God's help, the crucified Christ and God) on 60 bi-polar scales that had been elicited from subjects who were asked to complete the phrase "the ... crucified Christ". They found six interpretable factors in the item mode, covering a general evaluation, a specific evaluation, (e.g. relaxed — tense), traditional Christianity (divine — human), familiarity, activity and traditional pietism (supernatural — natural). The concept mode distinguished the persons in the deity, non-religious and religious concepts and human or divine action. The two factors in the person mode were not, however, interpreted. (If this study were to be replicated, some of the factors might be moved towards the content-free dimensional model outlined by Peterson and Scott (1983) whose fundamental measures of the dimensionality of a domain of objects are based separately on paired comparisons, ratings, and descriptive check lists.)

Brown and Forgas (1980) used a free response method to elicit the concepts or elements that are associated with "religion". The 33 elements so derived were then rated by another group of subjects on 16 semantic differential scales taken *a priori* from previous work (although those scales might also have been elicited). An INDSCAL analysis of the data yielded three dimensions that were identified as institutional — individual, positive — negative control, and known — unknown. Those dimensions align with the orientations to religion that Brown (1964) found in a content analysis of the answers from a modified sentence completion task that had been designed to test the robustness of Allport's contrast between extrinsic and intrinsic forms of religious orientation. An institutional — individual orientation that had been conjectured by Allport and Ross (1967) reappeared, using Jeeves's (1957) items. The other dimension in that study of orientations contrasted self-serving and extrinsic orientations to religion against a committed or intrinsic involvement with it, which parallels dimensions defined by negative control or punishment through religion, and positive or immediate responses to religion.

An important aspect of these results is the extent to which they cover the implicit conceptions of religion held by subjects who are heterogeneous with respect to their religious memberships and their beliefs, and which go beyond the doctrinally-based concepts that most investigators have relied on, but which still tap into the recognized categories of belief and knowledge, practice, experience and the consequences of religion.

Gorsuch's (1984) solution to the problems of structure identifies religion as *both* uni-dimensional *and* multi-dimensional. He argued in Gorsuch and McFarland (1972) that in our culture, religious people are distinguished from non-religious people by a general dimension that "can be measured with reasonable consistency by most scales concerned with credal assent and related beliefs and attitudes". These scales also subdivide religion conceptually and empirically on the grounds of doctrine, participation, change, and orientation or motivation. While the actual factors depend on the items, subjects, and analytic procedures, the higher order analysis of the factors reported by King and Hunt (1975) has produced second order factors that define organizational activities, religious despair or hope in life, and the salience of religion.

Maranell's (1974) study of eight separate populations, which found two religious factors that were defined by fundamentalism and theism and by Church orientation and ritualism was reanalysed by Gorsuch (1984) who found "a general Christianity second order factor subdividing into theism (to which doctrines belong) and Church orientation factors". He added that, "those first order factors could be further subdivided". In Maranell's study there were gross differences for denomination (when, for example, Unitarians were compared with Trinitarians), age (the older being more religious), political conservatism (the religious people being more conservative), and sex (with females expected to be more religious). Gorsuch notes that the first order factors identify exceptions to conclusions about religion in general, so that, for example, "correlations with bigotry scales were positive for the variables representing the church orientation factor but generally negative for variables representing the theistic-Christian factor".

The received elements that are commonly used in studies of religious responding limit subjects' responses to the customary meanings of most statements about religion. They also define the traditional and social structures of religion with which individuals interact. Parallel to those elements are the spontaneous conceptions of religion that Brown and Forgas (1980) drew on, which as we have seen are structured into institutional or orthodox and individual or personal aspects of religion, into its tangible forms and as positive or negative evaluations that entail releasing or controlling perspectives.

Religion and personality

The generality and cohesiveness of any higher order religious factor, and perhaps its political implications, can be clearly found within the domain of personality measurement. The MMPI, for example, includes 11 specifically religious items that form a separate factor (Johnson *et al.*, 1984), although unlike the religion scale on the Omnibus Personality Inventory, that factor is not scored separately. Religious issues were also found to be important in the *Authoritarian Personality* (Adorno *et al.*, 1950) and in Rokeach's (1960) work on the *Open and Closed Mind*, both of which span the political and personality domains, showing the close theoretical links between religious orientations and personality. Others have found religion aligned with such negatively evaluated characteristics as submission and dependence (Dreger, 1952); Ranck, 1961), low self-esteem (Stark, 1963), self-reliance (Prothro and Jensen, 1950), and social conformity (Goldsen *et al.*, 1960). Dittes (1971c, p. 371) was able to conclude that "the generally consistent report is of the correlation between orthodox religious commitment and a relatively defensive, constricted personality". Brown (1962), however, found that measures of authoritarianism, rigidity and intolerance of ambiguity loaded on a factor that was independent of religion, and Francis (1985) found no significant relationships between religion and Eysenck's personality factors.

If Dittes' conclusion were a valid one, it could draw on a contrast between the traits of dominance and control that need to be balanced against the care and affection that is both a female *and* a "religious" trait. Such a conclusion could also be explained in terms of the *awareness* and readiness of religious people to disclose their inadequacies in answers to personality scales, since religion itself aims to meet the needs, and give comfort to those who are weak or threatened. Religion and psychology both focus on inadequacy, helplessness, and weakness; but when they are being applied they try to overcome these weaknesses in different ways, by a process of conversion or salvation (Sarason, 1981) on the one hand, or by therapy (Kilbourne and Richardson, 1984) on the other.

William James (1902-1960, pp. 269-271) identified the practical consequences of saintliness with asceticism, strength of soul, purity and charity, which are also aligned with ideal female traits. Allport (1960) found the attributes of a mature personality in engagement, compassion, emotional security, functional intelligence, self-insight and directedness which he synthesized into an intrinsic religious orientation. The intrinsic and extrinsic orientations to religion that Allport identified emphasized another structural level of religion that, as Donahue's (1985) meta-analysis argues, may define the way that any belief system operates with reference to dogmatism and bigotry. The intrinsically religious are committed and low on dogmatism, while extrinsic religiousness "does a good job at measuring the sort of religion that gives religion a bad name", being positively correlated with prejudice, dogmatism and trait anxiety, and with fear of death but not altruism. These relationships between religion and personality are most unlikely to be linear.

Intrinsic religiousness therefore confounds the characteristics of those who are low in prejudice and of those who are religiously unsettled, so that people who are low on intrinsic religiousness can be either non-religious *or* extrinsic in their orientation. These orientations to religion do not therefore correspond with the simple distinction between religious belief and disbelief that has been a staple in the psychology of religion.

Other approaches to the structure of religions go beyond the simple distinction between the open or closed organizational structures which sociologists have identified with Churches and sects respectively. (Dynes, 1955, has produced measures of those orientations.) Following in that tradition, Wallis (1984) has classified the new religious movements as accommodating, rejecting, or affirming the world (p. 6), but "with some world-rejecting cadres of world-affirming movements" (p. 125), and commentators, who may be hostile or sympathetic to them, offering external or internal accounts of what they involve (p. 133). Stark and Bainbridge's (1980) finding that sects arise from schism and cults from innovation identifies these organizational structures in terms of their origins and history, and parallel the subject variables that psychologists use.

In a roughly similar way, psychologists who are concerned with intellectual or personality development have distinguished immature from mature forms of (religious) thinking, belief and attachment (cf. Godin, 1971), although these forms of accepting or using religion are not independent of what religious texts have been thought to prescribe and from which religious traditions and individuals can each select narrowly or broadly to identify the beliefs they find they are able to accept.

Religious and psychological structures

These psychological structures that have been identified refer to a content of religion that is widely recognized and to which reactions have been assessed. They are therefore convergent, and if the measurements were made on different assumptions (with an emphasis, for example, on disbelief rather than belief) the outcomes would be quite different, and could give findings similar to that for the strategies used in a Prisoner's Dilemma game being dependent on whether it is presented as a problem to be solved or as a competition (Abric, 1984). In this simplistic sense the religion that is seen by those who are inside it is different from that seen by outsiders, not only because they have less knowledge, since even insiders do not all have comparable knowledge or responses. The components of a religion and the experiences it selects or elicits are not, therefore, necessarily evaluated in the same way by those who are inside and those outside of it. Kim and Rosenberg (1980) therefore argued that evaluation rather than acceptance or rejection is the central proces in any judgment process.

Figure 1 shows how the major components of religion might interact, from an outsider's perspective. An insider would recognize the same components, but they would be differently evaluated and finer distinctions would be made within any sub-category. This model could be compared with the explicitly content based "map" of King (1967), which reduces to subjective beliefs and feelings, and religious involvement or participation (King and Hunt, 1975) (see p. 77). Any view of religionism can be fitted into the traditions within which people become aware of religion, and the doctrines they are offered and can accept, would modify or reject.

Thouless, who defined personal religion as "a felt, practical relationship with what is believed in as a superhuman being or beings" in 1923 was not inclined to defend that view in 1971 (p. 11) because of its focus on the supernatural. In 1971 he distinguished a religious attitude from scientific naturalism, in that the "world of space and time in which our bodies live is not the only part of our environment to which we must be adjusted". Religious people, he said, "believe that there is also some kind of spiritual world which makes demands on our behaviour, our thinking and our feeling" (p. 12). This is probably the defining characteristic of "religion".

A defect of the psychology of religion is the extent to which it has focussed either on responses to specific doctrinal statements of beliefs, or on non-doctrinal but widely recognized beliefs. It may be, however, that among most Westerners, religion is socially represented by doctrinal variants of basic Judeo-Christian truths except for the few who have been influenced by non-Western religions and their derivatives, which Western psychology has hardly touched except in terms of meditational and other technologies, and the effects of the new religious groups that carry those beliefs into practices directed at personal and social adjustment. The further one enters (or belongs to) a conventional religious structure, the more specifically it is construed. The further away one moves, the more general religion appears, the vaguer it becomes, and the more readily it disappears into social and linguistic structures. That conclusion interacts with the distinction between conservative and liberal orientations or constructions, since each person restructures what they encounter to make it acceptable and intelligible. If we believe in God, we must fit ourselves into the available "texts" and traditions, with their own definitions. These reactions of acceptance or rejection have been assessed by the numerous scales that are available and which rely on broadly evaluative judgements, so that religious responsiveness is now accepted as a quantifiable, if a latent, social variable that is accessed through its content.

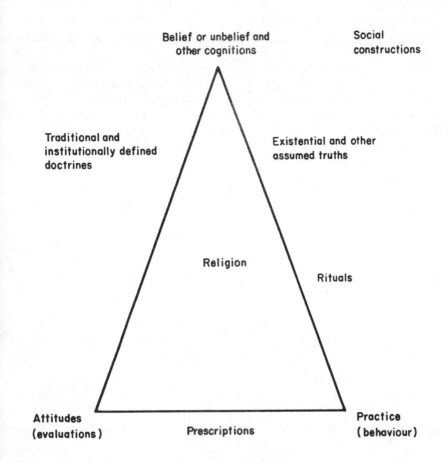

Fig. 1 *A schematic diagram of the components of a religionism factor.*

Summary

Any detailed analysis of religious structures rests on some knowledge of religious doctrines and the modes of response to it. So King and Hunt worked within the Methodist tradition and Strommen studied Lutherans. In a broader context, Broen worked on fundamentalism and nearness to God and Lenski distinguished involvement with and orientations to doctrinal orthodoxy and devotionalism, while Donahue (1985) argued that all these analyses should be at a higher level and in terms of a religious attachment and not as responses to specific objects (whether the Bible, God or the Church).

Individual differences in religiousness that have been identified include liberal-conservative and intrinsic-extrinsic orientations although the evidence for personality differences and for specific behavioural and other consequences or the effects of adopting a religious stance are not clear. Sacred and profane, natural or supernatural, magical or scientific categories are neglected aspects of religiousness, but whatever categories are adopted the aim has been to establish links between psychological variables and the traditional, organizational, or theological features behind what people *believe*.

6   Understanding the religious dimensions

> ... whether there be knowledge, it shall vanish away. For we know in part, and we prophesy in part ... When I was a child, I spoke as a child, I understood as a child: but when I became a man, I put away childish things. (1 Corinthians 13, 8 and 11)
>
> ... after 75 years of research psychologists interested in religion are confronted with an avalanche of descriptive and correlational data but few promising theories explaining why people think feel and act as they do with regard to religion. (Batson, 1977, p. 415)

Some conception of the stages of religious development has been an implicit feature of traditional theories and explanations of religion in general, and of Christianity in particular. These stages carry assumptions about the proper or mature forms of religion and of how to be (or become) a believer. Bowker, however, concluded that, "There is no conclusion" (1973, p. 181) to this problem. Assertions about the truth of particular religious claims lurk behind these theories, since the religious perspective itself is an important mode of understanding. Contrasted against that view is, for example, Marx's judgement that religious belief is fallacious, or Feuerbach's argument that anthropology is the key to theology because it is about man and the nature of man. Marx's views about the origins and functions of religion within societies that dominate their members, who are alienated from what they have themselves created and compensate with a fantasy world that offers later rewards for the oppressed, showed how religion justifies and preserves the existing social order. Freud's explanations of religion as an illusion were similar, although dervied from a psychological theory of unconscious defence mechanisms. As Ernest Jones said, "the religious life represents a dramatisation on a cosmic plane of the emotions, fears and longings which arose in the child's relation to his parents" (1926).

Other theories about "our sense of God" (Bowker, 1973) have not only relied on psychological but also on the social processes that construct reality (Berger and Luckmann, 1972). Durkheim, who recognized that religion has always been fundamental to society, looked for its primitive or elementary forms, and believed that some view of the sacred is an essential part of any society. Because of the complex and fragmented character of modern societies several other foci of integration have tried to displace religion. Work, sport and even the search for health can be included here. In line with that, Weber gave religion a structured role in providing common patterns of meaning through the myths and symbols that rationalize our interpretations of the world.

Theories of religion

Pratt (1920), in his *Religious Consciousness*, examined religion both socially and individually, since both perspectives are involved in it in a manner that is similar to the Cartesian dualism of mind and body, although Pratt also pointed to the important role of the "subconscious" as a fringe of the mind (p. 50), tracing it from Leibnitz to C. S. Myers (pp. 45–46), for whom the unconscious was the channel for telepathy. Pratt himself was unimpressed by that, saying that it "immediately suggests round squares and true falsehoods" (p. 55) and that an "appeal to the unknowable to explain the contradictory is not very enlightening". Of alternative, "physical approaches" to unconscious material, he said that they "have groped and grubbed and worked their way through a mass of abnormal and often very unpleasant cases, mining what facts they could; while the Myers school has been borne often on the wings of intuition to conclusions far more interesting, and, if true, metaphysically far more interesting" (p. 46). Tylor's theory of animism postulated another form of these primitive psychological mechanisms for religious thinking that is not dissimilar from Piaget's concept of egocentricity, in which a child's necessary immaturity forces magical, sometimes transcendentally mystical solutions to natural problems which are inadequately understood (cf. Houssiadas and Brown, 1980). Wundt, however, took a wide sweep across cultural history and identified a sequence from primitive religion and totemism to a period of Gods as heroes and finally to a religion based on humanity. Jaynes's (1976) modern version of this developmental or evolutionary theory identified the separate functions of the right and the left brain which came to be coordinated by the rationality of language (at least in right-handed people). It is a short step from there to the discovery of religion within the brain's biochemistry (perhaps in β-endorphin: Fischer and Falke, 1984). A feminist perspective on religious control treats general arguments like these as a remnant of patriarchy (Ruether, 1983).

Any religious explanation entails a particular perspective on religion and social science, but it is hard to find single explanations that can fit into the whole of religious phenomenology and do not give an implicit priority to social or psychological processes, unless it is itself explicitly partisan and derived from some other coherent system.

In considering the current theories, I will look only at work that is primarily psychological and refers to Christian traditions. In doing this, the popular plausibility of the derivatives of psychoanalytic theory will be apparent, although those views are not well-supported empirically beyond psychoanalysis itself. We must therefore distinguish what have now become common-sense explanations from the formal psychological theories that guide research. The psychoanalytic explanations approached religious beliefs and practices from the point of view of wish-fulfilment, the control of drives or needs, the balance of primary and secondary process thinking, object relations, the genesis of conscience and an ego-ideal, or the economics of libidinal and aggressive urges ... "[so that] religion can be approached as a symptom. Psychoanalysis said more forcefully what James had noted when he said that people *use* their God" (Homans, 1970, p. 117). Stratton (1911) had, however, noted differences between religions that involve problem solving rather than information processing. That contrast links to the orientations, not to say the motives for and the meaning of whatever it is that religions provide. The obviously social sanctions of any religion that individuals carry may be passive or more active, and provide an important basis for classifying religious people.

Perspectives on religion

Pratt (1920, p. 13) divided the attachments to traditional or historical religion into primitive credulity, intellectual belief, and emotional belief, and he derived rational and volitional, or mystical orientations from William James's *Will to Believe* (1912), while a suspension of disbelief suggested practical or moral orientations that formed another category (p. 14). Baron von Hügel had earlier argued that in religion "external, definite facts and acts are found to lead to certain internal, deep, all-embracing emotions and experiences" (cited by Pratt, 1920, p. 18), which recognizes that we are reactive and responsive, and can produce creative and adaptive, or destructive solutions. But religion forms only a part and not the whole of life, although Troeltsch insisted that there are reciprocal relations between the whole and these parts (cited by Wiles, 1976, p. 96). One test of a religion might be made against its success in making social and personal transformations or applications of whatever it involves, as when Schweitzer (1948) argued that the evidence of history suggests that each period creates Jesus to accord with its own character. When the current theologies of liberation make life and death the universal points of reference for religion they fit with our scepticism, which has also forgotten about limbo.

The outsider's perspective is apparent in any psychological analysis that is designed to make a believer's "life of faith" intelligible, and an involved existential stance does not allow specific religious beliefs to be interpreted simply in psychological or pathological terms. The fatherhood of God or the life to come cannot be interpreted by their manifest content to find the motives or reasons for holding those beliefs.

On the other hand, Elkind (1970) argued on Piagetian grounds that accepting religious solutions to questions of ultimate meaning is a result of normal mental growth. One strand of that argument expects that increasing self-awareness and criticism allows received practices or beliefs to be reinterpreted abstractly or metaphorically so that those who do not develop in that way are therefore in some sense immature. Hunt (1972), who identified the forms of religious meaning as literal, antiliteral and mythological, also cast each of those perspectives into the social constraints of a religious membership or alignment. That was reinterpreted in linguistic terms by Orlowski (1979), although religious institutions sustain and sanction the religious beliefs that take their meaning from a theological system with its own context and tradition, which can itself be interpreted.

Any theory of religion must recognize the separate yet coordinated contributions of persons, society and theology. Each of those levels mandates and explains some aspects of the belief and practices prescribed by a religion. Taking any of these components separately seems to reduce religion to pathology when the stress is on psychological factors, to civil religion when the stress is social, and to history when theology alone is emphasized. Continuing religious traditions maintain their own perspectives that specify and limit the credibility of the particular beliefs their insiders recognize. The increasing lack of credibility Catholics give to the formal proscriptions against "artificial" contraception is an example of that process.

Outsiders do not understand the corporate nature of faith. As Mitchell (1981) argues, "When we look at traditions, whether political or religious, which have a continuous history, what we find is a range of beliefs and a variety of interpretations. Not all individuals or groups within the tradition accept, or have in the past accepted, all of these, but all have accepted some of them" (p. 12). Any system of religious belief carries that ambiguity through the various levels of its meaning, and interpretations of what is involved must be made within a discourse that allows assumptions about what can be taken seriously.

Psychologists make similar assumptions about the most fruitful data and theories, which depend on their own traditions or models. They are not immune to the limited horizons and a neglect of others' perspectives that characterize the closed-mindedness Rokeach (1960) identified. Functional analyses of belief necessarily separate the content of any knowledge of the world from the secondary advantages which may accrue from, for example, gaining access to a group or following a leader who "knows".

Any study of a religion therefore entails implicit and explicit assumptions about the processes that may be involved, whether they are psychological or social, and about the "correct" procedures that are required to test a theory or give an explanation. Table 6 sets out some characteristics of three dominant psychological approaches to religion, comparing them with a broadly theological perspective. Although that perspective is confessional in the sense of being intelligible to believers it also involves an informal psychological analysis, because it applies to people, that is also to be found in the entries for Buddhism and Taoism in Harré and Lamb's *Encyclopedic Dictionary* (1983).

Table 6   *Three approaches to the psychology of religion, aligned with a theological approach that follows Wiles (1976)*

Approach	Behavioural positivism	Socio-personal integration	Humanistic phenomenology	Confessional theology
Religion as	External (or pathological)	Tradition	Transcendental	Revealed
Man as	Mechanistic	Consensual	Unique	Free
Psychological epistemology	Causes	Norms	Experience	Prayer and life within a community
Method	Observation	Description	Introspection	Participation and reason
Data	Behaviour	Social action	Consciousness	Texts and faith
Aim	Prediction and control	Explanation	Interpretation	Understanding
Emphasis	Nomothetic (Lockean) science	Cohesion	Idiographic (Leibnitzian) self-help	Completeness
An exponent	Dunlap (1946)	Allport (1950)	Strunk (1962)	Wiles (1976)
A focus	Mohammed	Christ	Buddha	Yahweh

The psychologies implicit in religious or theological systems have been explored by those advocating an explicit alignment between psychology and theology (cf. Malony, 1985), although that approach raises the question whether, or in what way, a non-believer can ever understand a believer's "truth" except by some reductionism or a translation into other terms that are usually psychological. Although psychology is still expected to be able to find explanations of religion, and the psychology of religion is itself agnostic, psychologists are not necessarily non-believers (cf. Beit-Hallahmi, 1977). Tension among the advocates of different psychological approaches or theories often extends beyond pragmatic or evidential considerations to strongly held beliefs and meta-beliefs about the nature and procedures of science itself.

Not necessarily eclectic approaches

Writing of the overlapping theories of prejudice, Allport (1954, p. 208) noted that in them "we have at our disposal a ring of keys, each of which opens one gate of understanding". Such eclecticism is unusual, although Thoulesss (1971, p. 9) also said that we cannot expect to have a unique theory of religion. Even within a single tradition like psychoanalysis there are differences of opinion, for example, between Freud, Jung, Melanie Klein and Ricoeur as exponents of a depth or dynamic psychology, and differences can be found in the religious assumptions underlying the psychology of religion itself. While Freud treated religion as a category, for William James it was a quality, and phenomenologists like Heiler and Otto gave their primary emphasis to the meaning of experience. These are not just reinterpretations of religious meaning, but focus on separate aspects or forms of religious response that are articulated through social and psychological structures and processes, including the language that expresses thoughts, feelings, attitudes, beliefs, hopes and so on, and by the learning and habits, cognitive consistency, or dissonance reduction that maintains responsiveness. Recourse to experience, intuition, argument or a positivistic and value-free approach does not resolve these issues. While tough minded mechanists are prescriptive about the procedures that psychology should use and others advocate a personal or person-oriented approach (cf. Chapman and Jones, 1980), these camps are being bridged by the models now being developed within cognitive science (cf. Johnson-Laird, 1983). For these reasons, philosophical problems cannot be swept aside since they are not beyond science.

Granted the non-quantitative problems embedded in the psychology of religion and the explanations for the neglect of quantitative methods and theory in terms of the biases of the investigators, which were advanced by Capps *et al*. (1976b), we should look at the dominant theoretical perspectives that have been applied to it.

1. A long tradition of religious psychology has welded an explicit, usually humane psychology to Christianity. Examples of this genre extend from Alliott (1855) through Everett (1902), Stratton (1911), Grensted (1930), Weatherhead (1935), to Lee (1948) and Jeeves (1976), and range broadly across both religious and psychological perspectives. Lee, for example, was a psychoanalyst and an Anglican priest, while Jeeves is a neuropsychologist and evangelical Anglican layman.

2. The psychoanalytic-clinical or depth psychology model was developed by Freud and his followers who turned naturally to religion because of its archaic nature and moral base. Their interpretations were readily accepted, and not simply applied to religious expressions of pathology (Rieff, 1966). Capps *et al.* (1976a) have 99 references to "depth" psychology in their bibliography and they list nine titles to do with religion in the form "Freud and … ". Those who have adapted psychodynamic perspectives to religion include Godin (1967) and Vergote (1969) as Jesuits, Kunkel (1943) and Pfister (1948) as Protestants, Zilboorg (1967) as a convert from Judaism to Catholicism, Fromm (1950) and Erikson (1948) as neo-Freudians, and Ricoeur (1967) as a theoretician.

3. Closely related, but based in clinical practice, is the "pastoral psychology" model developed by Boisen (1936) who stressed "the role of religion in mental illness but emphasizes the importance of taking the religious contents and dynamics of the illness seriously" (Capps *et al.*, 1976, p. 243). Oates (1958) and Hiltner (1943) juxtaposed theological and psychological terms in sin and sickness, grace and gratitude, providence and trust, and Boisen understood the recovery from his own psychiatric illness as a successful problem-solving or conversion by which he found a new perspective on his life through a theological understanding which Homans (1967, p. 102) says linked neo-Freudian or Rogerian psychology with a neo-Reformation theology. While the Hartford Theological Seminary offered a course on the psychology of religion in 1899, similar courses now still have a pastoral or pedagogical rather than an empirical emphasis. The Academy of Religion and Mental Health was established in 1957 to foster this work which is in general "ego-based" (Pruyser, 1968). The Menninger Clinic and the Princeton Theological Seminary are important centres for this perspective which uses a "hermeneutic of appropriation" in which pastors and others involved in religion have turned to psychology for their ideas and techniques. The emphasis is individual rather than social, stressing compassion and self-directed change rather than power or anomie and alienation (Beit-Hallahmi, 1974). While pastoral psychology still focusses its interest on religion and mental health (Sanua, 1969; Bergin, 1983)

the recently developed university courses in "religious studies" may
now be trying to annex a phenomenology of religion that extends the
conventional boundaries of theological study to the non-Christian traditions and not only to psychology.

4. Behavioural models were developed from Watson's (1925) emphasis on
   "Behaviorism", in which the introspective material behind any public,
   measurable responses was judged as unsuitable for psychological analysis. Variants of Behaviorism have become the dominant academic
   "School" of psychology, and readily contrast against the dynamic and
   more recent humanistic perspectives that Sullivan (1962) identified with
   the observation of behaviour and inferences "about the experiences of
   the person's observation". Behavioural analyses are not strictly concerned with belief as such, except as it guides action. A constructive
   form of this approach is to be found in Gorsuch's (1984) analysis of the
   current measurement paradigm that has derived from Thorndike's psychophysical scaling procedures.

5. The existential, humanistic and phenomenological psychology that has
   already been examined broadly in Table 6 derives from the philosophies
   of Brentano, Stumpf and Husserl who stressed the creative and constructive potential of persons, which contributed to Tillich's (1952)
   identification of religion with "ultimate concerns". Despite its popular
   appeal this approach is naive about data, stressing instead the values
   that are to be aimed at. Those who are most sympathetic to religion lie
   towards the human end of any psychological continuum because of the
   "richness" and "irreducibility" of the religion they want to describe,
   just as those who are behaviourally oriented have their commitment to a
   general psychological theory that puts religion on a Procrustean bed.

6. Allport's social-personality model, outlined in *The Individual and His
   Religion* (1950), has been the single most influential perspective on
   religion in recent years. It balances persons and their contexts and
   recognizes religion as a normal social and psychological process.
   Although Allport did not identify a separate religion, in his work on
   prejudice he examined a range of theories that emphasize the distal or
   historical roots of prejudice, its proximal causes in ignorance, socialization or upbringing, the effects of specific teaching or indoctrination,
   the differentials of power, and personality-based explanations in
   ethnocentrism (or egocentricity), displaced hostility and similar
   dynamic mechanisms, as well as social theories that refer to inter-group
   relations and scape-goating, cognitive theories of stereotypes and
   beliefs about selected targets, and finally the biological theories that

either stress instincts or such drives as aggression. Each of these theories has some relevance to religion.

Allport's model contrasts against G. Stanley Hall's "Clark School" that dominated the psychology of religion at the beginning of the century, which encouraged research and published the *American Journal of Religious Psychology and Education* from May 1904, until 1915. Leuba, Starbuck, E. T. Clark and Coe were all aligned with that School, which invited Freud and Jung to make their first US visit in 1909.

7. European schools. While Allport's broad perspective, which was also carried by Dittes, has been dominant in the United States, Godin in Brussells, Vergote in Leuven and Sunden in Sweden have had a substantial influence in Europe. Godin applied Piaget's developmental psychology, and Vergote has worked within an explicitly dynamic tradition, although neither has responded only to those influences. Sunden was concerned with religious experience. William James's *Varieties* was translated into German by G. W. Wobbermin in 1907 and the *Zeitschrift für Religion-psychologie* began in 1906. From the German and French journals concerned with religion it could be concluded that the European perspective is more social than psychological, although Godin (1967) argued that Girgensohn and James were the two who had had the greatest influence in establishing the psychology of religion as a "science of observation".

8. Religious material is also used within general psychological models as a vehicle to explore basic processes like attitudes, decision making or values. No prior assumptions are made there about the specific meanings of religion in either social or personal terms, since the religious content is of little interest for its own sake. This approach can be found most clearly in Fishbein and Ajzen (1975), who take religion as one domain for the analysis of social attitudes, but it also appears in Chapman and Jones (1980) and in the standard list of psychological questions that Giles *et al.* (1975) propose as the basis for a psychology of religion that is centred on language and the maintenance of social interaction. (For example, when is religion salient in conversation and what are persuasive religious messages?) These general approaches to religion have been centred on its role in social interaction more than on its individual psychology; but in fact, most of the actual experiments in the psychology of religion are essentially social (cf. Deconchy, 1985).

9. Other social models draw on the structural and the functional approaches that are found in sociology and anthropology. While these

traditions focus on a religious content that is consistent and readily interpreted they resort to psychological theories to account for individual influences, whether in socialization, understanding and meaning, or group involvement (Heelas, 1985).

10. Homans (1967) argued that a dialogue model, in which theology and psychology contribute to one another independently, holds promise for progress because it recognizes the central role of transcendence for religion and the responsiveness of modern theologians to Freudianism and to other aspects of the culture. In a similar way Spilka's (1970) anti-reductionist approach would base the psychology of religion in "objective research" while recognizing explicitly theological values.

That these models interact and overlap is shown by Palma's (1978) advocacy of a "normative approach" that relies on G. W. Allport's work as the "paradigm", and by the argument that "normal" views about science are held "religiously" by science itself. Religious control and language have also given paradigmatic models for political analysis, although that could simply reflect the extent to which the "history" of the involvements of any group stretch back to the period when religion *was* dominant and powerful.

One can be a *bricoleur*, in Levi-Strauss's sense, taking up whatever can be useful theoretically and methodologically to advance one's analysis. This might, however, extend religious analyses too far, as when Pruyser (1974) offered experimental aesthetics as a model for a psychological analysis of religion. Religious processes must be deliberately investigated, whether in an exploratory or explanatory mode or with reference to behaviour, language or morality. Any theory is a filter that can gain understanding. While separate theories might be integrated and their convergence recognized, it is now almost a common-place for religion's supporters to assert that it is a complex, over-determined phenomenon, and for its opponents to adopt a reductionistic attitude to it.

Towards a coherent approach

The analyses or uses that psychologists have made of religious beliefs, belonging, behaviour, and experience are summarized in Table 7. Not only are measurements of religious behaviour ambiguous, but the reasons (not to say the "motives") to believe or belong (and not to do so) can hardly be determined without reference to the believer's own account, which moves any enquiry to its subjective context, where there is always more to tell.

Mancias and Secord (1983) write of a new, realist theory of science (following Bhaskar, 1978) that rejects the "covering law" model of scientific explanation with its assumption that explanation and prediction are symmetrical. An important feature of this approach is its integration of "subjective" and "objective" perspectives and the recognition that socially or ideologically relevant responses must be understood partly through existing social structures, within which they are reproduced, and which individuals transform by meaningful and intentional action. At the same time they are coercive, and limit how we can act. So religious language, actions, and beliefs presuppose individual skills, competence and habits, and a group or social tradition that sanctions and recognizes their meaning.

Table 7 *Psychological and social analyses of religious belief (which itself is tied to theologically acceptable doctrines)*

I. Psychological or personal focus
    (A) etic or participant analyses
        (a) immediately, as reasoned or self-evident truth
        (b) evaluatively, for conclusions about believers
            (1) positively (through support or "surprise")
            (2) negatively (through rejection or reconstruction)
    (B) emic or detached analyses
        (a) as an independent variable
            (1) functional adaptations (Katz, 1971),
                e.g. what can religious beliefs do, whether existentially or defensively?
            (2) attributionally (Proudfoot and Shaver, 1975),
                e.g. to identify:
                    (i) personality characteristics (both implicit and explicit),
                    (ii) social attitudes (usually conservative).
                    (iii) social position
            (3) structurally (Allport and Ross, 1967),
                e.g. as an orientation to, or focus of religion in:
                    (i) response patterns (Thouless, 1971)
                    (ii) content (Sanai, 1952)
                    (iii) explanations (Spilka *et al.*, 1985b)
        (b) as a dependent variable, produced by:
            (1) cognitive processes
            (2) experience
            (3) socialization or learning
            (4) group influences
            (5) psychodynamic processes (especially projection)

II. Social or sociological focus
    (A) institutional (e.g. Greeley's (1982) approach to religion as a social movement)
    (B) functional (e.g. Mol's (1985) approach that aligns religion with cohesive roles as in rites of passage)

III. Psycho-social interactions that differentially legitimate religious and other beliefs

---

In examining "religiousness", we must therefore distinguish between (1) religious people, (2) their beliefs and knowledge, (3) attitudes and other responses, (4) experiences claimed and (5) their sanctioning religious traditions and groups. Each of these components can be explored from psychological or individual and social perspectives. Although separate structures may be identifiable, when they subdivide, these components are always interrelated. Let us consider each separately.

(1) Religious people

Religion is obviously carried by people. In being religious they respond to, and reproduce or react against, their own religious formation and training. Those reactions are usually unable to modify these religious traditions. It is perhaps for this reason that early psychological theories of religion (Hall, 1904) explained it in terms of individual development and an increasing sophistication which may force changes on the believers because of a decentred awareness of the implications of any beliefs, or the unintended consequences of their action. But religious "people" have typically been studied through the personality characteristics that may facilitate survival within particular religious frameworks, and assume that those with a conservative orientation will readily accept the norms of a conservative group. Yet it is important to note that while there is no evidence that religious groups enforce particular kinds of personality, they do expect responses to conform with what is recognizably "religious", just as those who are *not* religious are assumed to be uniform in their negative evaluations and in their disbelief. Classifications as leaders and followers, members and non-members, Jews and Gentiles, sheep and goats, reinforce these pressures, and those who continue within a religious frame could develop defined characteristics because they are influenced by that alignment and accept the group norms. A longitudinal perspective could be expected to show some evidence of personality development or change, although the majority of personality studies have used one-shot or cross-sectional approaches to data.

(2) Beliefs and knowledge

The creeds and sacred texts provide the formal statements that are conveyed in religious teaching. We are taught to accept or reject them and we are given some knowledge of their basis and justification; we distinguish beliefs from facts, and use our knowledge about religious texts and history to justify our beliefs. A person's religious beliefs therefore depend on what has been received, which may be modified so that it makes sense. De Saussure's linguistic theory provides a useful model of these processes in his distinction of *la langue*, or a whole language, from *la parole*, as the parts of it that a person uses, and which develop an "internal structure" or schema with its own coherence. Religious or denominational groups similarly make their own doctrinal and practical emphases and differ in the coherence or the conformity that they demand from their members, who will themselves select what is important for them, whether deliberately or by assimilating what is congenial and acceptable, interpreting them in literal, anti-literal or metaphorical terms (cf. Hunt, 1972). Poythress (1975), who converted these alternatives of Hunt's into Likert scales, found eight religious response types involving mythological, mythological-anti-literal, literal-anti-mythological, literal-pro-mythological, strongly anti-religious, moderately anti-religious, slightly anti-religious, and non-religious. While most elements in belief are "found" (in the sense in which Duchamp turned ready-made objects into works of art by signing and exhibiting them), they can also be modified to be made credible or linked with other beliefs.

(3) Attitudes

Religious people also have *attitudes* as predispositions to respond positively or negatively or to evaluate stimuli and social "objects" they think are related to religion. These structured or patterned responses are usually identified with conservatism (Wilson, 1973), dogmatism (Rokeach, 1960) authoritarianism (Adorno *et al.*, 1950) or orthodoxy (Deconchy, 1980). All of those terms have both religious and personality overtones, and there is continuing uncertainty whether these attitudinal patterns also form personality traits, in the sense that they can reduce some of the variance between individuals. That "liberalism" has been a neglected component of religious attitudes reflects their more readily identified conservative nature. Hood (1983) has argued that more attention should be given to the methods and measures that have been used to assess fundamentalism because the "simplistic views" of it "feed into stereotyped modes of thought that may be more characteristic of the scientific study of fundamentalism than of fundamentalism itself". Implicit religious *and* scientific attitudes certainly drive many quite systematic studies of attitudes.

Apparent inconsistencies between attitudes and actions are not simply a result of error, and we may have expected too much consistency. Asch's (1946) research on the effect or evaluations of the source of expressed attitudes showed that the ambiguity of social responsiveness can be resolved by reassigning values on the basis of additional information. In the same vein, Thurstone (1954) said that:

> a man may be entirely consistent in what he says and in what he does about a controversial issue and yet both of these indexes may be dead wrong in reflecting his attitude. In order to determine a man's attitude in the sense of affective disposition about a controversial issue, it will be necessary for his friends to ask him privately when he is free to speak his mind and is not likely to be quoted.

Allport (1935, p. 824) made a similar point when he said that:

> Not only is the individual inclined to give a safe and conventional answer, but, strange to say, he is often sincere in his answer for he possesses two distinct sets of contradictory attitudes, one reserved for his personal and private life, and the other socially determined and quite honestly maintained in public. It is by no means certain that the inner, private attitude is any more fundamental or significant than the outer or public attitude. Both may be sincerely held.

As well as being statements carrying both public and private perspectives, attitudes are *used*, and they are not simply self-reports, descriptions or "read-outs" of affective states, or about the causes of behaviour. They are used socially and agreement with their traditional implications may be withheld. Taking a child for Baptism fulfils a social obligation and satisfies the requirements of a traditional Christian initiation, even when the meaning of that sacrament is not well understood. To withhold Baptism can alienate the parents who have a different view, and questions about whose consent is required for Baptism is only one issue that has divided the Church.

While Church records or observed behaviour that depends on external rules are not good guides to religious attitudes, these attitudes can, however, be used as:

(a) a basis for our communications about social alignments or to define a stance or an "attitude" in the original sense;

(b) evaluative statements of approval or disapproval, typically in the form "I feel that ...";

(c) as a guide to future action, or to clarify and account for past actions making them appear consistent (Snyder *et al.*, 1983; Lalljee *et al.*, 1984);

(d) as expressive, self-referential statements, in the form "I prefer ..." or "I favour ...", that are used for impression management;

(e) to convince, convert, witness, or explain oneself to others.

Uncertainty about the inconsistency of attitudes and behaviour has largely disappeared from the recent assessments of attitudes (Fishbein and Ajzen, 1975; Eiser, 1980); as Campbell put it, situations (and actions) are the hurdles attitudes must cross before they can be expressed, which could explain the apparent preoccupation with their quantification and group-based differences. Even the Churches ask, "How many people?" and "How much money?" which avoids difficult questions about how good they are or how strong their faith is that can only be answered with operational definitions of how it is to be assessed.

(4) Experiences

Conversion experiences, once *the* approach to religion, are now primarily interpreted as a response to pressure or persuasion, or as a behavioural process in which awareness or control is reduced (cf. Sargant, 1961; Lofland and Stark, 1966), or simply as a reasoned decision. Social pressures and the effects of situations themselves are thought to be more important in modifying our responses than are any internal needs (but cf. Hay, 1982). When religious action draws on particular states or interests it follows from what is prescribed or allowed for in particular social contexts. That involvement establishes a specific identity which in turn controls our experiences, and directs our attention, creativity and the concepts we form, as well as the beliefs and values that give meaning to our social and physical environment.

(5) Religious traditions and groups

Each denomination has historical traditions that emphasize and select from a broad repertoire of possible beliefs and forms of attachment, to identify those who are agnostic, heretical, committed and so on because of their differentiated acceptance or rejection of what has been received. So Methodism in Australia began with the Wesleyans, until the Primitive Methodists separated from them. They were reunited after the First World War and continued until 1976, when they formed the Uniting Church with many (but not all) of the Presbyterian, Congregational and Church of Christ groups. That the separate Churches continue to be critically important to some people and only nominally so to others is shown by the number of congregations that stayed out of the union, and by the fact that in the 1981 Australian census 3.4 per cent still identified themselves as Methodists, compared with 7.3 per cent of the population in 1976.

Religious traditions establish and maintain values, so that a high churchman needs the Church *because* it is the Body of Christ. Yet the acknowledged differences between religious groups like Quakers and Catholics cannot support psychological typologies in terms of personality, except stereotypically, any more than political parties show personality differences that are independent of prescribed ideologies and their solutions to social issues (cf. Christie and Geis's, 1968, analysis of Machiavellianism). Processes like defensiveness, anxiety, tranquility or commitment have nevertheless facilitated easy psychological interpretations of the ideological content that believers hold, which can only be broadly validated (Billig, 1978). It is slipshod to assume that they must have a psychological basis, because of our tendency to reify religious or political differences as typologics.

Religious groups have their own social structures, rules and conventions about both religious and secular matters, including their clergy and other elites. They sanction beliefs about, for example, who is among the "elect", whether election is achieved by faith or works, and who can perform the various roles or duties. These requirements limit the possibilities of religious belonging (Godin, 1964b), and form the group identifications that themselves implicitly control the confidence with which beliefs are held and expressed (Deconchy, 1982). Identifying oneself as belonging to a religious or ethnic group marks you off from the members of other groups (Turner and Giles, 1981), so that Gorsuch (1984) argues that in our culture, although religion is distinguished from non-religion, it readily breaks itself into theism, ritualism and so on. Fichter (1954) found that the structure of religious congregations (as face-to-face groups) can be aligned along a central-peripheral dimension, and Dittes (1969) emphasized that no group membership or identification implies that such people hold any particular religious beliefs.

That conclusion is reinforced by data from my students which show that they are almost equally divided between accepting their family's religious training or moving away towards their *own* position. One wrote that:

> I strongly follow the beliefs of a religion, but don't place much emphasis on the rituals and traditions within religions. I think the emphasis on them makes you religious while an emphasis on the beliefs and way of living doesn't. Rules are religious; following your beliefs etc. is just living in a certain way you've chosen. So while I don't think I am religious, others might.

That a person's religion is often indistinguishable from the traditions to which they belong avoids the incorrigibly subjective or idiosyncratic factors which older psychological explanations of religion found in sentiment, instinct, suggestion, or the unconscious. Those terms were adopted from self-referential perspectives on committed or traditional membership. O'Dea (1961) therefore aligned the dilemmas of institutional religion with its power, especially in conversion or coercion, with the administrative order that delimits the concrete from the spiritual, and in the mixed motives and misplaced concreteness it allows. From that perspective it is important to recognize the interests that are served by any analysis, which can foster or be an agent of the Church, or see the Church duping people to support its own position.

The appeal of religion

Religious people carry beliefs, knowledge, evaluative attitudes and other responses that reflect their religious membership and allow them to be recognized as "religious". Those explicit influences shape or prescribe the responses like prayer or meditation that can change those who practise them. But it is not clear to whom religion appeals, or who will be most appropriately studied beyond those who already belong, since those who are *not* religious are expected to disbelieve and evaluate religion negatively. For that reason it is impossible to treat individuals as if they were randomly assigned to religious groups. Even those who believe will select from the existing religious structures and express degrees of agnosticism about what they believe, and only about half of those who are converted at evangelistic meetings can be expected to be active church-goers a year later (Argyle and Beit-Hallahmi, 1975, p. 43).

None of the models, paradigms or approaches to the psychology of religion considers the actual psychological processes that are required to draw continuing support for any religious content. Since this is complicated by philosophical or theological problems about the nature of truth, we might begin to examine what is involved in processing religious or any other specific knowledge. That task has hardly been started since the general focus for the psychology of religion has assumed that being "religious" (or being converted) requires a response to some set of religious beliefs themselves. But one cannot investigate everything at once, and scientific theories are built up piece-wise. In the same way, experimental psychologists concerned with linguistic processing or human learning have until recently neglected individual difference perspectives in their work; Eysenck (1981, p. xii) argues that "experimental psychology cannot do without taking individual differences into account". Despite that, the positive or negative inducements or effects of religious belief are yet to be experimentally studied.

Maranell (1974), however, who developed a model of religion with eight independent dimensions (Church orientation, ritualism, altruism, fundamentalism, theism, idealism, superstition and mysticism, pp. 13–23), explored the effects of controlled changes on these measures as a result of social derogation, criticism or arrogation, suggestibility, and perceptual rigidity or perseveration. He found that ritualism and idealism scores were increased by social arrogation, and that while the suggestible people were ritualistic and the non-suggestible idealistic, those with high ritualistic scores were perceptually rigid (pp. 201–202).

Questions about the way religious or other material is processed psychologically must be resolved first at the level of religion itself, before it can be aligned with trust, playfulness or hope, the search for meaning, or in terms of disguised family relationships. Specifically individual theories of religious belief and action must recognize that religious beliefs pre-exist, but are maintained by those who react to them favourably, and on whom they have positive or negative effects.

McClelland (1961) explained the link between Protestantism and capitalism in terms of the general ideas, beliefs and values that are fixed through child rearing practices, delay of gratification, independence and mastery training, which form high levels of achievement motivation. Because capitalist enterprises need that orientation, they must maintain the link between individual and society beyond the period of child rearing through other values. Failing to accept the possible "truth" or validity of any religious or transcendental perspective could indicate a temperamental bias against the idea of such reality, in favour of a materialistic perspective, or in William James's terms, to a lack of imagination, or an unreadiness to grant that the natural order might be both simple and complex (as in the claims of Sir John Eccles or Sir Alister Hardy). Alternatively, it could be playfully made "user-friendly" through an animistic or anthropomorphic modelling that does not have to be taken literally (cf. Thouless and Brown, 1964).

While we do not know what establishes the credibility of particular ideas or models, we know that some beliefs *are* convincing to some people. But the psychology of religion remains silent about how these connections and their plausibility are formed, and how particular influences are recognized or rejected, despite the innumerable examples and case studies of saints and martyrs. Contemporary psychologists have neglected the evidence from leaders and true believers in favour of an interest in their followers, whose experience of religion is shaped by the models that influence decisions to drift, reject or accept. Bowers (1968) has, however, shown that leaders are themselves the followers of others.

Despite their hoped-for objectivity, the explanations found in the psychology of religion are not like descriptions in the psychology of mathematics or sport, which are concerned with how to do it, and how to teach, coach or eliminate errors. In fact there is a continuing debate among religious educators about whether (and how) religion *should* be taught, especially by those who are not "committed Christians", or whether the new multi-culturalism should require Christians to teach about non-Christian traditions, at least in State schools. While Argyle and Beit-Hallahmi (1975, p. 207) assert that the world we live in has had the numinous removed from it, with an implication that religion's effects are decreasing, there is little evidence for that, at least in the numbers who claim to accept religious beliefs. We must, however, leave sociologists or moralists to decide why sport, for example, draws more attention in newspapers, television and radio, than does religion, which may be simply because it *is* a minority interest. To describe a person as a sports fanatic is not like calling someone a religious fanatic, because of the tendency to interpret the *content* of religious beliefs directly. Sporting occasions can, however, be interpreted as if they were religious rituals, because of the deference to the players, the enthusiasm of the crowd, and the rule-governed nature of what they transact.

A perignostic or multi-axial analysis

Although religious truth is maintained by a tradition or its "texts", and by reason or personal experience, few other forms of social life have been subjected to such detailed analysis as religion, perhaps because like sport it is tangible and more immediate than politics. For that reason, religion lies within an *assumptive* or constructed world that is unquestioned by most people. Non-believers look for some theory — biological, psychological or sociological — which will explain the religious "illusions", and believers seek to understand the manner in which a group conceives of reality and their relation to it. While religion is part of the social life of believers and non-believers, it has the further dimension of truth for believers (Evans-Pritchard, 1965, p. 121).

Greeley (1972), who wrote of the "ritual procedure" of rehearsing the history of an empirical social science of religion "to affirm the unity of social scientists" (p. 30), identified three strands in religion:

(1) "the integrators, or the functionalist followers of Durkheim, concerned essentially with religion as a source of social integration";
(2) purveyors of meaning and explanation, like "the disciples of Weber (particularly Talcott Parsons and his students), concerned primarily with the meaning-providing role of religion in contradistinction to Karl Marx";
(3) the deprivationists like Sigmund Freud who see religion "as a source of comfort in response to the deprivation and suffering that society inflicts upon certain groups", and who stress that religion is "a response to suffering and discontent", or a "social comfort" (p. 21).

Greeley's own view is that a combination of belonging and meaning, as well as comfort, provides an "extremely useful tool for understanding American religion". The unity *or* diversity of religion is an important aspect of its explanations, and "Why?" questions continue to be asked, despite the explanations that have been found already. The analyses of religion are broadly classified in Table 8, which draws from Evans-Pritchard (1965) and uses the concept of "perignosis" which, like the multi-axial classification adopted by the American Psychiatric Association in their DSM III (1980), looks around at what is to be known and not straight through to a single diagnosis. The importance of not focussing on a single dimension or conclusion is no less important for psychiatry than religion, since complex and over-determined causes operate in both of these domains. Tisdale (1966), for example, writes that "not only is religion in many ways very private and difficult technically to measure, it is also exceedingly complex. Attempts to isolate its essential aspect have certainly been made frequently, but they often turn out to be too simplistic" (p. 4). In a similar way, Argyle and Beit-Hallahmi (1975) collected empirical findings (which are essentially social) "to test psychological and sociological theories about the origins, functions and effects of religious behaviour" (p. 1), which Argyle (1964) had earlier summarized in terms of the "seven psychological roots of religion".

The four separate domains of explanation identified in terms of academic disciplines and with some common-sense in Table 8 implicate biological, psychological, social and cultural processes, and cover internal as well as the presumably invariable or "dependable" processes (Woodworth, 1958) and macro-social perspectives on "world religions". Evans-Pritchard (1965) continually emphasized that while "theories of primitive religion" may not still be found acceptable "in their time they have played an important part in the history of thought" (p. 3), although they are now judged to have been wrong. He was especially severe on Jevons's (1896) history of religion, saying that "It is a collection of absurd reconstructions, unsupportable hypotheses and conjectures, wild speculations, suppositions and assumptions, inappropriate analogies, misunderstandings and misinterpretations, and especially in what he wrote about totemism, just plain nonsense" (p. 5). Exaggerated claims continue to be made.

At a biological level, it has been asserted in conversation that, "LSD is *the* basic religion before all the organized religions got started", and it is still common enough to believe that man was made in God's image (Genesis, 1, 26). Reynolds and Tanner (1983) have recently examined the "biological consequences of belief in God", including the impact of religious sanctions on contraceptive practice. At the psychological level, Pratt (1920) noted that, "The Eighteenth Century regarded religion as purely an individual matter, and even such recent writers as Max Miller and C. P. Tiele speak of the religion of primitive men as though it were purely a relation between the individual and the 'Infinite' whom he 'perceives' or 'apprehends'" (p. 11).

Sociological or social psychological theories that recognize the effects of social prescriptions on action, and the individual responses to them, are now common. Evans-Pritchard noted that, "A social representation is not acceptable if it conflicts with individual experience" (1965, p. 90), and that "consciousness determines the social being which determines consciousness" (p. 77). Nevertheless Freud's theory of religion as a compensation for frustration and stress, or as a projection of oedipal motivations, which has recently been criticized by Jules Masson (1984), is still more commonly used to explain disapproved forms of religion than are any explanations in terms of cultural learning, while a focus on the beliefs or actions of individuals has displaced an earlier search for the universal sources of religion in some facet of human nature. Freud's interpretation can, however, be dismissed on empirical and on logical grounds because of Vergote and Tamayo's (1980) failure, in their cross-cultural studies, to find the predicted identity between God images and parental images, when they tested the assumption that every believer projects their own fantasies into the Christian cosmology.

Table 8 *A template for the analysis of traditional theories about the origin or nature of religion (cf. Evans-Pritchard, 1965)*

Focus	Level	
	Necessary or General	Sufficient or Differential

Personal	*Biological or physiological processes.*
	instinctual
	Homo Ludens (Huizinga, 1949)
	brain physiology
	  (e.g. hallucinogens or
	  transmarginal inhibition)
		Psychological and mental states or traits.
		God is father (Freud)
		religion as a model of thought
		  (Levy-Bruhl, 1931)
		magic
		fear
		part of the inner life,

Collective	*Anthropological and cultural base*
	
	totemism
	"route maps from birth to death"
	  (Bowker, 1973, p. viii)
	in the social structure
	  (Swanson, 1960)
	acculturation or " 'ways through'
	  the limitations which circum-
	  scribe human activity" (ibid.,
	  p. 64)
		Sociological and group processes
		as social facts or control
		  (Durkheim)
		as institutions and practices

Interdependent	Socio-biology
	  (Reynolds and Tanner, 1983)
		Social-representation theory
		sense of dependence on a
		  spiritual or moral power
		  outside ourselves (cf.
		  Radcliff-Brown) learned as part
		  of cultural inheritance
		"a social representation is not
		  acceptable if it conflicts with
		  individual experience"
		  (Evans-Pritchard, 1965, p. 50)
		beliefs and practices that unite a
		  moral community

Thouless (1971) stressed the diversity of religious forms and expressions and the variety of their sources, although Dittes (1969, p. 605) noted that using formal statements of belief to express hostility, control, punishment or forgiveness is common-place. Christianity is itself an interpretative theory, and Pratt (1920), for example, pointed to the solutions that religion holds out for the victims of drink and the destitute through its concern with "the deepest questions and most abiding values" and "the promise of supernatural and unfailing assistance" (p. 158).

But even these social scientific theories cannot necessarily be taken as empirical generalizations. Niebuhr (1964, p. xi) argues that Marx "left behind his passion for empirical observation and analysis" when he examined religion and used his claims as "the ladders on which the empirical critic of the status quo climbed up to the heaven and haven of a new religious apocalypse which made him the revered prophet of a new world religion, as potent in the twentieth century as was Islam in the seventh." If Marx was only studying reality for the sake of transforming it, many psychological theories are similarly simple transforms or translations into another vocabulary of what "everyone" knows already, or has borrowed from the assumptions of others. Homans (1967) therefore argued for an approach that combined Freud's concept of transference, which he said can bring together Freud's psychology of the self and his psychology of religion (p. 105), with Tillich's (1952) concept of the "transference fad" in the *"Courage to Be"*.

Others, but especially Spilka (1976), have argued for a stand that aligns the theological themes of a balanced commitment to self, to others and to ultimate values with a positive self identity, positive relationships with others, and a sense of purpose and direction in life (p. 17).

These approaches are rather different from those in the late nineteenth century which tried to understand primitive religions as a key to the more complex (or developed) forms or which looked only at religious conversion. Evans-Pritchard's (1965) criticism of that search for origins emphasizes its failure. Sociologists, on the other hand, concentrated then on the functional relationships between religion and society, while psychologists focussed on the characteristics of carriers of religion in terms of instincts, experiences and the reasons underlying conversion to a new set of beliefs. But even Pratt's approach, of letting people's accounts of conversion "speak for themselves" (1920), led him to the conclusion that "conversion is a natural human phenomenon" (p. 128), and he cited Tolstoy with approval who, when he "found the external and superstitious religion of his childhood and of those about him inadequate for his needs" said that, "The truth is that life is meaningless" (ibid. p. 138). That William James had earlier accepted Starbuck's recognition of voluntary and involuntary conversions, Pratt thought was enough to justify the conventions of evangelical theology (p. 152).

A behavioural interpretation of the conversion phenomena is found in Sargant's (1961) Pavlovian-based theory that people are deliberately prepared for change by rhythmical stimulation, isolation or social pressure, which is independent of whatever actual content is to be presented. Another criticism of an appeal to conversion is found in the methods of the evangelists who arouse fear by stressing sin and the terrors that can be avoided by accepting Christ's saving grace. Religion readily became an omnibus that itself carries these perspectives and explanations.

The basic theoretical problem with religious belief involves some variant of the question, "Why believe in God?", which many believe cannot be answered directly, but only by an attributional or hermeneutic process. Existing evidence about the characteristics of those who believe in God and how they differ from those who do not hardly suggests where the best answers might be looked for.

Dittes (1969, p. 643) identified the dependent variables for belief as (1) intensity, including open-mindedness, (2) tolerance of ambiguity or dogmatism, (3) content (as for example, "the benignness of God") and (4) the "protection of belief" in evidence that is adduced. He also found three independent variables covering the support for beliefs in their reinforcement from objective reality, from the social environment, and intrapsychically in terms of the "pain of indecision over internally conflicting motives ... oedipal anxieties stilled by feeling and assurance of a loving father ... and ... attitudes of gratitude and thanksgiving that are fostered as a 'conforming response' to God's goodness". This analysis emphasizes both the richness that has been found in religion and its elusive nature, which Capps (1974) attributes to the way it is "woven into ordinary phenomena".

The explanatory system that one accepts reflects what is taken implicitly as the crux of religion: while Rokeach (1960, p. 48) identified religion as a self-centred doctrine, Giles *et al.* (1975) looked for the ways it influences social interaction. The differences of opinion there suggest that it is unhelpful to hope to find a uniquely "religious attitude" in whatever characterizes the religious dimension, the important elements of which can, however, be found in concepts relating to the transcendent, whether they refer specifically to God or to being surprised by "joy" (C. S. Lewis), "belonging" (Tillich) or the "Other" (Otto), or use psychological terms like "decentration" (following Piaget), delayed gratification, or concepts like identity, and even experience.

Religious codes

A less specific perspective takes religion as a "code" (Frye, 1982) that carries meanings which make sense, defines obligations that direct intentions, and the metaphors which express more than can be said directly. That use of "metaphor" can resolve the confrontation that is set up between religion and science when religion is treated either as an illusion or as concretely true. The metaphorical view appropriates or translates biblical categories existentially or through cultural and historical processes. If psychology hopes to make subjective meanings explicit, there must be an unestimated error term between metaphor and meaning similar to that in the relationship between attitudes and behaviour (Fishbein and Ajzen, 1976). Alternatively, a revised theory could take linguistically expressed attitudes seriously and find what it is that words can *do* (Austin, 1962) in various situations or contexts.

Strictly descriptive or phenomenological studies of the content of belief have often been interpreted too concretely when looking for abstracted similarities between parental images and God images. Thus Ferre (1962) asked, "Is not the religious believer (and non-believer as well) entitled to care about what reality is 'really' like behind the unmoveable veil of his images?", without being thought to be projecting, phantasizing, irrational, or assuaging guilt.

To call God "Father" or to regard the parables of the kingdom as metaphors, as I. A. Richards said, puts "two thoughts of different things active together and supported by a single word or phrase, whose meaning is a *resultant* of their interaction" (emphasis added). There could be some similarity, rather than an identity with the content of concepts *projected* on to the same screen, rather than taking the psychological arguments about God as a projected father concretely. Family metaphors are embedded in the language of Christianity, but we do not describe God as jailer, sorcerer, or murderer (although some might argue for their appropriateness), nor do we use lion or lover, both of which are terms that describe God in the Old Testament. While "Nature" is similarly metaphorical, our beliefs about it are not questioned and interpreted like religious beliefs (except perhaps when arguing when life begins, which has become a crucial religious debate). Metaphors can be explained, and while it is common enough to argue that the chronic use of metaphorical or allusive thinking is diagnostic of schizophrenia, our vocabulary necessarily develops by adding new meanings to extend our knowledge (Le Selle, 1975, p. 46).

Ricoeur argued that even "guilt" itself is a metaphor, symbolically captured by words like alleviation, wondering, captivity, chaos, blinding, fall, and situated in "the being of man in the being of the world", which is itself a metaphorical expression (Ricoeur, 1967, p. 357). It is inadequate to assume that concrete interpretations and mistakes inevitably lie behind our metaphors, since they (like animistic thinking) are hard to diagnose.

Statements of belief should not, therefore, be taken too literally, although the psychological (rather than behavioural) theories that would account for them grope for (and have interpreted) the meanings that both individuals and groups find for their religious myths and practices, as they look for the ways beliefs are used. We urgently need systematic studies of these "informal theologies" that people develop for themselves, as in the belief that we think like machines, which is comparatively recent and derives from Descartes who split mind from body and subject from object. Our theoretical models in science are also (mental) constructs to account for phenomena in the natural world (Barbour, 1974, p. 6). They must be taken seriously but not literally, because they are symbolic and social representations, which Moscovici (1961) defined as:

> systems of values, ideas and practices with a two-fold function; first, to establish an order which will enable individuals to orient themselves in and master their material social world, and second, to facilitate communication among members of a community by providing them with a code for naming and classifying the various aspects of their world and their individual and group history. Christianity certainly fulfils each of those functions.

Clear yet arbitrary social boundaries are drawn between what is accepted as "religious" and what is not, so that astrology is taken to be a religious equivalent by a few and an error by others.

The targets of the specific theories of religion are not always specified clearly. When Argyle (1964) identified the "seven psychological roots of religion" that relate to a fantasy parent-figure, conflict, anxiety and need reduction, identity development, solving intellectual problems, and biochemical processes, it is not clear which bits of "religion" each applies to. We could, however, add social learning and an external locus of control to a list of what have been the dominant independent and psychological variables on which religion in general depends. So Derek Wright held that "religious beliefs, and especially those of Christianity, are a way of domesticating the universe, turning it into a family affair in order to reduce anxieties and fears that the individual is unable to tolerate". Early analyses neglected the potent and direct effects of situations and social contexts, and the differential susceptibilities or predispositions of individuals, with parallel linear models to account for the changing responsiveness of individuals and the mediating effects of religious alignments themselves.

Jones and Nisbett (1971), among others, have found that actors generally attribute individual differences to situational or external factors while observers explain those consistencies in terms of internal or psychological traits and characteristics. The roots of religion that Argyle (1958) summarized were in those terms predominantly observer-derived and neglected the social ground on which they settle to produce the fruits or effects of religion that William James (1902) thought were its most important features. While religious doctrines and practices are socially defined, as transcendental metaphors they allow variable responses that have defined effects. Rather than continuing to make sophisticated interpretations about cognitive needs, the relief that religious doctrines offer, or the delusions of religious people, one might directly explore the consistencies in what is experienced or claimed by religious people.

When Argyle and Beit-Hallahmi (1975) distinguished psychological theories of religious *behaviour* from those that are "theologically-based", they divided the former into three levels covering theories of the origins of religion (which confuse traditional and personal processes), theories of maintenance "which attempt to explain why certain individuals or certain societies hold certain belief systems" (p. 180), and the "theories of consequences, which deal with the effects of religious behaviour for either individuals or social groups" (ibid.). Most of the theories they consider have already been mentioned (in Table 7, p. 101) although they stress the difficulties of validating any psychological theory that refers to projection, cognitive need, frustration and so on. At another level religion binds or involves reactions to universal experiences of evil, suffering and death, and how the world began. Religious or psychological interpretations of such existential and intellectual problems within the natural world, that have no "scientific" solution, turn religion back into a primitive science of existence with a "God of the gaps" as an epiphenomenal process that must be taken for granted and can only be directly tested experientially or subjectively (perhaps by the koan, "Show me Jesus").

Adult beliefs are innocently and insistently questioned by children who will accept religious or scientific explanations indiscriminately, and form philosophies that seem to centre on themselves. This phenomenon led Piaget (1931) to identify religious thought as a form of egocentricity, which Godin accepted for children while arguing that decentration, or as he put it "purification of our images", is a necessary step towards mature religious attitudes. Brown's (1962) replication of Thouless's (1935) finding that religious beliefs are held more confidently than are matters of fact, found U-shaped distributions of response certainty for belief and disbelief in religious propositions, although Sanai (1952) had reported W-shaped distributions for religious items because of the responses of those who were uncertain, a U-shaped distribution for responses to political statements, and a normal distribution for the answers to his factual items. The meaning that is found in any beliefs is, however, independent of the confidence with which they are held, despite the confusion that surrounds neutral categories, which can imply either "don't know" or "don't care". In an early study, however, when both of those categories were available, the overall results were no different from those when only a "don't know" was allowed (Brown, 1962).

Personality traits have been commonly invoked to account for the confidence granted to religious beliefs, neglecting their content, metaphorical meaning or the evidence that is believed to substantiate them. Although measures of conservatism, dogmatism and authoritarianism are correlated with confidence about religious beliefs, there are, of course, other orientations to religion. Here, as elsewhere, the findings depend on the questions that are posed and the samples that are studied (cf. Argyle and Beit-Hallahmi, 1975, p. 61), and we must recognize that religious beliefs are *received* and used, when they have been assimilated or rejected by individuals (Spiro and D'Andrade, 1958). A good analogy to that process is found in the difference between competence and performance in language acquisition and use.

Believers must learn how to use their religious beliefs properly, both generally and in specific contexts, distinguishing what may be said to family, friends, and at church from what is appropriate for funerals. Each requires a different register, which depends on the context. The beliefs themselves endure because they are socially supported, and not as Argyle and Beit-Hallahmi assert, "because the private fantasies and images of individuals correspond to these cultural traditions". That view is too covert, granted the broad acceptance of religious beliefs which Mol (1985) shows is wider for religion than for atheism, humanism or rationalism, as alternative systems. Strictly private religious fantasies and the constructions on them are not ordinarily uncovered although the psychiatric literature insists that they do become problematic for a minority. What are judged to be unusual beliefs or devotions can be publicly maintained by sub-cultures or strong leaders (cf. Richardson, 1980, on the "Jonestown massacre"). To survive, such movements must be moved into some tradition, where they join the work of Luther, Calvin, St. Theresa, Catherine of Sienna and other reformers. Successful religious eccentrics and reformers are, however, comparatively uncommon.

The early finding that adolescence was *the* time for religious conversion reflects the extent to which religion has been used for problem-solution and to define the purpose of life, a view linked with the Protestant doctrine that salvation is by faith alone, while Catholicism expects a steady and continuous religious growth. Evangelical conversion is therefore a social and religious process, with clear expectations about the appropriate age to make a "decision" or be confirmed, although educational and liturgical views about Christian initiation have changed to recognize a gradual growth into Church life (Brown, 1969).

The separate effects of cognitive development and deliberate teaching were teased apart in a study of beliefs about the appropriateness and the efficacy of petitionary prayer from the ages 12 to 18 (Brown, 1968). The results showed that beliefs about the appropriateness of these prayers vary across religious denominations, which teach their own doctrines, while the believed efficacy of such prayer, in different situations, depends on age, because there is little explicit teaching about that. But even these beliefs do not develop autonomously or spontaneously, and must be transmitted, and aligned with other knowledge. The alternative view takes the control of religious belief as an internalization of the parents' moral standards with the power to reward or punish (Nelsen and Kroliczak, 1984). In that way religion maintains "the adult's typical balance between desire, morality and action" (Ostow, 1959).

Beyond any set of theoretical mechanisms, religions do exercise restraint and control, working negatively through fear or positively as commitment, devotion, duty, and love (*agape*). Differences in their traditional doctrines and practices do not allow simple and direct interpretations of differences between Catholics or Protestants, because, for example, of the Catholic access to auricular confession or their use of fasting, the significance of which has recently changed (Douglas, 1978). Other demands have changed as well, and Catholics are increasingly asking to be dispensed from their religious vows for reasons that include a desire for freedom, disaffection and dissatisfaction, or simply to be able to lead a different life. Furthermore, religious sanctions have not stopped sexual attitudes and practices from changing, although being religious may mean that fewer aggressively delinquent acts are committed by Church members than by non-members (Argyle and Beit-Hallahmi, 1975, p. 148). Whether that reflects social and external rather than some internal control, in Rotter's sense, is not clear and is confounded by what is expected. Occam's Razor prefers simple explanations that can be substantiated, to complex arguments about intangible processes.

Theories about the personal consequences of religion that were discussed by Argyle and Beit-Hallahmi (1975, p. 201) in terms of individual integration and adaptation appear to favour an instrumental or pragmatic approach to religion, with its own accounting of the costs and benefits of belief. Prejudice, lowered creativity, a preference for long-term rather than immediate goals, and an "irrational" confidence or trust in authority must be set against the better mental, physical and social adjustment, greater confidence in crisis, clearer identity, and the social stability that derives from sharing religious beliefs and membership (ibid., pp. 201–203). But what is an appropriate test? Argyle and Beit-Hallahmi examined the theory that religion relieves a fear of death against data which show increased levels of religious responding with age and in beliefs about the pleasantness of the after-life (ibid., p. 196). Those findings are confounded, because those who are older grew up when religion was more strongly sanctioned than it is now, and their confidence could simply reflect that.

Summary

While most psychological explanations and theories of religion depend on interpretations of specific forms of religious practice or belief, general psychological theories have also been applied to religious material, since there may be nothing in religion that cannot be aligned with other beliefs, attitudes or practices (cf. Malony, 1976). Both of those perspectives try to account for the appeal of some beliefs to some people and at different times. The explanations in psychological terms usually involve motives like self-seeking, helplessness, or awe, or such cognitive processes as consistency, dissonance reduction or attribution. Social explanations make reference to training, socialization and other social influences. While being "religious" is unlikely to require a special psychological response, it is less a matter of processing new information than maintaining the beliefs and orientations that are made available within a system. The transcendental reference that characterizes every religion presents contradictions of plausibility which believers resolve in concrete or metaphorical terms, that are then focussed socially or personally and asserted with varying degrees of confidence. Religious belonging has secondary advantages in resolving loneliness and alienation.

The early theorists were ambitious in trying to explain why religious beliefs are held at all and how they might have developed originally. Later views looked at the integrative effects of religion and at the social correlates of religiousness in terms of sex, age, class, or orientation (Roof, 1972). Those analyses assume that religious believers share some characteristics because they are grouped coherently, although they are not all equally committed, since there are doubters and varied interpretations of the religious concepts that are pregnant for some, empty for others, and structure the feelings of a few. Although the characteristics of believers have been readily interpreted, William James insisted that they should be identified by their fruits. That, like the rest of religion, depends on what religious authorities and their texts allow. Those following too closely to the text appear to develop an extrinsic concreteness or absolutism, although negative answers to the questions "Do you believe in God?" are also categorical.

Because religious belief systems model the social order, they impinge directly on other frameworks or agreed meanings through their distinctive sets of values, attitudes, life-styles and social involvements. Greeley (1972) argued for the necessity of religion from the popularity and wide acceptance of religious beliefs, and he asked "why religion has persisted in the masses when some of the elite have seen fit to reject it" (p. 8). Those who reject traditional religions may, however, have found functional substitutes in their quest or search for beauty or clarity in art, literature or science (Back and Bourque, 1970).

Two separate stages in adopting a religious position have to be accounted for. The first involves the socialization or initiation into a believing stance and the other concerns its maintenance and consequential effects. Those who have their first encounter with a religion when they are adults, and are changed by that, are now found most obviously among those in "the new religious movements" (Richardson, 1985) because of the way so many have been immunized against conventional religious ideas. Although the early psychologists distinguished a gradual development from sudden conversion, even in the new movements it is hard to separate the effects of personal history, psychological dynamics, immediate situational and traditional influences on a decision to change, and the social or intellectual advantages of belonging. The majority holds its religious beliefs superficially, using them to deal with the crises that psychological methods seldom clarify. To show how religious perspectives or the belief content itself acts as a cognitive filter requires newer approaches, perhaps in the manner of Tversky and Kahneman (1974). Until the decisional heuristics used for religion can be identified it remains an explanatory or attributional system that is held within language. The evangelical Protestants in England (but not in France) kept religion there when they disallowed teaching sign language to the deaf who had to be able to *say* that they accepted Jesus as Lord.

7   The parameters of religion

... if that learned man [Mr. Casaubon] would only talk, instead of allowing himself to be talked to by Mr. Brooke, who was just then informing him that the Reformation either meant something or it did not, that he himself was a Protestant to the core, but that Catholicism was a fact; and as to refusing an acre of your ground for a Romanist chapel, all men needed the bridle of religion, which, properly speaking, was the dread of a Hereafter.
George Eliot, *Middlemarch*, 1871–1872, Ch. 2.

Opinion's but a fool, that makes us scan
The outward habit by the inward man.
W. Shakespeare, *Pericles*, Act II, Scene II, 56–7.

Religious and psychological fashions, as well as the interests of particular psychologists dictate where it is hoped the keys to understanding religion will be found. They have been looked for in conversion and religious change, in the images of God, in belief in specific doctrines like the resurrection, or in traditional, denominational and other affiliations. Some have focussed on a process like meditation, others on the characteristics of particular groups such as the members of a Catholic order (Hjelle and Lomastro, 1971) or on the consequences of belief in an after-life, on the Church as a social setting (Festinger, 1950), and the conditions that elicit altruistic behaviour (Batson and Ventis, 1982).

These studies of religion range from descriptive field-work (Saliba, 1974) to the controlled experiments in Deconchy's (1985) analysis of the different independent and dependent variables that have been used in which external validity is important, and in simulations that emphasize internal validity (Brock, 1962; Malony, 1985). Many different measures have been developed, so Embree (1972) used free associations and Hunsberger and Ennis (1982) wrote attitude items based on the Apostles' Creed. In all these approaches, whether religion is taken as a dependent or an independent variable, it is an undoubted social fact that both religious and non-religious people must come to terms with, because it can operate as a cognitive filter and as a focus of values, habits and social attitudes.

For some people religion embodies revealed or experienced truth and defines the context in which they live and move and have their being. For others religion is an illusion or fantasy. Religious beliefs and believers are not only evaluated for their own authenticity but for the way the beliefs seem to be used and the effects they appear to have on the happiness or prejudices of believers, who may be called a "child of God" or a Protestant, Catholic or Jew. Many who hold religious beliefs and attitudes, or parallel disbeliefs, may not realize the breadth of meaning others can find in what they conventionally believe. The difficulty of resolving the subjectivity inherent in what is believed and the intangible effects of belief on behaviour or action has led psychologists to emphasize the individual differences and personality factors that might influence the acceptability of different religious beliefs, practices, or institutions. The emphasis in most investigations is nevertheless on the beliefs professed, the social alignments that are claimed to support them, and on whatever concomitant effects can be identified.

Psychologists of religion

While the professional and religious background of an investigator may influence the issues that are taken up (cf. Malony's, 1978, collection of accounts of the "Christian experience of eighteen psychologists"), it is clear that Catholic psychologists tended to avoid the psychology of religion until the 1950s, except for some interest in spiritual guidance and mysticism and its relationship to psychopathology, especially in the work of Marechal (1878–1944) (cf. Misiak and Staudt, 1954, p. 217 f.). This focus avoided possible conflicts of interest between a dogmatic position and empirical data. Liberal Protestants and non-believers, on the other hand, found it easier to recognize the psychological basis of religion.

Although sociologists and psychologists have relied on similar data, their analyses and theories have been different, with sociologists being primarily concerned with religion and society (Glock and Stark, 1965), which transcends individuals, while psychologists emphasized individuals and their religion (Allport, 1950). Berger and Luckmann (1972) among others stressed the problematic relationships between individuals and the social order, which Durkheim resolved with reference to a symbolic reality that is a precondition for social integration. As Luckmann says, "For Durkheim man is essentially *homo duplex* and individuation has, necessarily, a social basis ... For Weber, on the other hand, the problem of the social conditions of individuation appears in a more specific perspective — that is, in the historical context of particular religions and their relation to historical societies" (1967, p. 12). Sociologists have therefore been interested in differences between social groups and in the nature of social deviance, while psychologists have looked at the variability within groups, at conformity, and at differences between individuals.

Psychologists of religion have not developed an analogue to the KAP model used in studies of fertility, which covers contraceptive knowledge (including beliefs, approval and implicit comparisons with others), attitudes, and practice (or experience), as well as the "vital" data and other background characteristics, which include institutional alignments (cf. Berelson, 1966). It is usually assumed with religion that, unlike fertility control (itself an important phenomenon closely linked with religious norms), there is an interaction between the beliefs a person accepts, the demands of a tradition, the social groups that maintain and sanction them, and each believer's position and role within some institution or tradition. These assumptions allow crude distinctions between believers, non-believers and disbelievers, and among the believers between church-goers and non-church-goers, both within and across religious denominations. The high level of general assent to religious beliefs means, however, that subtle distinctions between social groups are not easily detected, nor will they necessarily correspond to any psychological differences.

Sociologists, especially in the tradition of Max Weber, have been more concerned to categorize religious organizations, for example, as Church or sect (Troeltsch, 1931), the first being open and the other closed, and to examine the historical role of religious groups and individuals in producing social and religious change (cf. Hill, 1973). Phenomenologists of religion have described what it is that religious traditions make available (cf. Smart, 1969, 1971).

The place of religion

Historical perspectives on religion have plotted changed patterns of participation, first from parish records (Currie *et al.*, 1977) and more recently with opinion poll data. They cannot, however, touch subjective factors and reactions of change. That is only available for those who have articulated their own development in their diaries or other writing.

The regular use of survey methods in the 1930s, and the national and local surveys of religious attitudes, beliefs and practice that are now a feature of Western social life have allowed better base rates to be established than ever before. *"What do we Believe?"* is thus the title of a comparative study of national samples in the US in 1952 and in 1965 (Marty *et al.*, 1968). As sociologists, those authors warned against using "blunt instruments on delicate and subtle material" (p. 57) and of the difficulties in identifying the criteria for their validity, especially if the Church is taken to be a divine institution. They also note that many questions are so worded as to make them "religiously irrelevant to many". Questions and the items to be rated are nevertheless the tools by which what we believe is established. The independent social variables on which these beliefs hinge are identified by coarse categorizations as Protestant or Catholic, or by age, sex, education and region.

Marty *et al.* (1968) offered five major findings. The first is that "there is little evidence of major doctrinal change or major decline in religious activities among American gentiles, but there seems to be a rather notable doctrinal decline among American Jews while at the same time there has been an increase in religious activity in the Jewish group", that "there is some evidence of major structural strain in American Catholicism", that the religious school issue "is still a level one", that "there is a decline of anti-Jewish feeling among gentiles; and there is also a decline of anti-Catholic feeling among Protestants: but there is an increase of anti-Catholic feeling among Jews" and that "there is no evidence of a massive defection from religion among those under twenty-five" (pp. 111–112). In general these results show, "not that change has taken place in religious attitudes, but the degree to which traditional ideas appear to have held" (Marty *et al.*, p. 103) over a 12 year period, despite the extent to which traditional beliefs were being challenged in the 1960s by men like Harvey Cox (1965) and John Robinson (1964).

Behind the broad spectrum descriptions and analyses of religious beliefs lie quite specific analyses of, for example, religion and prejudice in the work of Glock and his collaborators in the United States (Glock and Stark, 1965), and Mol's (1971, 1985) social analysis of religious belief in Australia. Despite the growth of religious pluralism, bigotry is still an important feature of religious attitudes in both countries.

To identify the relevance of religion in popular culture, Greeley (1968) explicitly compared present religious and political behaviour, on the grounds that, as he says, "almost every informed student of the subject seems to believe that the American political system is vital and effective". He enquired into the involvement in voting and in church-going, whether Governments and Churches are believed to be doing a good job, the amount of discussion of politics and of religion, financial contributions to political and religious organizations, employment by political groups, and general knowledge. Religion always came out ahead in each of these comparisons. They concluded that "the religious data require our being cautious indeed concerning assertions of the present irrelevance of religion for the personal lives and the institutional commitments of most Americans." They added that religion predicts attitudes and behaviour better than does social class, and that the stability of religious attitudes and behaviour is shown in the Gallup polls. Despite their evidence for the continued survival of religion, Greeley (p. 14 f.) notes that religion has had little influence on other comparable contexts that have "emerged in the last 400 years", so that phenomena once interpreted religiously are now explained scientifically, while the development of abstract thought "means that myths are no longer self-sufficient and must be interpreted". Yet the scientific and technical society has not revalued the human crisis of confidence about meaning, and religion has become more explicitly individual, "so that free choices are possible among consumers in the supermarket, religion" (p. 15).

These developments have left religion providing a "faith" or system of meaning about ultimate questions that can both comfort and challenge, and offering systems of belonging that assign mystical powers to social groups whose membership is now more voluntary and independent than it may have been previously. Since we can decide about our own religion, it has, argues Greeley become both more central and explicit so that we are, therefore, *more* religious. (An important religious issue centres on the forms of approval or disapproval of an ideology that insists on continued Church growth.)

Mol (1971), on the other hand, gathered profiles of belief for separate countries, and on the basis of a detailed analysis of religion in Australia he argues that our faith is no longer essentially Christian, although it continues to be linked with Churches, denominations and specific religious groups and with ethnicity and social background. As a consequence, people are usually born into their religion and do not change into it (nor are they often changed by it). Although the Church is no longer the social focus for a town or suburb, and many do not know where or what their parish church might be, they continue to accept formal religious beliefs. (Incidentally, they often do not know their electorate or their M.P. either.) That religious institutions have survived despite post-war changes in Church order and in its power is a surprise to some people. Others believe that these changes have been made in an attempt to adapt to a changed social environment.

Population censuses can define the limits of religion at social or national levels, and reflect the geographical or social patterns that may limit basic attitudes. Although the Australian census has been conducted somewhat irregularly during this century there has been a consistent five-year cycle since 1961, with an optional question that asks "What is your religion?". Public opinion polls taken regularly since 1941 have also included questions about religious allegiance, attendance at Church services and attitudes, and Mol's (1971) survey of religion in 1966 was based on a "random 0.067 per cent dwelling sample of 60 per cent of the Australian population", giving 4,201 respondents, with a 12 per cent no response rate (p. 308). Mol identified six religious categories: orthodox believers (17 per cent), unorthodox believers (eight per cent), public believers (ten per cent), believing secularists (16 per cent), secularists (20 per cent), and consistent secularists (16 per cent), with the other 13 per cent being "mixed", and perhaps inconsistently pro-religious. Australian Gallup poll data suggest that in 1970 only about five per cent claimed no religion while in the 1983 Australian values study, about 13 per cent claimed no religion.

Australia, like other Western countries, appears overwhelmingly Christian, although the actual questions that are asked to assess this give different estimates of the percentages who are religiously active. Hogan's (1979) analysis of this material shows that more males are "secularists" or that "women are more conventionally religious than men", and that the secularists tend to be younger, although these differences are "not great". Despite regional differences the secularists are in the cities, and Hogan found that although there is no effect of social class, secularists are also better educated. Hogan concluded from his survey material that, "Catholics are steered toward the conservative end of the scale; the smaller Protestant denominations are even more strongly steered in that direction. The No Religion respondents are very strongly steered to the liberal end of the scale," and "the early Catholic-Protestant division in Australian politics appears now focussed on Christians versus securalists." But he concedes that survey measures are crude and that results must be accepted as "suggestions" or hypotheses for further study. Yet they are an important basis for generalizations about a society and show that consistent patterns and agreements exist, especially about basic social values.

From an American NORC survey, Roof and Hadaway (1979) aligned such value differences with denominations, as social groups, and they developed a classification of "major mainline, liberal mainline and fringe denominations", finding that switches of denomination occur "among the five mainline Protestant denominations themselves (Methodists, Presbyterians, Disciples, Lutherans and Baptists)" and that "about a third of all switching out of these denominations (for Disciples even more) to other mainline groups, with 7.4 per cent overall switching to 'None' and 13.0 per cent to the fringe, to other main Protestant groups (66 per cent) and Sects (5.4 per cent)". Their findings about those moving to the "None" category broadly support the Australian data, but these moves are seen as an "expression of disillusionment not simply with the church but with the *status quo* more generally", while "those who switch to the sects are less educated, have lower incomes, tend to be more conservative in moral values, are less optimistic about people, and express less confidence in American institutions".

Social factors

Religions are set within broad social contexts in which demographic and attitudinal factors dictate or influence how "religious people" can react to institutional religion. The upwardly mobile move towards liberal groups, others turn from established Churches to fringe groups and those who are alienated defect from institutional religion. Those changes, which may be deliberate or personally motivated, also involve broadly social attitudes and the contexts within which religious institutions operate. As Roof and Hadaway conclude, "People switch religious preferences not simply for doctrinal reasons but also because of the undue commitment and behavioural styles associated with religious identities", which draw on "the symbolic functions of religious identification". That presumably raises a psychological question. The apparent move away from active involvement with religion is broadly taken to be a form of secularization, or "the process by which sectors of society and culture are removed from the domination of religious institutions and symbols" (Berger, 1967, p. 113), although that is not the only meaning of "secularization", as Hill (1973, pp. 228–251) shows. On the other hand, some religious people simply hide their religion. That a majority habitually claim some religious affiliation while the Churches reinforce traditional values and beliefs, is emphasized by Mol's analysis of the discrepancies in membership claimed for the Uniting Church, formed in Australia in 1977 from the Methodist and the Congregational Churches and two-thirds of the Presbyterian Churches. This union should have covered about 12 per cent in the 1981 census, but only 4.9 per cent said they belong to the Uniting Church. Mol argues that that figure identifies its active members and the remainder, including the three per cent who said they were Methodists, were the nominal adherents, although some of them may have retained that identity on principle. The increase in the "no religion" category in that census from 6.7 per cent in 1971 to 8.3 per cent in 1976 and 10.8 per cent in 1981 suggests that many nominal adherents have cut that religious tie, which Price (1981, p. 4) argues does not show an increase in atheism, but a decision to clarify their position and not drift unthinkingly by "putting in the census schedule the long discarded religion of their childhood".

That one's social background influences these responses is shown by the fact that more men, and more younger and better educated people gave "no religion" in the census. Vernon (1968), who compared the characteristics of those with "no-religion" and those who are politically "independent" says that "no religion" might imply "non religious" or that they are sceptical, agnostic, atheistic, neutral, or even "hostile to religion". Each of those terms involves more than a mere disbelief in religion, although Allport and

Ross (1967), who identified a group that is indiscriminately pro-religious, neglected those who are indiscriminately anti-religious. Vernon's data show that 25.9 per cent of his sample of people with no religious affiliation accepted belief in God with at least some uncertainty and that another 25.9 per cent nevertheless agreed that they had had a feeling that they were "somewhat in the presence of God".

Those with "no religion"

We must therefore distinguish those with no religious affiliation from those who are neutral to religion and from those who actively disbelieve. Vernon's review of the literature led him to conclude that those who are not religiously affiliated do not differ from those who are so affiliated in their social behaviour, prejudice, security or anxiety, and marital adjustment. As Vernon says, "Theory about the functions of religion, then, may involve unwarranted interpretations if 'religion' is interpreted to mean 'organized religion'." In a similar way, Kotre (1971) showed that lapsed Catholics are not strikingly dissimilar from Catholics who continue their active practice, although each group gave different reasons for their position. The reasons for remaining in a religious organization are not simply the converse of the reasons for leaving, or for not affiliating at all, and may involve different conclusions about a core of beliefs. The psychological functions or the social categories that are identified or associated with religiousness are not necessary features of a religious structure. Dittes (1969, p. 616) emphasized the extent to which church attendance itself is an age or stage related phenomenon, citing Bender (1958), although consistent linear relationships should not be expected between separate measures of religiousness and any social variables, but especially with age.

Hunsberger and Brown (1984), in a recent study of 836 Australian students, found that those who still belonged to the religion in which they had grown up had significantly higher scores than those who had given up any formal affiliation in their agreement with the religious teaching of their parents, the importance of such teaching in life, current frequency of church attendance and bible reading, and the frequency of prayer before the age of 15. They also had a stronger belief in God, in the divinity of Christ, in the Bible, in miracles and in the existence of the devil, as well as in the frequency with which they turned to a religious source for counselling, saw and were in touch with both parents now and during their childhood. Their reported happiness and adjustment in life, conventionalism and agreement with their parents' position on social issues relating to alcohol, premarital sex, politics, education, money, hard work and overall philosophy of life, as well as scores on a measure of Christian orthodoxy, and in their parental bonding score

(Parker *et al.*, 1979) were also all different. Those who had lapsed had higher scores for living away from home, rebellion against the parents, Higher School Certificate or matriculation examination results, a liberal political orientation and their enjoyment of intellectual discussion and debates on religious issues. There were no differences in sex, year at university, or parent's education. A stepwise multiple regression analysis following a factor analysis of these data found that an "intellectual orientation" was the first variable entered as a predictor of lapsing or not, followed by the "emphasis placed on religion in childhood". Five other factors that added significantly to the variance explained each accounted for only about one per cent of it. They were "relationship with mother", "childhood relationships with parents", "contact with parents", "agreement with parents on moral issues" and "the importance of hard work". The over-riding importance of these parental factors replicated Hunsberger's (1980, 1983) earlier Canadian studies in which "personal happiness and adjustment" was also a significant factor. Different alternatives were chosen as their strongest influences by those in various religious traditions. Orthodox and Jewish students identified their home as the strongest influence, 46.6 per cent of Roman Catholic chose school while 21.9 per cent of Anglicans and other Protestants chose the "Church" for that.

Overall, this study shows that both Australian and Canadian students who have lapsed from religion are primarily reacting against the religious training they received at home, although "intellectualism" also had a greater effect on the Australian than the Canadian students, which could reflect their reaction against the religious anti-intellectualism that is evident in New South Wales, while the Canadian students might find it harder to withdraw themselves from their parents' religion. This intellectualism factor explained 5.8 per cent of the variance, and the emphasis on religion in childhood accounted for only 4.5 per cent of the variance. Because the other significant factors had each accounted for only about one per cent of the variance, a great deal of what is involved in lapsing from religion is yet to be explained.

Bender (1958) reported on a group 15 years after graduating from college, whose scores for the religious and political values on the Allport-Vernon-Lindzey study of values were equal, whereas during college, the political value had been highest and the religious value score was lowest. Furthermore, he notes that a further follow-up 25 years after graduation showed that 12 of 86 men were attending church more frequently than they had ten years before, while 16 had become non-attenders. One person who had not attended church is reported to have said, "I define religion not in terms of belief (I am an atheist) but in terms of concern, for search of values, for one's own integrity ... For me the equivalents for love of God are reverence for life; people are precious." Others are quoted as saying, "I set an example for my children", "You can't lose by going", "You meet the right kind of people at church", "I like our Minister". Non-attenders said they found it "not worthwhile", "unrewarding", "not exactly inspiring except for the music". Reasons like that are still being offered. Bender advocates the concept of a "religious impulse" as "a more generic term than religious faith, having humanitarian characteristics such as the search for wisdom, the brotherhood of all men, the meaning of being, a reverence for life"; he identified that impulse, which is similar to Yinger's non-doctrinal religion, in nine attenders and six non-attenders from a sample of 96 men. Such an impulse is less tangible than is the excitement, immediacy or sociality of watching or participating in sport or other entertainments, but perhaps not music.

Gorlow and Schroeder (1968) collected the reasons for participating in religious activities from 175 active Church members, and then asked 100 undergraduates to make Q-sorts of a reduced set of 87 of those reasons. A factor analysis of these ratings yielded seven interpretable factors, identified as humble servants of God (which accounted for 16 per cent of the variance, and was most highly correlated with frequent church attendance and being a Roman Catholic), self-improvers (also accounting for 16 per cent of the variance but negatively correlated with church attendance and interest). A "religious egg-head" (or intellectual) factor that accounted for 11.4 per cent of the variance was related to family education and background. The other smaller factors involved God-seekers (5.8 per cent of the variance), family guidance seekers (3.7 per cent), socially oriented servants of God (3.6 per cent) and moralists (3.3 per cent). The two major factors in that study align with intrinsic and extrinsic religious orientations respectively (cf. Allport and Ross, 1967), although Gorlow and Schroeder find a parallel with Monaghan's (1967) autonomy-seekers in their first factor, and with his comfort-seekers in their second factor. Social participators were thought to reflect the religious motivation of members of a fundamentalist Church. Church attendance is not, however, a simple phenomenon, and the reasons that are offered for going to church regularly, irregularly or not at all necessarily overlap.

Mol's (1971) Australian survey of religion showed consistent differences between regular and irregular attenders of Anglican, Catholic, Methodist and Presbyterian Churches in terms of their frequency of praying (55 per cent of the regulars said they prayed daily, compared with 20 per cent of the irregulars), a feeling of being in God's presence, "a sense of being saved in Christ", and a "feeling of being punished by God for something they had done" (except for the Methodists). Those responses all support the need to maintain a broad perspective on the way religion is expressed.

These perspectives include self descriptions or identities as "religious" or belonging to a denomination, that are consistently linked with demographic variables and secular alignments because of the involvement of religion with the society at large. For that reason alone most people usually answer the question, "What is your religion?" with a denominational identifier, whether in the census, on admission to hospital or in conversation, even if they question the legitimacy of that query. Those answers provide the profiles of denominational membership which change with reforms, an increasing tolerance of religious differences, and secular pressures. Despite that, denominational identity remains the most common religious differentiator.

Religious belonging

Religious belonging is somewhere behind a religious identity (Brothers, 1964). Fichter's (1954) analysis of the degrees or states of membership in a local religious group moves from the nuclear members through modal, marginal and dormant members, although there has been little psychological analysis of the consequences or even the reasons for those levels of forms of attachment. This is partly because the samples that psychologists study "have generally been late adolescents, for whom issues of autonomy versus institutional loyalty and conventional orthodoxy would seem to be especially keen" (Dittes, 1969, p. 610). The differentiations are most clearly marked among adults.

Argyle and Beit-Hallahmi (1975, p. 11) concluded that "there appears to have been a decline of weekly church attendance from 25 per cent for England in 1900 to about 15 per cent in 1965. This decline has varied between denominations." Jews are the lowest on these measures, followed by Protestants, with Catholics and members of fundamentalist Protestant groups the highest (ibid., p. 19). There are also national differences. Britain, has 40 per cent and the USA has 70 per cent of adolescents saying they attend weekly, and 15 per cent and 42 per cent of adults in these countries give that answer (ibid., p. 64). While those figures refer to the 1960s, the Princeton Religious Research Center's *Report on Religion in America* in 1982 concludes that since 1958 – a peak year for church attendance – the decline in church-going has been sharpest among Catholics. "Attendance at Mass fell 22 points – from 74 to 52 per cent – between 1958 and 1978, and currently stands at 53 per cent. Since 1973, Catholic church-going has remained fairly stable. In contrast, church-going among Protestants has remained fairly constant since 1958", with 41 per cent attending "during an average week in 1981" (p. 44). They also report sharp differences by age groups, with more older people attending weekly. Catholics and Lutherans are the most frequent church-goers (p. 45); 68 per cent nationally claim membership in a

Church or Synagogue (p. 41). "The most likely to say they are members of a church are women (73 per cent), non-whites (71 per cent), adults 50 years of age or older (76 per cent), persons living in the Midwest (73 per cent) and South (75 per cent), and married persons (72 per cent)."

Morgan-Gallup poll data in Australia show fairly consistent patterns in the frequency of church attendance from 1950 to 1981 (23 per cent having been to church within a week in 1950 and 22 per cent in 1981), although there are great differences between the Anglicans (11.9 per cent had been "last week" in 1981) and Roman Catholics (37.4 per cent) (cf. Bouma, 1983, p. 21).

Argyle and Beit-Hallahmi (1975) report "a clear, positive relationship between social status and church attendance in the USA" (p. 161), and although "social class affects the way in which religiosity is expressed" (ibid.), members of the middle class are those most likely to attend. Argyle and Beit-Hallahmi interpret these findings in terms of social participation and general life-style (pp. 164–165). Specific religious differences could also be referred to liturgical demands, the involvement with a group and its members' involvements with the broader community. Religious sects are isolated and draw most of their support from those in the working classes, whereas many Church activities support middle-class values through their secularized rather than specifically religious activities and orientation. The congruence between religious and class values deserve further investigation, although it is unlikely to force revisions of these broad conclusions. Argyle and Beit-Hallahmi note, however, that "recent surveys show that there are now no class differences between denominations" (p. 16) which probably reduces any differences in the levels of active participation.

Wherever one turns in Christianity, except among the office-holders, there is a predominance of females. Argyle and Beit-Hallahmi (1975, pp. 71–79) interpret this psychologically as a congruence between religiousness and such "female" characteristics as less aggression, greater guilt feelings and their religious socialization. "With God presented as a father figure, girls should be more concerned with a God that is presented as a fatherly male" (p. 77). Moberg (1965) casts some doubt on the generality of such a conclusion. Vergote and Tamayo (1979) also show that concepts of the God figure are more closely aligned with female, or at least with maternal characteristics. It could be that the sex-role characteristics that define girls as loving and comforting, while boys are planners and controllers, make it easy for religion to be a feminine trait (Terman and Miles, 1936), with the soul itself taken to be feminine (Jung, 1958).

The most parsimonious interpretation is that women are expected to be more religious, and they therefore constitute the majority of active Church members since it is easier for them to be religiously involved. Their other roles and responsibilities are reinforced there so that "non-working women, the young and the old, who are not involved in work activities, are all higher on religiosity" (Argyle and Beit-Hallahmi 1975, p. 79, following Berger and Luckmann, 1972). The 1983 Australian Values Study reinforces these findings by showing that the most active religious support comes from married women who do not work, and who have young children. The British findings, however, show that increasing age itself accounts for most of that variance, and has the greatest impact on religious involvement (Abrams *et al.*, 1985, p. 96).

These results all relate to the social context, and the ways Church allegiance competes against and draws on other social processes and activities. It could also be that religion is more scientifically interesting in social than psychological terms, since it so strongly reflects demographic, ideological or economic processes. Yet religion also depends on the people who respond to it. A few will be self-selected, others will be recruited, but most are directly trained into it, and with a religious attachment that involves a social identity and *some* (if minimal) linked social activity. The former has been assessed by asking for repeated answers to the question, "Who am I?". The latter by measures of religious activity.

Godin (1964b) argued that belonging to a Church is inherently ambiguous because of the varied *meanings* that are found, or embedded in Church-related behaviour with its "exterior signs", whether as actions or verbal statements, being elaborated whenever they are to be accounted for. There is always more to be said, and our external judgements as observers are necessarily juridical, so that Godin asks, "What does one think of a Joan of Arc dying at the stake, 'lapsed into heresy'?", and of those "innocent witches" (cf. Cohn 1975). Psychohistorical, psychoanalytic and even psychotherapeutic material can only be approached superficially by making group comparisons, and difficult questions might be resolved only when an individual is in a diclosive mode, as in a priest's posthumously published statements about his loss of faith while maintaining the exterior signs of belonging for many years "because of the help and comfort that he was able to continue to give to his neighbour" (Godin, 1964b). That is like the burn-out phenomenon which is now identified among clinicians and social workers.

Religious attitudes and behaviour

The inherent unreliability of answers to single questions limits their usefulness, but religious responding is not restricted to religious practice, social identity, or even to claims about them that are the target of such questions. Religious beliefs and attitudes, feelings and experiences that are difficult to address in that way should also be included. Responses to these questions relate to internal states as the variables that are set between social or religious "objects", other phenomena (including people, situations, traditions, doctrines, and groups) and the cognitive, affective and behavioural responses and intentions that are attached to them.

Fishbein and Ajzen (1975) argue that links between attitudes, beliefs and behaviour have either been ignored or are simply assumed to depend on attitudes. As we have already seen, attitudes can be assessed in several ways. Ostrom (1969), for example, looked at the relationships between a set of 12 indirect measures of religiousness and direct self-rating scales of Church-related behaviour, including frequency of church attendance, prayer, and Bible reading, money donated and a willingness to attend religious discussions:

> Each of the 12 attitude scales was correlated with each of the eight behavioural measures; thus there were 96 attitude-behaviour correlations. They ranged from – .06 to .68, and most correlations were below .30. The only behaviour that could be predicted with reasonable accuracy from the attitude scales was church attendance. More important, there were no appreciable differences in the predictive validities of the three attitudinal components, and taking all three components into account would not improve prediction of behaviour (ibid., p. 343).

Nevertheless, correlations between the Thurstone, Likert, Guttman and self-rating scales were high, averaging 0.65. Eiser (1980) resolved that problem with reference to the content of these items, which are typically in a generalized form while questions about behaviour are of necessity specific. Furthermore, the items to be included in most scales are identified *a priori* (even if they are only retained when they form a uni-dimensional scale). Fishbein (1967) has argued that the intention to perform an action is a function of an attitude to some piece of behaviour and to the subjective norms concerning that behaviour. Our attitudes to objects therefore influence behaviour only indirectly, as when they are used to justify some action.

Helping to make decisions, and assigning meaning to actions are important uses for attitudes and beliefs, that operate independently of any actual behaviour. Not to act in a way that is consistent with one's attitudes often depends on the lack of an opportunity for action, and verbal reports about one's actions must be less reliable than what is actually done, although attitude measures become more reliable when they involve behavioural intentions.

Attitude-behaviour discrepancies are therefore artifacts (Eiser, 1980, p. 52), that can be resolved by further information, or by recognizing that knowledge, intentions and beliefs may be more important than behaviour itself. This is especially so in a domain like religion. Wicker (1971) examined factors that could limit or inhibit expressions of behaviour, with questions about "the effect on a subject's worship service attendance if he had weekend guests who did not regularly attend church?'' and ''How would a subject's contribution be affected if the congregation voted to spend funds on a project of which he disapproved?'' Fishbein and Ajzen's (1975, p. 346) summary of these results in Table 9 shows that ''none of the four predictors is significantly related to all three behaviours. With respect to church attendance and contributions, judged influence of extraneous events was found to be the best predictor, and adding the other variables did not improve the multiple correlations with behaviour. The prediction of participation in church activities was largely unsuccessful.''

Table 9 *The prediction of church behaviours from attitude and other variables (adapted from Fishbein and Ajzen, 1975, p. 346)*

	Product-moment correlations				
Behaviour	Attitude toward own Church	Perceived consequences of behaviour	Evaluation of events	Judged influence of extraneous events	Multiple correlation
Attendance	0.31**	0.19*	0.31**	0.42**	0.50**
Contributions	0.22**	0.05	0.37**	0.45**	0.53**
Participation	0.11	0.20**	0.06	0.14	0.23

*$p < 0.05$; ** $p < 0.01$.

Although those studies were directed at clarifying attitude-behaviour relationships in general, and not to the nature of religion itself, they emphasize the care that is needed in any study of religion to ensure that the items or questions are appropriate and specific enough to be answered. Religious behaviours are not all equally important, nor are they equally public and approved. Fishbein and Ajzen (1975 pp. 348–349) noted that ''a nonsignificant correlation of – .04 was obtained between perceived attitude toward taking an active part in church activities and evaluation of spending more than 30 hours a week in church activities'' (p. 350).

Good predictions of actual behaviour can only be made when attitude and behaviour ''variables are measured at the same level of specificity'' (ibid). ''Attitudes to an object do not necessarily draw the linked behaviour, which can, however, be assumed or *believed* to be related to religiosity or religious attitudes'' (p. 355). As Thurstone pointed out, ''overt action ... [may] ... take quite different forms which have one thing in common, namely, that they are about equally favourable toward the object'' (1931, p. 262).

Attitudes and the objects or institutions to which they relate involve a range of consistent responses since the essence of an attitude is a positive or negative evaluation of an attitude object. In a similar way beliefs draw on the truth-value that is assigned to statements or propositions, while behavioural intentions reflect attitudes or beliefs about some actual behaviour that runs in accordance with a set of rules. Forming a wish, desire or demand simply expresses one's current bargaining position. If I state a belief, I can take into account possible dissent by saying that I'm a militant believer, if I hope for some change, and when I posit knowledge I am dismissing out of hand any of the negotiation I expect when I state a belief. Action that is in accordance with the rules allows my behaviour to be independent of, or discrepant from, both attitudes and beliefs. To assume that attitudes, beliefs and behaviour must always be consistent therefore neglects the social pressures that dominate action (Ostrom, 1969).

Repeated or habitual actions can, however, converge on some "multiple act" criterion that might involve prayer before or after meals, taking a religious course for credit, donating monies to a religious institution, and dating a person against one's parents' wishes (Fishbein and Ajzen, 1975). When Likert and Thurstone's scores from items like that were intercorrelated with five separate verbal attitude scores it was found that the correlation of the multiple act criterion score with each of the separate attitude scores was as high as the intercorrelations of self-report, semantic differential and Thurstone scales, but lower than for the scores on Guttman and Likert scales. These correlations ranged from 0.605 to 0.714 for the multiple act criterion, but the mean correlations for the single act criteria were from 0.121 to 0.149 with the verbal scales.

Although measures of religious behaviour and attitudes have been used repeatedly within both the psychology and the sociology of religion, traditional church attendance, prayer, and bible reading show the highest base rates of religious responding (cf. the Princeton Religion Research Center's Report, 1982, pp. 41–50). The items that fail to discriminate between religious (and non-religious) groups or individuals probably do so because they lack any clear evaluative implications, and not because those with negative religious attitudes will throw stones at church windows or would refuse to return the greetings of a minister or priest. While such actions *could* be regarded as "religious behaviours", they and their linked intentions are constrained by other values and social rules about how we ought to act, even if we are not religious.

Except for those whose religious observance has become habitual, changes in religious responding over time must be expected (cf. Feldman 1969). We must also recognize conflicting demands on the time that is available, our changing attitudes, and the subjective as well as socially referenced norms about religious behaviour. Fishbein and Ajzen (1975 pp. 301–302) emphasize the levels at which behavioural predictions can be made, and that we continually attempt to *understand* others' behaviour. As they say,

> to predict such a single-act criterion as a person's attendance at the 7 a.m. Mass at St. Mary's Cathedral on the coming Sunday morning, the measure of intention has to refer to exactly the same behaviour. That is, the person's intention to attend the 7 a.m. Mass at St. Mary's Cathedral this coming Sunday has to be measured. Similarly, the repeated-observation criterion 'number of worship services at St. Mary's Cathedral attended in the course of one year' requires a measure of intention such as 'How many worship services at St. Mary's Cathedral do you intend to attend during the coming year?' To predict a multiple-act criterion, it is usually necessary to obtain an even more general measure of intention. A multiple-act criterion based, for example, on observation of several religious behaviours at St. Mary's Cathedral (e.g. number of worship services attended, amount of money contributed, singing in the church choir, and teaching Sunday School) could be predicted from the following measure of intention: 'I intend/do not intend to act supportively toward St. Mary's Cathedral'.

It is because of such complexity that psychologists of religion have been more concerned to understand than to predict Church-related behaviours (Godin, 1964). Perhaps this also depends on the philosophical idealism on which the psychology of religion is predicated and the indirectness of relationships between religious attitudes and behaviour. The Church statistics that continue to be produced (for example, about Baptisms or the number of communicants (cf. Bouma, 1983, pp. 22–23)) may be administratively useful, and might themselves help to draw further support, but they hide a great deal of information about religious commitment and understanding, except in sects and closed groups that impose stringent demands on their members (and from whom that information is not readily available anyway). The unwillingness to strike people from parish lists means that a person's own account of their Church membership is probably as useful a guide as any other, although it could simply reflect idiosyncratic ideals or norms about the appropriate frequency of church attendance and other religious demands. Formally prescribed conventions will not necessarily be accepted or observed.

Religious beliefs

Strommen *et al.*'s (1972) study of 5,000 Lutherans aged between 15 and 65 in 1970 is probably the most thorough analysis that has been made of the religious "beliefs, values, attitudes and behaviour" of a group, except perhaps for the cross-national "European Values Study" (Abrams *et al.*, 1985; Harding and Phillips, 1985) that is currently being analysed. Strommen *et al.*'s first conclusion was that age, occupation, level of education, sex or financial status are less important "in predicting a Lutheran's attitude or his behaviour ... [than] ... knowing what he values or believes". This depends on a basically transcendental view of life that is God-directed rather than self-directed, in which the supernatural is more important than the natural and dualism than monism, with Jesus Christ "at the heart of what they value and believe". The faith Lutherans accept is conservative and historical, with an emphasis on "doctrines of eternal life, providence and sanctification", and an experienced "sense of faith, devotion and practice of piety". They are not exclusivistic in their attitudes to other Christians, despite the fact that their faith "makes exclusive truth claims". There is, however, tension between recognizing the humanity and the divinity of Jesus ("Youth accepts the humanity of God more readily than do adults") and between orientations to the law and the gospel as "more than theological constructs" (pp. 286–289). Beliefs about social issues and the mission of the Church are clearly stated although "the greatest reservoir of discontent for the Church is linked with a lack of emotional certainty of faith, namely doubt", with prejudiced attitudes a "limiting factor in the ministry and mission of the Lutheran church that is mediated by the misbeliefs of Lutherans" (pp. 291–292). Their age trends show that older people favour "a stable and predictable world, whereas younger Lutherans place less value upon orderliness and the preservation of the past" (p. 293). They also found age-related disagreements about social issues, although regional differences and congregational size have little effect on them. "More Lutheran women than men reflect a gospel orientation" and are "stronger practitioners of their faith".

Strommen *et al*. (1972, p. 177) argue that some religious involvement itself produces further religious involvement. Their best indicators of congregational activity were high worship attendance, older age, with college age youth the least active, a strong orientation to the transcendental meaning of life, close friends in the congregation, frequent family devotions, high Sunday School attendance, a willingness to serve, and believing oneself to be as religious or more religious than one's parents (p. 177). Several times Strommen *et al*. emphasize the enormous range of possible variables that can be involved with religion. Most of those variables that are involved reflect common-sense knowledge rather than a formal theory.

Sociological analyses like that of Mol (1971, 1985) focus on sex, age, parental influences or ethnicity as antecedent or independent variables that seem to structure religious responses about core normative issues like belief in God or church attendance. Beyond those factors, traditional and individual differences must be taken into account since both Catholics and Protestants know that their respective Churches expect them to attend services regularly, and that while Catholics find their Church condemning "artificial" means of contraception, not many now accept that prohibition for themselves. On the other hand, the Protestants who do not use contraception do so for their own rather than for normative reasons. The weights assigned to these normative, attitudinal and intentional factors are not uniform across individuals (cf. Fishbein and Ajzen, 1975, Ch. 7), and depend on the meanings that are found or assigned to the components of a religious system, or to experience, moral judgements and education. Tension with other aspects of one's society means that religious rules are not necessarily followed, nor are they always tolerated, so that we can expect some who profess belief or go to church to play that role hypocritically. Survey methods do not penetrate these masks and although a revival may draw people in, it seldom produces deep changes, although it can help to make contact and present a challenge to a new group of people.

Another set of limitations on our enquiries is made by accepting theological dicta and judgements, which themselves disallow a complete reductionism, although we can increase our understanding of them with psychological interpretations. Even then a consensus is needed to decide that religion is mere fantasy, or really true: so Cohn (1975, p. 262) drew attention to the tens of thousands of witches who perished in Europe who "would not be primarily victims of village tensions but victims of an unconscious revolt against a religion which consciously, was still accepted without question".

Strommen *et al.* (1972) concluded that the few differences they found between the generations were due to the differing interests or concerns of the young and the old, and not to any profound psychological problems they confronted, unless a concern among adults with death, serious illness and financial hardship is pathological (p. 247). Those differences could also reflect the change in the religious training that young people are now given and in the concerns of these people themselves. Those who grew up in the 1920s were more completely exposed to religion, and it was harder to escape from it than it was in the 1970s. And religious groups are still looked to for social support by those people now. It is unwieldy to interpret changed preoccupations, or an increased need for support, in terms of a necessary link between religious belief itself and the closeness of death. Argyle and Beit-Hallahmi (1975, pp. 55–57, and p. 197) cite a study by Osarchuk and Tatz (1973), which among others supports that view, and they conclude that, "Apart from the complications introduced by belief in hell, this group of studies provides very strong support for the theory that fear of death is a basis for religious beliefs" (p. 198). Beliefs about piety, trust, the delay of gratification, concern for others, and discrepancies between rhetoric and action, an openness to change, understanding, mission, and the role of the clergy, as well as feelings of alienation, pessimism and purposelessness are among other differences between the young and the old that Strommen *et al.*

(1972, p. 260) found. Those effects all help to define the contexts within which religions operate and the values that they invoke, and they are necessarily precursors to religious conviction.

Religious values

Rokeach's (1968) study of the terminal and instrumental values of a national sample in the United States found clear differences between religious and non-religious groups, and between separate, but broadly defined religious groups like Christians and Jews. Yet Rokeach concedes that it was hard to interpret the different value patterns of those narrowly defined religious groups and sub-groups. Although people who are intrinsically religious may be more tolerant than those who are extrinsically religious, "salvation" and "forgiving" are the dominant values for both of those groups.

A recent study (Feather, 1984) of Rokeach's values, the Protestant work ethic, and conservatism, aligned those attitudes to the values "salvation", "being obedient" and "self-controlled", and negatively to the importance of "a world of beauty", "mature love", "being broad-minded", and "imaginative". These results, despite being derived from a student sample, emphasize again the link between broadly religious and conservative orientations. Wilson (1973) similarly attributed a fundamentalist religious orientation to the ideal conservative, as well as an anti-hedonistic outlook and a preference for restrictions on sexual behaviour. As Feather notes, these characteristics appear "antithetical to individual enterprise and innovation involving as they do respect for authority and the status quo". But there is an ambiguity even there, in that there are both conservative but also revolutionary ways to be religious. Despite that, the "religious syndrome" still aligns with stability, maintenance of the social order and orientations to accomplishment or achievement, to future rather than immediate satisfaction, orderliness, and away from excitement, freedom and imagination. Control dominates both the external and internal worlds of religious people, and simple and direct codes of conduct (whether in rules, laws, morals, duties and obligations, following Wilson, 1973, p. 264) offer predictability, discipline and order. But it is not only religious people who are still being socialized into those orientations.

Psychological perspectives on religion must look behind the gross social variables of age, sex and class to styles of commitment and other patterned responses. While those who are religiously committed are a sub-group within the religious spectrum (Wright and D'Antonio, 1981), it is probably better to ask *how* people are religious than to ask *if* they are religious (Yinger, 1970), since most people still *say* they are religious. English surveys have shown that between six and 22 per cent deny any Church membership, with between 16 and 20 per cent denying any belief in God (ITA, 1970).

Church-based religion

Dissatisfaction with traditionally organized religions contribute some unreliability to the estimates of religiousness. Despite a greater awareness of Eastern religions and the "new religious movements", the place that is occupied by Christian traditions in the West has altered little, and the interpretations have changed little in recent years. Spilka *et al.* (1981) showed, from the citations in psychology text-books, that religious attitudes provide the usual approach to psychological studies of religion, perhaps because they are the most readily quantified or measured (Gorsuch, 1984). As I have argued, religious attitudes are constrained by religious institutions and ideologies, and by being kept within language they support religious behaviour but are not bound to it.

Roof (1980) distinguished Church from non-church religions, and Yinger (1977) identified a non-doctrinal religion that "rests upon the persistent experience of suffering, injustice and meaninglessness". Brown (1981b), however, showed in a study of responses to Yinger's scale and to Martin and Westie's (1959) religious fundamentalism scale that the first main factor involved Christian fundamentalism, while the others contrasted powerlessness and alienation against suffering and meaninglessness, independently of fundamentalism. "Religion" still conveys that limited Christian perspective to us before any other.

We have already seen that many studies have examined the structures of religious attitudes and beliefs, contrasting them against other social attitudes and beliefs. With religiously heterogeneous subjects, typically of student age, it is usual to find a single religious factor that is aligned with church attendance and agreement with traditional religious beliefs. Brown (1962) found that this religious factor was independent of personality measures and of any preference for certainty itself. With a different set of measures, Wearing and Brown (1972) found a single factor that covered religious fundamentalism, belief in a personal God, the frequency of prayer and church attendance, the religious value measured by the Allport-Vernon-Lindzey Study of Values (1960) and belief in both an evil power and in a supreme being. In that study the second factor related to honesty and morality as determinants of one's career. The third factor was defined by the family's religious denomination and the duration of Sunday School attendance, and the fourth by (a high) frequency of the mother's church attendance. The fifth factor was similar to Rokeach's (1960) anxious dogmatism.

In a massive international study carried out among the employees of a multi-national company, Hofstede (1984) found that both Western and non-Western religions coherently mediate different social structures of power distance and differences that stress equality, pluralism, and a "foxes" or a "lions" approach to social stability (p. 104f.) He has proposed a model of stable culture patterns in which religion, together with family patterns, role differentiation and social stratification, education, political structures, the built environment and "theory development" are consequences of, and reinforcers of, social norms and values, and historical processes.

Another study which identified the central place occupied by religion is Coan's (1974) analysis of the optimal personality which extracted 17 factors from the responses of 556 subjects to 130 items. The first factor concerned religion, with a conventional outlook contrasted against "various alternatives". It was defined by items like, "The really important life is the life after death", "Every man's basic duty is to serve God", "Mankind cannot survive without faith in God", "The universe is governed by a divine Being who possesses infinite power, infinite knowledge, and infinite love", and "Religion is unnecessary if one has a code of ethics" (with a negative loading).

We find in these, and other studies (including Sanai, 1952; Brown, 1981b) a general "religionism" factor. Its specific content changes and it does not involve great sophistication about religiousness, but it is defined by the coherence of responses to statements about religion, whether they are for or against it, and by doctrinal statements. Dittes (1969, p. 609 f.) similarly emphasized that "attitudes toward the Church, including reports of church attendance or consent to conventional theistic or Christocentric statements" contrast against items which assess social attitudes that do not directly relate to religion.

It is of some importance that this general religious factor, when assessed by found or prescribed items, has been aligned with social stability, conservatism and authoritarianism. It reflects the truth as many people construe it, and gives assent to an explicit religious position. Church-sanctioned religious doctrines and values inform and lie behind these religious attitudes, which Strommen *et al.* (1972) tapped as a single dimension of religious orthodoxy with items about miracles, eternal life and the devil. Glock and Stark (1965) identified a similar factor, which they say is common to all religions, that is linked with value statements about service and an ethical life. Christian doctrines of the Trinity, justification, redemption, creation, and the divinity and humanity of Jesus, were included in Strommen's study because, as they say, these doctrines answer questions about "What is it for?" (Strommen *et al.*, 1972 p. 80) as an element of the "relationship-with-other" (p. 81), or as a sense of otherness. Their second dimension, which involves "self-development", could be the kind of realization that Wright's

(1972) analysis tried to link with the social, but also personal uses of religion. As Strommen *et al*. argue (p. 101) the basic questions now are not "how?" or "what are the origins of religion?" but "whether?" and "what is religion for?". These questions must be answered with reference to belief, rather than in relation to truth, wisdom, or justice.

Stark and Glock (1968) assessed religious *orthodoxy* with a cumulative index based on belief in God, in the devil and life after death. In a national sample in the USA, they found great differences within Protestantism that were aligned with specific denominational affiliations. None of their non-Christians agreed with all three of those items, but five per cent of Congregationalists, 15 per cent of Episcopalians, and 44 per cent of Southern Baptists did. They note, however, that "the overall Protestant and Catholic differences seem relatively trivial in that 32 per cent of all Protestants scored high while 29 per cent of the Roman Catholics did so" (p. 63). Their general conclusion, that an "overwhelming proportion of Americans today do not adhere to a pristine orthodoxy" (ibid.) warrants further investigation, because it stresses a difference between religious beliefs that are acknowledged and the secular influences that are expected or assumed to bear on them. Stark and Glock also measured "particularism" (defined as believing that only those who believe in Jesus could be saved, and that Christians are currently the chosen people of God), which showed patterns similar to those for orthodoxy and ethicalism.

In an important psychological study, Deconchy (1982) showed that the beliefs expressed depend on the social context in which the data are gathered. One feature of such orthodoxy (as he calls it) is that not only are variant religious beliefs accepted, but the orthodoxy is recognized as having a necessary instability in the way it is expressed. Deconchy showed that a questionnaire derived from outside an orthodox religious system will be answered convergently. The same questionnaire presented from within that system will be answered divergently.

Dittes (1969, p. 610) similarly emphasized inside and outside perspectives on religion. His inside perspective relies on responses to religiously sophisticated items from religiously homogeneous groups, and the outside perspective involves information about "institutional affiliation" and "belief in God" from those who are religiously heterogeneous. The homogeneity of variance in the beliefs and participation that religious insiders report does not allow religionism to emerge as a single factor which is broken up because of the subtle religious distinctions that are being made by those who are religiously involved. The studies by Cline and Richards (1965) and Keene (1967b), with their sophisticated items and heterogeneous, cross-sectional samples, each therefore found a large and general religious factor, which in the case of Cline and Richards had its loadings "more exclusively for females than for males", with the males' responses loading on an "activity" rather than on a "belief" factor. As Anthony Burgess recently noted, "What everybody fears with any new religious group is a repetition of the James Jones horror in Guyana. Religion is always dangerous: that is why Anglicanism is probably a 'good thing'" (and, we can add, why we must learn *how* to believe).

Keene's first factor involved "committed-like items, institutionally loyal behaviour, extrinsic-like items, and the mystical and moralistic". His second factor draws on a conservative-liberal contrast, and the next interpretable factor involved institutional religion. These approaches to religiousness converge on what it conveys publicly, and the coherence of those religious and ideologically related attitudes is likely to be mediated by a social conservatism, or by the extent to which Western attitudes to *social* issues are referred back to the dominant and broadly Christian traditions within which we operate. That tradition is found in, for example, the concept of a Protestant work ethic which now shows little denominational variation, so that both Jews and Catholics score highly on it (Furnham, 1982).

Whether specific items refer to doctrinal beliefs, habits or attitudes they show greater variability than do scaled scores. This psychometric phenomenon is an important feature of our responses, since we can adjust our beliefs when they are threatened, or when given the opportunity to alter them, which indirect measures can readily detect. When a scale's items are rather bland slogans, religious attitudes form an independent but interpretable cluster (Ray, 1982). Wilson (1973) deliberately used that approach in his conservatism scale, and showed that religious items form a separate cluster. That was also found by Marino (1971) who, with creativity tests that measured verbal fluency and different uses of common objects, concluded that Catholic students in the US and in Northern Ireland showed "less originality, ideational fluency and spontaneous flexibility" than did Protestants, although there were no differences between the responses of Catholics and Protestants in Eire and Scotland. Such a difference supports the earlier findings of Knapp and Goodrich (1957) that Catholics were disproportionately under-represented among American scientists and scholars. That could reflect social status and the educational opportunities that are available to them, rather than creativity itself, or teaching methods and the content that is taught. It is widely believed, at least by non-Catholics, that a Catholic training has constraining effects. Religious groups necessarily operate within other socio-political structures that can influence their adherents, and lack of creativity is less likely to be a direct result of religious *beliefs* than of whatever social controls support the beliefs, and the ways they are presented. In fact, Godin (1972) argues that understanding religious beliefs can be a spur towards intellectual maturity.

Ploch (1974) noted that not only do the names given to the variables identified in studies of religion reflect the operations by which they are constructed, but the error term is usually larger than the effects interpreted so that "less variance is explained by the model than by variables outside and independent of it". Those variables are likely to be social but they are not unaffected by strictly religious doctrines. Shaw (1970) showed with an inventory that assessed theological, psychological and illness-related beliefs about behaviour, that fundamentalists favour theological explanations while non-religious people scored higher on the psychological and the illness beliefs. That finding is consistent with the assertion that religious beliefs *become* categories by which we can explain, interpret and cope with the natural world (Brown, 1964). In that way they can be used to resolve, for example, the incompatibility of explanations within the domains of religion and of science. Shaw (1970) argues that the causes and the cures of illness are understood by religious people through terms like will, sin, prayer and virtue, which is a language that takes those who use it away from biological or psychological explanations.

Other religious concepts

Beyond the concepts of God, which we have already examined, other specific religious concepts have been rather neglected, although Gustafsson (1972) used a free association method to explore concepts and images surrounding "the cemetery" (and its link with death). He found it "a highly charged emotional symbol inspiring at times fear and sadness, at other times quiet reflexion". That conclusion was supported by the answers to direct questions and semantic differential ratings, and Gustafsson (1972) said that the cemetery "is frequently used as a spot for meditation, sometimes even preferable to a church", and is more commonly used for this purpose by young non-believers (61 per cent) than believers (23 per cent). "For some believers . . . [the cemetery] . . . means the rediscovery of the order inherent in their faith and their very existence; non-believers find in it their own lack of hope and the bitterness of a finite existence; both groups experience peace and tranquility."

Magni (1970, 1972) has explored "the fear of death" itself, almost by definition a construct that is avoided. He correlated scores from other attitudes to death scales in Lester (1967) with MMPI profiles, and found that the separate scales had low intercorrelations, concluding that the manifest and latent content of these reactions have different meanings and constraints.

Welford (1946) used a rather different approach. In a study of prayer he looked at the believed appropriateness of prayer to solve problems, and the preferred forms of words, finding that more frequent church-going "increased the stress upon the mode of expression of the prayers as opposed to the ideas contained in them . . . (and that) most non-church-goers showed a preference for the most simple and direct of prayers", while clergy and ordinands preferred liturgical prayers, and disliked those that were preferred by the non-church-goers. This again could reflect a conservative preference, or simply their familiarity with liturgical forms. Welford (1948) also looked at the preferences for passages of prose in Biblical or secular language. He found that these "preferences indicated that the liking for biblical language falls off when it is used to express non-religious subject matter", which he said, reflects a "repertoire of preformed patterns of response emanating from a more or less 'structured' background".

In a similar vein, Rosegrant (1976) examined the effect on religious experiences of a period of "wilderness solitude" during an Outward Bound school, in relation to the stress felt, attitudes to nature, and the sense of community. "Meaningful experiences" occurred more consistently with a communal orientation and "mystical experiences" were reported when stress was added. These studies all emphasize the coherence of specifically religious responses.

Maranell (1974) has reported an integrated, multi-variate analysis of religious attitudes in which the responses of university professors in both secular and religious institutions were subdivided according to region and age, and by political conservatism and socio-economic status. From these findings (pp. 155–157) he concludes that, "Southern professors are more superstitious than northern professors", that "Professors in denominational schools are more church oriented, more ritualistic, more altruistic, more fundamentalistic, more theistic, and more superstitious than professors in public colleges". In short, that religious variables cohere with social variables, so that, "Professors in small colleges are more fundamentalistic and more theistic than professors in large colleges and universities", and that behavioural scientists were less religious than physical scientists while fine arts professors had the highest scores on religion. This supports Malony's hypothesis of a "scholarly distance" which allows those furthest from the scientific study of religion to be academics who are most strongly committed to it. When his eight separate scales were factor-analysed at a second order Maranell found two religious factors, one concerned with theistic fundamentalism and the other with a principled morality because of its high loadings on altruism, idealism, Church orientation and mysticism.

Dittes (1969, p. 611) referred to King's (1967) analysis of the constituents of religion as "the most thorough mapping yet of religious space". The 11 factors, (which we have already looked at on p. 7f.) cover credal assent and personal commitment, congregational participation, and personal religious experience, as well as personal ties in the congregation, openness to religious growth, dogmatism, extrinsic religious orientation, financial behaviour and attitudes, and the salience or importance of religion. Dittes notes that others have gone "inside" these separate facets, so that Ashbrook (1966), for example, examined institutional affiliation, Gray (1964) took apart traditional and activist attitudes to the Church, Monaghan (1967) identified authority-seekers, comfort seekers and social participators among Church members, and Broen (1957) distinguished nearness to God from a fundamentalism-humanitarianism factor. Shand (1953) had found that fundamentalistic factors contrasted righteous-formalism against a practical fundamentalism, and that the two interpersonal factors covered a personal and an ethical or concerned belief in God.

Although the broad religionism factor can be broken down into theoretically sensible components that cover religious practice, experience, belief, knowledge and attitudes, Gorsuch (1984) asserts that higher order factoring of this material reclaims the single religious variable. It seems as if that single religious factor, while sanctioning a conservative or institutional perspective, is not necessarily inconsistent with individual and even radical attitudes to religion, and of literal as well as metaphorical interpretations of the beliefs.

This again involves a conservative-liberal distinction within the psychological and theological meanings that are identified by those who rely on the claims or assertions of an unquestioned authority and by those who look for the kerygma or the truth behind the myths (Bultmann, 1953), which Dittes (1969, p. 60) identifies as a contrast between super-ego and ego types of religion. The former is concerned with correctly following the rules while the latter is sensitive to meaning and situational demands. The former entails a priestly stance while the other is prophetic, which also contrasts an explicit and differentiated religion against what is subjective and diffused, or what is consensual and extrinsic against a committed and intrinsic orientation. Furthermore, the former is official and the other radical, the one is "religion" and the other "religionless" (Bonhoeffer, 1953). (Martin Buber said somewhere that, "Nothing is apt to mask the face of God so much as religion".) Both poles can be easily found, although the conservative and authoritarian varieties of religion seem to be more common because they depend on external rather than internal control.

The results of several inductive studies support this basic contrast (e.g. Allen and Spilka, 1967), which as Dittes shows was also drawn by Amos and by Hosea, when they distinguished sacrifices from steadfast love and burnt offerings from knowledge of God (Hosea 6, 6). Perhaps those opposed orientations have been recently brought together again in the enthusiastic (Knox, 1950) or chiliastic forms of religion that are embodied in Pentecostalism (Malony and Lovekin, 1985).

Religious orientations

The *Authoritarian Personality* (Adorno *et al.*, 1950) and Gordon Allport's work on *The Nature of Prejudice* (1954) both found that at least some forms of religion support ethnic and other prejudices, which led Allport to distinguish an extrinsic orientation to religion from the intrinsic orientation, in which religion is lived and not simply used as a support for needs. Hunt and King (1971), reviewing the development of these concepts, modified the original Allport and Ross (1967) measure, and noted that Allport's initial formulation did not refer to a single continuum, but had universal-parochial, unselfish-selfish, relevance for all of life or not, ultimate-instrumental and associational-communal responses as its components. They concluded that, while this concept had become central to the psychology of religion, it points to a paradox. Religion can explain at least some of its own characteristics within its own categories, but they can also be accounted for as a component of personality. Dittes's (1971a) paper in the same symposium on religious orientations aligns Allport's intrinsic-extrinsic contrast with the sociologists' Church-sect distinction, and with priestly and prophetic religious roles. Donahue (1985) emphasizes the negative characteristics that define extrinsic religiousness, and concluded that the relationships between these orientations may correspond with the other findings of curvilinear relationships between non-religious and religious measures, as in the close link between intrinsic religiousness and commitment.

Gorsuch and Venable (1983) recently developed an "age universal scale" to measure these religious orientations, especially within a developmental context, to identify the motives behind religious behaviour. Their extrinsic items include, "I go to church because it helps me make friends" and "I pray mainly to gain relief and protection", while one intrinsic item is, "It is important to me to spend time in private thought and prayer" and another is, "I have often had a strong sense of God's presence". An obvious problem centres on the convergent way these theoretical perspectives have been operationalized as acceptable items, although among 230 students Gorsuch and Venable report alpha coefficients of 0.75 for their extrinsic and 0.68 for the intrinsic scale, with a correlation of -0.28 between the scales. Batson and Ventis (1982) reformulated the single extrinsic-intrinsic contrast into means, end and quest orientations.

Religious attitudes are readily linked with other social attitudes through social prejudices and political or economic conservatism: that led to a recognition of a contrast between a committed, highly personal religious stance, and the more consensual and instrumental or self-directed and institutional perspectives on religion which accounts for those who accept an extrinsic perspective being the more conservative or prejudiced. That distinction depends not simply on church attendance, religious denomination or belief, but on the meanings or uses that are found for whatever form of religion is adopted, as when Dittes argued that an extrinsic religion depends on the resolution of assumed threats from either external circumstances or internal impulses through control, social support and the clues to identity. Those who respond in this way show a syndrome of (negative) personality traits that includes suggestibility, rigidity, intolerance of ambiguity, a search for closure, and authoritarian control. Another view of extrinsic religion has it quite simply as an unthinking, even concrete acceptance of traditional doctrines. The intrinsically religious are assumed to show more positive traits. Spilka's reformulation of these contrasting orientations was in terms of a committed-consensual dimension, and Strommen *et al.* (1972) contrasted orientations to the law, with its guarantees, and to the gospel (p. 138). They rejected, however, the argument of Glock and Stark (1965) that Christian beliefs *cause* prejudice, because of their finding that prejudice was not related to their first general religious factor (p. 202), but to their measures of misbelief and heresy, although they did align prejudice with an orientation to the law, through a rigid personality. Since our usual measures focus on the consensual aspects of religion, with responses biassed towards agreement with them, it is likely that the extrinsic orientation will be the more prevalent. Following Rokeach's (1960) work on dogmatism we should continue to disentangle the typical belief contents or ideologies from any underlying or assumed personality styles, or forms of attachment to them. Eysenck's use of tough-mindedness as a personality/social trait in politics provides another example of that search.

The earlier classifications of religious forms were in terms of susceptibility to conversion (James, 1902), with reference to an institutional orientation (Clark, 1958) or to the characteristics of religious groups themselves (Wach, 1944). To use or interpret such social differences in psychological terms either assumes that people have deliberately or necessarily chosen the denomination they belong to, or that belonging to a Church actually moulds (rather than reflects) psychological functions and styles. That might happen, as when Clark (1958) distinguished primary religion based on an authentic experience from secondary or habitual religion, and from the tertiary religion that relies on another's authority. It is, however, more parsimonious to assume that religious groups allow or foster particular identifications, and that in doing so they prescribe or limit their members' opportunities for religious expression. Blaise Pascal offered the simplest typology when he said, "The two foundations, one inward, the other outward" (*Pensées*, number 470). Hunt and King (1971) showed that simple contrasts like this evolved into the functional intrinsic-extrinsic dichotomy that cuts across classifications of group members in terms of the traditions they accept.

Fig. 2 *Schematic classification of religious orientation (adapted from Brown, 1964) and showing the percentage of response in the main categories. (The italicized categories are conjectured).*

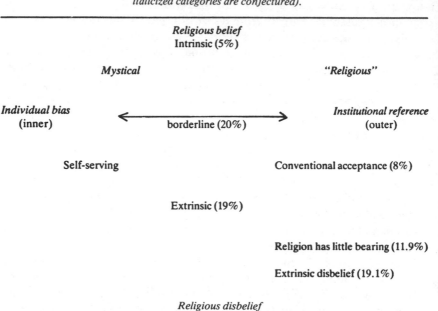

Religious belief
Intrinsic (5%)

Mystical   *"Religious"*

Individual bias   ⟵—————————————⟶   *Institutional reference*
(inner)   borderline (20%)   (outer)

Self-serving   Conventional acceptance (8%)

Extrinsic (19%)

Religion has little bearing (11.9%)

Extrinsic disbelief (19.1%)

Religious disbelief

The classification of religious orientations in Fig. 2 was based on completions of the sentence stems, "For me as an individual, a set of religious beliefs ..." and "In my everyday life, religious beliefs ...". Data from 319 Australian university students were independently classified by three judges, who found a simple division into intrinsic and extrinsic forms of religion impossible to use. A set of seven categories was therefore evolved, which these judges were able to agree on when classifying 90 per cent of the responses. This open-ended approach to the meaning of religion was later followed by a study that has already been referred to (Brown and Forgas, 1981), in which a group of students listed what they thought were the components of religion. In hindsight it is unfortunate that the ratings of those elements were made on scales that were provided and not on scales that were elicited, which necessarily ties the subjects' interpretations of the elements to a conventional and external perspective. But the first INDSCAL dimension involved external-internal, institutional-individual, and personal-impersonal ratings of the concepts authority, clergy, dogma, rituals and scripture, as opposed to peace of mind, faith, personal goodness, gives purpose, and experience of God. The second dimension involved the rating scales positive-negative, warm-cold and unorthodox-orthodox, and set the concepts "gives purpose to life" and brotherhood, against vengeance, heathen, dogma and ritual. The third dimension was defined by the scales known-unknown and tangible-intangible and put Church institutions, and authority against life after death, mystery, God as being, and miracles. These dimensions were unrelated to denominational membership and to holding any specific beliefs, and they are similar to the results of Muthen *et al.*'s (1977) Swedish study, with its three mode factor analysis of six religious concepts rated on 60 scales by 120 subjects. The factors they obtained related to orthodox, traditional and institutional processes and contrasted an individual's religious behaviour against divine action.

It seems clear that what is commonly identified as "religious" is understood first in terms of judgements about institutional demands, which are evaluated and assessed as tangible or intangible. The "religion" to which we have attitudes is not only a well-differentiated social domain, but its content is structured by what is institutionally prescribed, especially in the doctrines. Only secondarily does it relate to what is individually important. That *evaluations* have, applying the work of Kim and Rosenberg (1980), priority over our knowledge or over the content of our beliefs, and are independent of them, could account for the non-linear relationships that have been found between a conservative stance and church attendance (Dittes, 1969; Allport, 1964). Those who attend church weekly *or* very seldom, have, in general, more liberal attitudes than those who go to church irregularly. Those who have "moderate" levels of Church involvement might simply be "conforming" and particularist (Stark, 1963) although they could also be constrained by other social influences, so that those with an intense religious involvement are likely to show a broad range of specific responses.

The uses of religion

These results show again that conservative attitudes to religion are predominant (cf. Brown, 1985), except among those who are the most committed. Convictions about the immediacy or openness of religion and religious experience are unusual because we inevitably seem to prefer whatever it is that we know (Zajonc, 1968). Psychologists themselves have avoided studying the newer religious movements, sects and cults, preferring the "culture-affirming mainline churches" (Kelley, 1979), with occasional excursions towards evangelical and pentecostal groups and the efficacy of meditational techniques. This focus has given an undue priority to the institutional and cultural factors that the Churches carry, and the appearance that their value patterns and underlying attitudes do not favour individualism and freedom. Kelley's (1972) argument about the growth of conservative

Churches depends on the appeal of their organizational strictness as evidence for their seriousness and strength. The confidence that flows from this is compelling to some and alienates others, so Kelley (1979) argues that those recognizing a religious need "would tend to be attracted to a religious group that seemed to take itself seriously by insisting that it knew what it was doing and that its members practice what they preach ... what matters in religion is not so much its doctrines and tenets as how it gathers ... and protects them and supports and strengthens them". We might add the importance of the control they produce over actual beliefs that conform with their prescribed doctrines. For these reasons, says Hoge (p. 192 in Kelley, 1979), the conservative Churches stress evangelism, distinctive life-styles and morality, disallowing individualism. But the reviews of Kelley's book on the growth of conservative Churches (Thompson, 1974; Longino, 1973) show that there is as much disagreement about the validity of the arguments which favour the conservative Churches (cf. Hood, 1983) as there is about the new religious movements which some regard as pathological and others as adaptive and therapeutic organizations (cf. Richardson, 1985). Psychologists, like those in the other social sciences, are not immune to their own (and others') ideologies and prejudices.

Kelley implies that every religious group or individual must decide what they are serious about and then act on it. As he says, "If they are anxious about authoritarianism they can make the preacher stay outside while they decide" (p. 343). In this way Church groups might "cease to be a dependent and become an independent variable" (ibid.), which emphasizes the dilemma between freedom and authority in religion. To enforce what is prescribed obviously has some effect. The problem of meaning, which Kelley thinks is central to religious motivation, might be resolved if preaching about goals solicits commitment and discipline produces attitudinal or behavioural conformity. That raises questions about the kinds of religion that are accepted or expected, and the group alignments that can be maintained. A contrast is set between the strictness of small religious groups, and the leniency of mainline Churches which emphasize relativism rather than absolutism, and invite theological discussion about which is truer to the gospel, if not in general. The conservative Churches, on the other hand, use effective behavioural mechanisms to *take* control and shape responses and they emphasize their consensus and the ways their demands are being met, and encourage talk about faith and belief.

Longino (1973) has identified the values that are involved there. "In an age when science, technology and human resources are rapidly opening new vistas and unimagined horizons to the potential for individual and cultural fulfilment, Kelley is suggesting that seeking maturity is too threatening. Instead of coping with ambiguity and possibility, he says the churches should treat men to the security of a warm blanket and the milk of certitude on which to nurse." The different perspectives on how to realize, or preach the gospel have generated tension in Church life over civil rights in the US, about peace and cultural relationships within Southern Africa, and about the proper aims of missionaries in Central or South America. Convergence among the clergy and laity is needed to maintain either a mission or doctrinal purity, although those who are committed to revolutionary goals show as much faith in the actions they advocate as those who would avoid the Faith, and they stress on orientation to the world rather than to "the Church". An Australian study (Blaikie, 1983), suggests that clergy who stress their role in this world rather than in other-worldly terms are more likely to experience difficulties in dealing with their parishioners.

Denominational differences

Denominational groups differ sociologically and also in their history. So Davidson (1972a, b) links Baptists with a more vertical or supernatural perspective than the Methodist Church which is, he says, more likely to appeal to working class than to middle class congregations. Ploch (1974), however, argues that more sensitive analyses of within group variation are needed. To do that he re-examined Lenski's argument in *The Religious Factor* and Glock and Stark's *Christian Beliefs and Anti-Semitism*, and noted that the Catholic Church has not, like the Protestant Church divided into denominations. Within group variance is therefore confounded because there is no clear basis for clustering Catholic sub-groups, and the variance among Protestants over-shadows any Protestant-Catholic differences.

Mainline religions reinforce secular or broadly social values, and the conflicts between them and religious values can be resolved privately (by not letting your right hand know what your left hand is doing), switching into a hostile mode, even if that is in the name of religion, or focussing on one or another set of values. Bandura (1977, p. 43) notes that, "over the years much destructive and reprehensible conduct has been perpetrated by decent, moral people in the name of religious principles and righteous ideologies. Acting on moral or ideological imperatives reflects not an unconscious defense mechanism but a conscious offense mechanism." The recognition that our values and attitudes are taught both implicitly and explicitly has resulted in the development in religious education of "values clarification" as a specific teaching device "which tends to 'hide' the ethical agenda of the clarifier" (MacDonald, 1980, p. 398).

"Religion" is itself a word or concept that draws on stereotypes and prejudices. As a social category, religion is therefore analogous to race and nationality. Ready judgements about "Jews" or even "Atheists" threaten inter-faith or inter-denominational relationships, and are found in judgements of disapproved behaviour, attitudes or beliefs. Scalings of denominations therefore draw on social distance and explicit judgements, with rejection and similarity the latent variables. A similarity scaling of Christian denominations (Rokeach, 1960, p. 297) found that members of all the major Christian groups ranked "as least similar to themselves Jews, then Mohammedans, then atheists". Further data led Rokeach to suggest "that not all phenomena of bigotry or rejection of outgroups are necessarily attributable to personality ... The rejection of a particular outgroup is traceable to at least two independent sources. One is sheer similarity (and whatever gives rise to it). The other is openness or closedness of systems" (ibid., p. 300).

Rokeach also found that Catholics, Protestants and Jews 'lean more to the right than to the left of centre" although he had a small group of non-believers to the left of centre. "The right-oriented Catholic group scores ... [are] ... relatively high on right opinionation, dogmatism, F, and ethnocentrism" (p. 113), while the left-oriented non-believers are "relatively high on left opinionation, total opinionation, and dogmatism" (pp. 113–115), but relatively low on Fascism and ethnocentrism.

It is not known to what extent people reject other religious groups primarily for their doctrinal position or on some analogue of ethnicity. That problem aligns with the experimental work on impression formation, and the controversy over additive (Triandis and Fishbein, 1963) and averaging (Anderson, 1967) solutions. Triandis and Triandis (1960), however, showed that religious identity is an important criterion in judging the similarity of others, while our judgements of one another reflect our theories and knowledge of the way people are typically identified. This involves a simple attribution, which has become a dominant concern for cognitive social psychology. While Proudfoot and Shaver (1975) suggested that attributions could account for the religious interpretations of conversion or mystical experiences, and for religious testimonies, religious systems certainly interpret or explain the causes of natural and other events (including the origins of religion itself).

As well as explaining religious prejudice, group solidarity is maintained by contrasting one group against other groups (Tajfel, 1982), as when Allport found that church-goers were more intolerant than non-church-goers and that religious people are less humanitarian than non-religious people. Group solidarity could also explain the greater dogmatism of religious people. Allport's explanation of this relied on those extrinsic in their religion finding that in-group support reduces their insecurity.

Other consequences of religion

When religion is taken as an independent variable, its consequences for (political) judgements about, for example, other Churches or their union, might be mediated by exclusiveness or particularism (Stark and Glock, 1968), or by prejudices about their members' sexual behaviour, mental health, moral judgements and behaviour, or attitudes to death.

Any historical perspective on questions about religion and mental illness is complicated by the earlier dominance of religious explanations over these disorders, and the assumptions that if religious excitement did not precipitate mental illness, it could at least be a symptom of it. Farr and Howe (1932), who analysed hospital records from a number of American states for 1848 found that "religious excitement was the diagnosis in from 14.7 to 0.8 per cent of cases, with a median of 7 per cent". Among the 500 consecutive cases that Farr and Howe themselves examined, 13.5 per cent were judged to have a definite religious content, two-thirds of whom were diagnosed as manic-depressive. Lowe (1955) concluded that the delusional content of psychotic patients was "often" taken from religious doctrines, while Daly and Cochrane (1968) noted that in Britain "religiosity" was common among female middle-aged hospitalized patients. It is clear that the content of psychotic delusions tend to exaggerate reactions to cultural pressures, so that few patients now present them (Bergin, 1983).

A different perspective on the psychopathologies that embrace religion considers the extent to which religious practices, especially when they involve ecstacy or some other enthusiasm, are themselves symptomatic of an underlying pathological state. William Sargant (1961) interpreted them as the result of a deliberate manipulation, in which regular rhythmic stimulation moved some into an ecstatic state. He argued that those with a particular kind of neural or personality structure were therefore more readily influenced by pentecostal practices. Glossolalia or speaking in tongues, as one of the gifts of the Spirit, has been readily interpreted as an abnormal state, and although there is no evidence that those in the Pentecostal Churches show different personality patterns, they may have suffered social frustrations or other deficiencies that are compensated for by their pentecostal membership. This again rests on the balance between social control and the deliberate acceptance of a tradition, social context or specific group.

Boisen (1936) rejected psychopathological interpretations of religion in favour of a benign recognition of its social sanctions. In fact Wills (1984) found good evidence that:

> those belonging to a church have lower disease rates than those who do not, and that this difference exists regardless of denomination, time, or place. There are, however, several possible reasons for this effect. People could go to church to pray for guidance and strength, to assist in helping persons who are poor or distressed, to meet people, to participate in a regular and socially respectable activity, to do something they find enjoyable, or for other reasons.

These are all activities that may help to immunize against both physical and psychiatric disorders, although those who have a frank pathology might over-react to religious demands. But even the most scrupulous can be protected within a religious community.

Our problem is, therefore, not why some people focus their pathology on religious delusions or do not know how to hold religious beliefs appropriately, as much as why others (including some psychiatrists) identify positive religious attitudes and alignments as illusory. The shortage of good data on such matters makes us victims of untested theories on the one hand, and prejudice on the other. Over-generalized psychological interpretations, whether of individuals or social movements, in terms of group belonging or shared attitudes, beliefs and practices, are too easy. Yet lay psychological theories continue to assume that Pentecostalism attracts "certain kinds of people" or satisfies "psychological needs". The insiders' perspectives on the testimonies of those who are involved suggests that the "Baptism of the Spirit" *is* a form of conversion experience that supports or maintains behavioural changes directly or by the "gift" of tongues and other practices. Adverse reactions to the social and religious history of Pentecostalism, to its enthusiasm and its apparent emergence in times of religious persecution (Knox, 1950; Worsfold, 1974) depend on interpretations or assumptions of what that movement entails, while only a social consensus can check the validity of these (or other) religious claims.

A sympathetic or unsympathetic stance informs every religious enquiry that has been mounted, despite our ideals of objectivity. The aim may be to understand a movement or phenomenon, to discredit it, or to make a detached analysis of its quaintness. Whatever the stance, and the explanations advanced, we cannot disregard the fact that those who *are* Pentecostal report their experiences as compelling (even if they have simulated them). Those experiences are, moreover, "discerned" or recognized as valid and godly, or as demonic. Such judgements are hard to test, and their practitioners refer to biblical sanctions for their "discernment", itself a gift of the Spirit, and have an extensive vocabulary to describe these experiences, and the ways their lives have been changed by them. These reports must be accepted (or rejected) at their face value or tested on some other ground. It is impossible to know how those who claim religious experiences would act differently without the favourable attitudes they can express, nor how they have been prepared for change and how permanent that may be. Some prior acquaintance with what those religious experiences involve must however, be assumed.

Pentecostal glossolalia

There are two major questions about the psychology of Pentecostalism. One concerns the characteristics and responses of those involved with or drawn into the movement. The other relates to the explanations that are given for it, both by those who are and who are not involved. There has been little serious interest in the first question and much speculation about the second. The two questions come together whenever an interpretation is offered. Informed observation suggests that outsiders' explanations of Pentecostalism usually draw analogies with abnormal states, with the phenomena being located either *inside* the individual, or *outside* in conformity to social pressures. Alternatively the attachments may be regarded as legitimate, or as an illegitimate religious activity that is either heretical or psychotic.

Any evaluation of a person's response to Pentecostalism should, however, recognize the context within which that person operates, including attitudes and religious influences. Pentecostalism is now widespread and no longer restricted to the Apostolic or Pentecostal Churches. Those who are involved with it claim the New Testament as their authority and model, by which the validity of their practices is established, and have the belief that God speaks directly to or through them. The techniques for invalidation include direct denials of any validity, social rejection or asking, "What does he think he is doing?".

The most obvious response of those who are directly involved with Pentecostalism is glossolalia or speaking in tongues. This uses a special or conditional language privately or publicly (or both) for worship and prayer, and occasionally to transmit prophetic messages that are interpreted by someone with the gift of prophecy. The gift of tongues is one of the gifts of the Spirit, with healing and perhaps prophecy the most psychologically interesting of the others. The mere occurrence of glossolalia is accepted as evidence of this gift, which should be asked for. To use such "tongues" does not appear different from using any other special religious language and is continuous with non-religious uses of language, except that what is said is not written down. While children *invent* pseudo-languages, adults say they are "lost for words" or have "become incoherent". Samarin (1972), who asked subjects to produce an artificial language, argued that glossolalic speech is structurally similar to that of invented material, and he concluded that a linguistic analysis showed these (special religious) languages to be superficial imitations of how any foreign language is thought to sound. Yet Pentecostals continue to cite instances of glossolalic tongues being understood by other native speakers as their own language. Glossolalia has been linked psychologically with such forms of dissociation as visions, trances and paranormal experiences, although it is unlikely that even speaking in tongues is a strict dissociation because it is sensitive to volume and length of utterance, and can be stopped and started voluntarily.

One interpretation of the act of using these tongues has treated them as a releasing experience. Certainly those who speak in tongues do not regard them as abnormal or unusual in their proper religious context, and they also enjoy it. The "outsider's" analysis can only rest on what those who are involved appear to be, or say they are, doing. Yet in a study of attitudes to glossolalia in an Anglican parish in New Zealand that was carried out because some parishioners thought it was being taken over by Pentecostalism, with the tensions that entailed, I found that 34 per cent who had *not* spoken in tongues thought it a sign of abnormality, while none who had spoken in tongues said that.

A benign form of the "abnormal theory" of religion suggests that if the use of tongues is not pathological, it is adaptive, because it facilitates and guarantees membership in a group, and can satisfy individual needs or express personality traits. Adjustive or adaptive theories of religion are a common way to account for religious beliefs and behaviour, tested by comparing measures of adjustment or personality among those who belong to theoretically different groups. No strong evidence to support that theory has, however, been produced. Despite that, sociologists use such adjustment theories to explain the appeal of sects and outlandish religious groups (e.g. Lanternari, 1963). Psychological comparisons of those who have and have not had a religious conversion show that those who have been converted are more extroverted (Stanley, 1964), and in a study of the members of two prayer groups of Pentecostals, one in an Anglican Church and the other in an Apostolic Church, I found that those who use tongues were also more extroverted (using the EPI). This was, however, the only personality difference that emerged between these groups.

Religion and personality

Very few substantial personality differences have been found in other quantitative studies among religious people.

Neuroticism has, however, been theoretically linked with religion in the continuing argument as to whether religion involves instability (Vine, 1978; Wilson and Miller, 1968), stability and adjustment (Stanley, 1964; McClain, 1978), or bears no relation to it (Brown, 1962; Heintzelman and Fehr, 1976). Siegman (1963), who applied Eysenck's personality theory to the links between introversion, religious attitudes and social learning produced ambiguous results, although it is likely that since introverts condition more easily than extroverts they are therefore more readily socialized, have tender-minded attitudes and a concern with ethical and religious ideas, which act as barriers to the immediate satisfaction of aggressive and sexual impulses. So Wilson and Brazendale (1973) found a negative relationship between extroversion and religion, while Powell and Stewart (1978) found a positive relationship and Pearson and Sheffield (1976) found no relationship. Francis (1985) argues that these disagreements depend partly on the lack of agreement among the personality theorists themselves and their measures. He therefore examined the problem by staying within Eysenck's theory, which identifies neuroticism with emotional lability and over-reactivity. Francis's data from 403 boys and 685 girls aged 15 or 16 shows for the girls but not the boys a small but significant correlation between scores on Francis's (1978) attitude to religion scale and neuroticism. When sex differences were partialled out, however, that relationship between neuroticism and religion disappeared. A similar effect was found between extroversion and religious attitudes (r = − 0.15). Francis notes that Eysenck later identified impulsivity and sociability within extroversion, and revised his EPI accordingly, and in a further study with that measure, Francis *et al.* (1981) found small but consistent relationships between introversion and religious attitudes. In agreement with Bagley *et al.*'s (1979) findings Francis concluded that neurotic introverts have the highest religious attitude scores followed by neurotic extroverts, stable introverts and stable extroverts, although those interactions between religion, extroversion and neuroticism disappeared when sex differences were controlled. But as Bergin (1983) says, "To make so much of 5% of variance overlaps (much less in Francis's data) between personality and religiosity is not good theorizing." A positive relationship between lie scores and religious attitudes among young people has also been reported (Powell and Stewart, 1978; Francis *et al.*, 1982), which is explained in terms of their defensive conformity and social acquiescence. On the other hand, religious education teaches children to recognize the correct answers, which they will not necessarily follow in practice, as Hartshone and May's (1982) data on cheating in an arithmetic test showed. That emphasizes again a difference between public and private orientations to religion which can, however, coexist. I have already emphasized that our typical religious measures allow a ready dissimulation with a socially acceptable and so apparently conservative stance.

Francis *et al.* (1982), allowing that the lie scale measures a lack of insight, argue that the more insight 15 and 16 year olds have into their own thought, the less favourably disposed they will be to agree with the content of religious items. Maranell (1974), however, found that it was only his dimensions of superstition and ritualism that correlated positively with pathology (0.28 and 0.21 respectively). This suggests that insight, a wide latitude of responsiveness, and a decentration from socially desirable responses could distinguish mature from immature religious responses. That is consistent with Godin's (1971) analysis of the "developmental tasks" which face someone coming to terms with the "meaning" of doctrines and beliefs, as opposed to accepting them concretely. These tasks involve developing an historical consciousness, recognizing symbolic functions, reducing a magical (or concrete) mentality and developing an attitude of faith, finding a release from the moralism that dominates many religious attitudes, and "the continuous purification of Christian beliefs beyond the ambiguity (or metaphors) of parental images". These might all be more easily achieved by introverts, but whether this is so and whether continued involvement with a religious group and its doctrines and models affects personality functioning can only be established by well controlled longitudinal studies. It also depends on what "personality" is thought to involve and the effects that can be assessed.

On the present evidence, religion cannot be said to be an unequivocal function of personality, although arguments about that interaction will no doubt continue, not least because outsiders believe that the members of particular groups appear to share personality characteristics. That is, of course, a classical attributional problem.

The most direct studies of the effects of religion on personality have followed up those converted at religious "crusades". Bergin's (1983) analysis of these data concludes that:

> converts are functional or as better off (sic) than nonconverts, even though the subgroup of sudden converts is sometimes more disturbed than gradual converts or nonconverts ... the studies are consistent in indicating that conversion and related intense religious experiences are therapeutic, since they significantly reduce pathological symptoms.

This has also been reported among the members of new religious movements (Galanter *et al.*, 1979; Galanter and Buckley, 1978; Richardson, 1985), and in traditional Churches (Ness, 1980), but one wonders if those effects could ever influence personality traits rather than some present state.

There seems little doubt that religious appeals, even when they are judged to be primitive or regressive, can have dramatic results on behaviour and on mental status, despite questions about the permanence of the alignments that follow conversion (and few people *have* to stay in psychotherapy), and the benefits of "trading psychiatric symptoms for identification with a fundamentalistic subculture" (Bergin, 1983). One does not have to believe that fundamentalism is a good thing to recognize the confidence about the present and the future that it gives some people. Furthermore, the effects of a gradual process of religious conversion could be similar to the effects of psychotherapy.

Szasz (1978) has interpreted any therapeutic change as a form of conversion, faith healing or thought reform. That those effects are not unambigious is emphasized by Strommen's (1972, p. 462) observation that religion "attracts, reduces, increases and heals mental disorder". Spilka and

Werme (1971) similarly drew attention to the fact that religion can express emotional disturbance, be a haven from stress or a source of stress, as well as a means to achieve social acceptance, growth or fulfilment. But when we look at these effects on individuals in a common-sense way we too readily invoke what Tversky and Kahneman (1982, p. 23) refer to as a "Belief in the Law of Small numbers", to make unrepresentative observations and unwarranted generalizations.

Hannay (1980) argued from a medical perspective that religion is both a "culture maker" and a stabilizing factor, and found that those who attended church less than once a month, and had a "passive allegiance" to it had significantly more symptoms, whether physical, mental or social. He also reported that "increasing age and the female sex are associated with both active religious allegiance and higher frequencies for mental and social symptoms, although when age and sex are controlled that effect disappears". Increased religious observance had the greatest stabilizing effect for those belonging to non-Christian religions who, in that study, had had their "cultural base" in the Church of Scotland.

Recruitment into religious groups is an important phenomenon, especially in the light of the common finding that the religious identification of the majority is stable through their lives, despite fluctuations in religious practice and in the intensity of belief. If one is satisfied with a particular allegiance there is little need to search for another. While social influence and knowledge are important features of attitude change, the search for renewal in the Churches, and for authentic forms of expression, has given a strong impetus for change. That search has led to explorations of dreams, drugs, psychic phenomena, astrology and Eastern religions, as if the best way towards truth is by an exploration of the self. Keniston (1968) noted that those who are most committed to our technological society distrust these paranormal methods and believe that revelations from those sources are tokens of mental illness, because of their emphasis on feeling rather than knowledge. And the criteria by which to judge the authenticity of religious experiences are less those of science than of intuition and subjectivity. It is not clear whether culturally sanctioned evidence for direct contact with God includes an increasing membership, as some sign of social approval, which hides the constant tension for any religious believers who do not accept what is offered without question. While religion involves relating some sense of the infinite to all that is finite, only the latter is accessible to psychological or social analysis. As Berger (1967, p. 282) put it, the "public rhetoric may bear a different relation to social reality than what has not yet been captured" about the issues of wholeness or trust, and the dilemmas of life and death, good and evil.

Summary

The parameters of religious functioning have been established by taking the common-sense criteria of what religion involves in terms of belief, belonging, practice and experience and relating estimates of their incidence to personal, social and institutionally defined variables. In general, socially and traditionally relevant variables are more closely linked to religion than are any personality-based measures. Despite that, the reasons that people give to explain or account for the nature of their religious involvements suggest that religions are built or constructed in a way that makes them both personally and socially relevant. Neo-Pentecostalism offers a good example of the ways in which a coherent religious phenomenon holds these separate aspects of religion together.

8   Religious belief and disbelief

Vladimir:	Ah yes, the two thieves. Do you remember the story?
Estragon:	No.
Vladimir:	Shall I tell it to you?
Estragon:	No.
Vladimir:	It'll pass the time. Two thieves, crucified at the same time as our Saviour. One —
Estragon:	Our what?
Vladimir:	Our Saviour. Two thieves. One is supposed to have been saved and the other . . . (*he searches for the contrary of saved*) . . . damned.
Estragon:	Saved from what?
Vladimir:	Hell.
Estragon:	I'm going.
Vladimir:	. . . But one of the four says that one of the two was saved.
Estragon:	Well? They don't agree, and that's all there is to it.
Vladimir:	But all four were there. And only one speaks of a thief being saved. Why believe him rather than the others?
Estragon:	Who believes him?
Vladimir:	Everybody. It's the only version they know.
Estragon:	People are bloody ignorant apes.

(Samuel Beckett: 1956 *Waiting for Godot*, Act 1, pp. 12–13.)

I can believe six impossible things before breakfast. (*Alice in Wonderland*.)

In the *Psychological Abstracts* and its Thesaurus, "belief" is referred to "religious belief", perhaps because that is its most obvious domain, where beliefs are supported by traditional, ideological, and immediately social or personal factors. Our religious and other beliefs about the world are usually well settled and seldom deliberately questioned; as Stuart Hampshire (1959, p. 15) put it, beliefs "constitute the generally unchanging background to active thought and observation". Because we can disbelieve in God who might exist, or in Santa Claus who probably does not, beliefs are not constrained by the possibility of their realization, so that to examine a person's beliefs is not like drawing a blood sample for later analysis. If two people read a novel which one takes as true and the other as fiction both can find sense in what they read despite their different cast of mind, as Hume put it in

1757. Their talk about the novel is not a sharing of reality or even a mind-play, but sharing the ideas and beliefs each has constructed.

Needham (1972, p. 90) argued that, "The touchstone of firmness of belief is betting, and the degree of subjective conviction can be gauged by what the subject is prepared to stake". Blaise Pascal had formulated that as follows, "Let us weigh the gain and the loss involved by wagering that God exists. Let us estimate these two possibilities: if you win, you win all; if you lose you lose nothing. Wager then, without hesitation, that He does exist" (1960, p. 94). A group of students who evaluated the credibility of that argument for God's existence rejected it in favour of a formulation in terms of emotion, rather like Freud's (1928a) view that "a believer has certain ties of affection binding him to the substance of religion".

Explanations of belief

The broadly psychological theories that have been advanced to account for religious beliefs usually draw on the perspectives of cognitive psychology, which argue that we strive for an integrated understanding of the world, or in terms of clinical or personality theory to assert that our religious beliefs correspond to, or are supported by and resolve emotional needs. That "volcano theory" draws on the primacy of unconscious processes and the mechanisms of defence to produce the projection and compartmentalization that has been so consistently identified in religion. But in 1924, James Joyce had asked, "The unconscious? What do they know about the *conscious* mind?"

A third theory draws on the social or contextual influences that prescribe and support the beliefs we are offered, and that we accept as a consequence of those social influences. Typically we believe without being able to supply many reasons for our beliefs, which have become customary or habitual, with some of them going well beyond or against any evidence. So Wittgenstein (1966, p. 56) said of religion that "if there were evidence this would in fact destroy the whole business". Pascal had similarly noted that "Man is naturally credulous and incredulous" (1960, p. 62). Only the leap of faith takes one from unbelief to belief (MacIntyre, 1957, p. 209), and Hampshire maintained that "a belief is something that *can* only be abandoned by the subject as being false" (1965, p. 85). But to say, "Yes, I believe", is not a decision to *do* anything, or even a statement about a disposition, and each of us is the final authority on what we believe. Despite that, many people believe that we can detect the beliefs of others, making those attributions with reference to their actual behaviour and social alignments.

The perplexing events at Pentecost were interpreted naturalistically by those who said the Apostles were drunk, while Peter referred it to a prophecy from Joel. Those who now speak in tongues use the events at Pentecost as their authority to justify the reasonableness of their particular beliefs and actions, thereby increasing their coherence. From an outside perspective those beliefs operate as selective filters, while the religious insiders might believe that they flow from God. Neither group recognizes that they can depend on age, sex, and so on (Deconchy, 1985, p. 134). Any explanation depends on the perspective that is adopted, and while beliefs present both philosophical (Stich, 1984) and psychological problems, common-sense accepts them quite simply as mental states and part of an inner life with its own structure and coherence. Bertrand Russell identified belief as the central problem in the analysis of mind because of these mentalistic and behavioural implications, which are still unresolved, but which psychological data might be able to clarify.

As mental states, beliefs align with thoughts, desires, fears, hopes, plans and goals, and not with action or social interaction. They are directly identified from propositions in the form, "I believe that ..." or "I do believe in ...", or from some rating of their truth or probability. Beliefs can also be elicited by asking open questions like, "What do you believe about ..." and even "What think ye of Christ?" (Matthew 22, 24). Each person carries innumerable beliefs about the self and the world, or as the Apostle's Creed put it, "I believe in ... all things visible and invisible". Beliefs are learned or deduced, and relate to objects or concepts and to their relationships and uses. Systematic measures of religious beliefs have been validated against differences in the beliefs of the members of groups which are expected to disagree, as when Catholics are compared with Protestants, or believers with "non-believers" and disbelievers, and by the coherence or internal consistency of their responses (cf. Robinson and Shaver, 1973).

Religious belief

Belief or disbelief about God forms the core of religion. The Gallup Poll International continues to ask national samples about that particular belief. In 1949, 95 per cent in Australia said "yes" to it. By 1969 this percentage had dropped to 87 per cent and in 1983 to 79 per cent. There was a similar drop in the United Kingdom from 84 per cent to 77 per cent to 70 per cent: in France, it went from 66 per cent to 73 per cent and then to 62 per cent. The 1969 Australian study showed that 82 per cent of men but 93 per cent of women expressed a belief in God, with a similar difference for belief in heaven (57 per cent of men and 73 per cent of women), life after death (41 per cent and

53 per cent), hell (31 per cent and 30 per cent) and in the devil (30 per cent and 37 per cent). More Catholics than non-Catholics said they hold those beliefs, so that 64 per cent of Catholics and 24 per cent of non-Catholics seem to believe in hell.

Table 10   *Mol's (1985) criteria for the types of believers in Australia*

	Believe in God	Pray daily	Regular church attenders	Percentages
Orthodox church members	yes	yes	yes	17
Private believers	yes	yes	yes	8
Public believers	yes	no	yes	10
Believing secularists	yes	no	no	16
Vacillating secularists	occasionally	no	no	20
Consistent secularists	no	no	no	16
Unclassified	?	?	?	13

These expressed beliefs show less consistency than the doctrines themselves might imply, and a belief in God does not necessarily entail a belief in heaven and even less in hell or an after-life. (Perhaps the concept of hell appears bleak and pessimistic now, leaving "God" a slogan that is to be approved, like "motherhood".) To assume that religious doctrines are held consistently is unwarranted.

Mol's (1985) study of religion in Australia showed that a much larger proportion of people say they believe in God without doubt than attend church regularly, or pray daily. From those discrepancies he identified the six "types" of behaviour shown in Table 10.

Mol noted that Black's (1983, p. 155) data about members of the New South Wales Humanist Society suggest that although they believe that "superstition and dogmatic religious beliefs are barriers to human progress and unity" their membership fell from 737 in 1974 to 401 in 1977 partly because of their political platform and their stand against supernatural beliefs. Mol also found that 80 per cent said they never acted "on the advice of their stars, although 11 per cent did so occasionally and 2 per cent often did".

While some belief about God is both in principle and in fact at the core of religion, it is easier to specify the promises that maintain belief and the religious beliefs that are prescribed than to find the beliefs that are actually held. This is not simply a methodological problem, although it might be solved by disentangling what is accepted privately from what is publicly professed.

The simplest view is that our beliefs rest on some ground or evidence, whether that is an external authority or an experience that carries conviction. This is especially the case for beliefs about the transcendent and the paranormal, which are questioned by those who are sceptical or have doubts on whatever grounds. A limited certainty or reinterpretations of the meaning of such beliefs are among the techniques that find sense in what is claimed or received, and by which "believers" are identified. But Thouless (1971, pp. 70–71) concluded that religious "scepticism seemed to be uncommon, and the alternative to religious orthodoxy seemed to be an equally dogmatic and convinced rejection of religious belief". Deconchy (1982) defined such orthodoxy in terms of the "thoughts, language and behaviour, controlled by an ideological group to which a person belongs, and the power structure which is accepted". Thouless (1954) also distinguished obligatory religious doctrines from those that may be optional (such as a belief in angels) and from those that are tolerated or permitted, which believers may exaggerate as Father, Jesus or Spirit-centred forms of Christianity, that have their basis in tradition, or morality (ibid., p. 14), and which can be expected to vary from group to group, because they are supported by meta-beliefs about appropriate authorities to sanction beliefs, whether about destiny, self-efficacy, natural justice (as in Lerner's, 1980, just world hypothesis) or benevolence. These higher order beliefs have been assessed by quite specific statements, like "People are trustworthy" and "Businessmen are honest", while Lerner's finding that an optimistic belief that the world is fundamentally just, over-rides contrary evidence about the ubiquitous nature of evil, suffering and injustice that Yinger (1977) thought formed the basis of a general (non-doctrinal) religion.

Holding religious belief remains the most obvious way to *be* religious beyond religious practice and claiming a religious identity, and religious believers are identified as fundamentalists or liberals, open or closed-minded, on the basis of their talk and how they answer questions about what they believe.

Belief, knowledge, values and attitudes

Abelson (1973) identified the features that distinguish belief systems from systems of knowledge in terms of the non-consensuality of the elements in belief systems, and their concern "with the existence or nonexistence of certain conceptual entities". Belief systems "often include representations of 'alternative worlds' with a utopian character and rely heavily on evaluative and affective components or assessments and the episodic material of personal experience or folklore, unboundedness or openness and confirmation through subjective proof with variable certitude or credences''. Abelson also emphasized that "it would be fruitless to try to settle once and for all what is *really* meant by a 'belief system' ''.

Belief systems are well articulated and depend on some overriding perspective. Abelson remarks that while youngsters blame the generation gap on adult respectability and insensitivity, "adults develop concepts around adolescent rebellion and immaturity", and psychologists find a "communication failure between generations". Believers are aware that others think differently, unless they are so naive (or closed-minded) not to contemplate or allow alternative realities; Spiro and D'Andrade (1958), however, identified "cultural belief systems" as those that can only be detected by a decentred perspective.

Rottschaeffer (1978) distinguished a cognitive system with its content of more or less temporarily fixed and usually formalized sets of beliefs from a psychological system which involves the "connections among beliefs and connections between the beliefs and behaviour of individuals and groups". The cognitive characteristics of such systems are organized in terms of their intelligibility, truth or correspondence with facts, and their explanatory power, since as Rottschaeffer put it, they provide "a coherent, often causal, account of the data relevant to the system".

"Knowing" also requires presuppositions and assumptions, whether that knowledge concerns God, ESP, witches, atomic structure or subatomic particles. Those assumptions form the central organizing categories or kernels of a system in which the elements can be independently assessed as true or false and evaluated as good or bad, with the whole structure held in balance (Heider, 1946) or made to appear consistent (Festinger, 1957; Osgood and Tannenbaum, 1955). Abelson and Rosenberg (1958) described that coherence as an example of "psycho-logic". The depth at which any information is processed influences the boundaries that are fixed for these psychological structures, which are now seen as socially as well as personally based. For those reasons, Abelson says that "belief systems necessarily implicate the self-concept of the believer at some level, and self-concepts have wide boundaries ... whereas knowledge systems usually exclude the self". While "beliefs can be held with varying degrees of certitude, one would not say one knew a fact strongly". Abelson postulated information modules that are characterized by a tendency to completion, ease of learning and long-term retention, which can also resolve inconsistency and protect beliefs against disruption. That is analogous to the functions of doctrinal and ideological systems in reducing complexity by ordering and classifying the information to which they relate.

Religious beliefs are unlike scientific assumptions, since they cannot be tested against observations in the natural world but are established by an authority or consensus, by their claims and perhaps by the differential peace of mind or confidence detected among their believers and non-believers. They also carry untestable but not exhaustive explanations about, for example, divine intervention.

A neglected psychological problem involves the factual claims that have been offered to support religious belief. Many have tried to establish or rebut the historicity of religion (e.g. Schweitzer, 1948; Hick, 1977), although Goulder (1974, p. 650) writes that St. John's inspiration was similar to a scientist's sudden insight. But he also noted that, "Historical study is the implacable enemy of such a view of inspiration: when we remove the mist, we remove the mystery". Science and religion both involve *constructions* of reality in intellectual (or theological) and social (or historical) terms. The variety of these possible constructions makes it unlikely that only one version can be true, and psychologists have hardly begun to examine the responses to our "sacred canopy" of theories that have been built by contemplating human suffering or the grandeur of the world and can draw from Eastern or Western traditions that span the theism of Christianity and the atheism of Theravada Buddhism. Systematic comparisons, however, are hard to make because of uncertainty about appropriate dependent measures and the fact that not only are religious beliefs widespread, they are well protected and not expressed when it is thought they might be disapproved.

Religious ideas are also like the persistent myths that are realized when they are lived by, and which some can accept only if they are reinterpreted, while others reject them because they cannot find any meaning in them. What is believed about God can therefore influence the explanations of other religious (and non-religious) beliefs, and I have found recently that while God's agency may be seen in all events, God is more readily invoked to explain positive than negative events, and that a person's actions are less likely to be seen as having been caused by God than as responses to natural events or crises. Any religious attachment depends on some acquaintance with the tacit consensus about the language and the rules governing when and who can make religious claims in particular circumstances.

The classical test of the claims of any religion is to become a believer and by applying its techniques appropriately, to achieve sanctioned experiences of the transcendent. That process of discovery may generate dogmatic certainty.

Fishbein and Raven (1962) distinguished attitudes from beliefs in terms of the evaluations and the affective or motivational properties inherent in attitudes and the probability of occurrence and other cognitive aspects of belief. They noted that semantic scales like harmful-beneficial and wise-foolish assess attitudes, while possible-impossible, probable-improbable and true-false will assess beliefs. Fishbein (1967, p. 394) later linked attitudes to beliefs as a summed function of the strength of each belief about any object and of the evaluations of these beliefs. Beliefs are also organized along a central-peripheral dimension, with the most central beliefs, about ourselves and our physical environment, based on our earliest experiences with others and with the environment.

Harré (1983, p. 157), however, identified beliefs with a meta-awareness of the thoughts, feelings, plans, and their revisions that are shared in conversation, and which validate congruent experiences and responses to stimuli and contexts. In that analysis, beliefs bind inner states into language and social traditions. Religion fits there through its reference to ultimate and moral values, and in the way it can be used to excuse our actions. Informal observation suggests, however, that religion becomes a "conversational" matter only in some social settings, which can make it a specific or rather isolated social phenomenon. Harré also argued that the sense of a personal being relies on the talk of a mother to her child setting up the categories within which experience can be understood. That could be paralleled by the way in which the language of sermons, bible reading, prayer and ritual establishes and maintains religious categories, and the forms that are preferred (cf. Welford, 1946).

Bem (1970, p. 6) has referred to our most central beliefs, including beliefs about the self, as being at a "zero-order", while Rokeach (1960) called them "primitive beliefs". Bem noted that "most religious and quasi-religious beliefs are first order beliefs based upon an unquestioned zero-order faith in some internal or external source of knowledge" (1970, p. 7). These beliefs carry implicit tests of their truth, so that any higher order beliefs depend either on primitive beliefs, or they are defined by an external authority that helps a person form "a picture of the world he lives in" (Rokeach, 1960, p. 40). In Rokeach's system, peripheral beliefs fill in the details of one's world view, or our cognitive map, while our intermediate beliefs have a degree of absoluteness. "Some are convinced that there exists one true cause, one true bible, one elite, or one chosen people. Such absolute beliefs, by the way, do not qualify as primitive beliefs because the person who believes them knows that there are others who do not" (Rokeach, 1960, p. 44).

Disbelief systems run in parallel to belief systems, and rely on their own authorities. The specific content of any belief-disbelief system is independent, in Rokeach's analysis, of their open or closed cognitive structures. As he put it, "The relative openness or closedness of a mind cuts across specific content; that is, it is not restricted to any particular ideology, or religion, or philosophy or scientific view-point" (ibid., p. 6). Open or closed systems are defined by Rokeach in terms of their organization along a belief-disbelief continuum, along a central-peripheral continuum and with broad or narrow time perspectives (ibid., p. 55). The emphasis that is given to particular beliefs therefore depends on the ideological system that carries them, on the person who believes or disbelieves, and on the isolation of irrelevant beliefs. So the Resurrection, which conflicts with what we know about death, must either be rejected or reinterpreted if a belief in death and in resurrection are both to be retained. Keeping inconsistent ideas together, as in a computer's random search for solutions, is seen by some as a characteristic of cognitive functioning that allows compossibility or the preservation of cognitive consistency.

Abelson (1959) identified the techniques for resolving belief dilemmas as denial, bolstering, differentiation and transcendence, in which elements are built up to larger units with their own superordinate organization, while Rokeach (1960, pp. 35–39) discussed differentiation, articulation and comprehensiveness or narrowness as the organizational principles of belief systems. Moralists (and some psychologists) are constantly on the look-out for other examples. Simplification and alienation have both been offered as evidence for the "misuse" or the failure of beliefs, so that Soderstrom and Wright (1977) cite Maslow's judgement that "the ultimate disease of our time is valuelessness", and argue that decisions about values lie between God, social institutions and personal responsibility. Their thesis, that "a mature religious commitment will aid youth in their search for meaning in life", was assessed by grouping people as true believers, mainliners, unbelievers, humanists and fundamentalists in terms of their spiritual and moral commitments. They found that unbelievers and those with an extrinsic religious motivation or an uncommitted religious orientation had relatively low scores on a meaning of life scale, and concluded that "religious integration is indicative of greater meaning in life", and that "these integrative factors (in religious commitment) may be subsumed theoretically under the concept of mature religious commitment". Recent work in Australia supports the finding that those who are religious consistently express a greater sense of well-being.

Most studies of religious belief rely on ratings of belief statements in terms of their probability or likelihood, and the results are analysed within the context set by conventional attitude measurement models (Fishbein, 1967). This allows more systematic explorations than the free response methods which can elicit only what is thought to be relevant to that particular social interaction or enquiry: what is disclosed to a priest (rather than to a friend) about one's beliefs or state of mind is different from disclosures to a general practitioner or psychiatrist. These professionals will reach their own conclusions about the meaning of what is said, perhaps identifying a spiritual crisis or an endogenous depression, a mystical experience or a psychotic withdrawal. Few have successfully aligned religious and psychiatric perspectives on issues that involve the supernatural, good or bad spirits and their discernment, or conversion (Pearson, 1977), since those problems can be understood in either religious or psychopathological terms. While modern Western society is sceptical about the validity of the prophetic utterances of visionaries and mystics, earlier psychiatry accepted demonological and religious explanations of insanity; in the eighteenth century there was still a tendency to regard millenial prophets and fanatics who foretold apocalyptic dooms as mentally deranged. The boundaries between religious, psychological and other explanations, are still blurred and depend on higher order beliefs or judgements about what is normal, true or appropriate, and the "scholarly distance" that scientists would keep from religion (Malony, 1977).

A religious focus

Fullerton and Hunsberger's (1982) measure of "Christian orthodoxy" that rests on "tenets" found in the creeds was validated by its internal coherence and against questions about "church attendance, prayer and scriptural reading ... to assess the scale's relationship with more overt indices (sic) or religious orientation." They concluded that, "Belief in the fundamental principles of Christianity, as measured by the Christian orthodoxy scale, appears to be the major covariant of reported devotional behaviour. This is to be expected, but strengthens the impression that the scale is valid." A more secure validation was made by finding a significant difference in the mean scores of 77 apostates and their matched controls who were still religiously involved, and by the fact that for the apostate group the scale formed a single factor that accounted for 41.7 per cent of the variance, and for 70.4 per cent of the variance in the matched controls, where all items loaded at least 0.75 on that factor. This 24 item scale taps traditional beliefs (e.g. "God exists as Father, Son, and Holy Spirit"), all but one of which ("Most of the religions in the world have miracle stories in their traditions; but there is no reason to believe that any of them are true, including those found in the bible") make reference to God or to Jesus. It shows the high level of agreement that is expected of belief in, or agreement with a core of Christian doctrines. This and other belief scales (cf. Robinson and Shaver, 1973) cannot, however, establish the extent to which any beliefs claimed are deeply held.

    Caird and Law's (1982) inventory of non-conventional beliefs, Christian beliefs and "ways to live" (following Morris, 1956) identified as independent factors general Eastern and theosophical beliefs, including reincarnation and the statement "I believe there is a Divine plan and purpose for every living thing", on which the Buddhist and Hindu items, spiritualist beliefs, alternative life-styles, and an "interest in psychic development" were loaded.

A separate analysis of their specifically Christian beliefs found factors covering Roman Catholic beliefs, general Christian beliefs and secular attitudes to religion, including, "It makes no difference whether one is a Christian or not as long as one has goodwill towards others". In a higher order analysis of those separate scale scores, factors they called non-Christian religions, Christian versus secular, spiritualist and psychic, and Humanistic-Rationalistic were identified. Caird and Law argue that although Christianity is the dominant religion in Australia, its believers are influenced by other belief systems that are organized in general terms around "conventional religiosity", "non-conventional religiosity" and "non-religiosity". This implies differences between those who accept the conventional views of religion, those who dissent from it and those with no religion. Other features of that analysis were the extent to which the beliefs accepted correspond with formal group-based alignments or traditions, and the distinction they found between an "active orientation to life" and conventionally accepted religious beliefs.

Those findings return us to the question of religious orientations and the different kinds of religion. While it could be that those who hold particular beliefs might share some personality characteristics simply because of that, such similarities could depend on the status or the institutional links of those who hold these beliefs more than on any effects of the actual beliefs themselves. To believe that the natural order can be disrupted, or that it is better to avoid than to confront life's difficulties is to accept propositions that are self-fulfilling, and "primitive" (in Rokeach's sense). The implications of these beliefs for individuals can cause them to be identified as irrational.

Zingle's (1965) inventory of "personal beliefs" included items like, "I find it very upsetting when important people are indifferent to me" and "I get terribly upset and miserable when things are not the way I would like them to be" which drew immature or ego-centric responses. Martin *et al.* (1976) found significant relationships between similar measures of "irrational" or ego-centric beliefs and locus of control, and they argue that those who believe that life's events are a function of chance, luck or external controls accept more irrational beliefs than do those believing that they themselves have control. Sosis *et al.*'s (1980) findings about beliefs in astrology parallel that conclusion.

Behind these beliefs about control lies an attitude to religious and similar beliefs that must be distinguished from the "religious attitude" that requires accepting and not merely evaluating a religious system.

Religious belief and personality

It is widely accepted that as well as serving a need for knowledge and understanding, any system of belief offers a sense of control and helps to ward off or cope with the chaotic and threatening aspects of reality (Rokeach, 1960, pp. 67–70). While the separate domains of belief have their own content and coherence, procedures that might assess those structures independently of their content have been neglected by psychologists, who have preferred measures based directly on items with a specific content, in the way, for example that Furnham and Lewis (1985) have analysed the structures of economic beliefs. Scott's (1969) work on the content-free structure of natural cognitions which was developed from knowledge and beliefs about nations, has not yet been applied to religion.

Rokeach's dogmatism and opinionation scales, which are "content-reduced" have been applied to denominational differences by Kilpatrick *et al.* (1970). They found only small and inconsistent differences between them, with Catholics more dogmatic than other religious groups, although in the American South, Protestants had higher dogmatism scores than both Catholics and non-religious people. Rokeach himself reported systematic differences in opinionation, dogmatism and F scale scores between Catholics and Protestants in a Michigan State University sample, but not between Protestants and non-believers (1960, p. 110), but he failed to replicate those differences in a New York college sample (ibid., p. 112). When Argyle and Beit-Hallahmi (1975, Ch. 6) summarized these and other links between personality and religion they concluded that they do not involve differences in belief itself, but between-group or class differences embedded in Catholic, Protestant and Jewish membership, or differences in their teaching. One exception they allow is in a link between "religiosity and suggestibility": "While churches may encourage acquiescence, it is also probable that suggestible people will like firm guidance about beliefs and behaviour, and will be more affected by evangelists. Secondly, the guilt and intropunitiveness of Protestants may be due to the church's teaching" (ibid., p. 100). Such causal interpretations need to be directly investigated, although the wide nominal support that religious beliefs receive stops one from being confident that strong causal relationships could be found, although that itself is a common belief derived from Freud's "structural corpus of beliefs, emotions, intentions and approriate cognitive processes" (Harré, 1983, p. 158). The clearest case might be expected in the links between a belief in God as father and experience or beliefs about one's real or ideal father. This has not been empirically established (Vergote and Tamayo, 1980), and has also been criticized by the women's movement for its patriarchal implications. Despite that the traditional metaphor continues.

The clinical literature that has been preoccupied with personality differences between believers and disbelievers does not offer general support for any consistent relationships, and it is not clear that psychiatric patients are an appropriate group from which to establish such links. Bergin's (1983) meta-analysis of these studies suggests that there is no consistent link between religion and poor mental health, while a great deal of informal evidence shows that many Christians have withstood extreme hardships, even martyrdom, because of their confidence and their faith — which a nonreligious perspective considers foolhardy. Such obedience to principle is itself not specific to Christianity, and depends on the situation and its context more than on personality traits (Milgram, 1974) or beliefs. While the beliefs of some allow the death of a child or close relative to be interpreted and understood as the will of God, other authorities sanction suicide bombing and similar attacks in the name of their group.

Indirect evidence and observation suggests that religious beliefs and explanations are assumed to involve personality when they appear to have a disintegrative effect, and those with optimistic and positive or coherent religious views are thought to be unremarkable, until their religious beliefs begin to be questioned. (Hell-fire preaching and the sale of indulgences could itself have generated the anxiety and fear that was detected in religious people.)

When the effects of religion on group involvement have been examined, that view of "religion" tends to be non-specific and even denuded of content, as when civil religion (Bellah, 1967), a commitment to ultimate concerns (Yinger, 1970) or invisible religion (Luckmann, 1967) are identified as its modern variants. To regard religion as one among other systems of meaning pushes any relationships with personality further away by that redefinition of religious consciousness. Religious fundamentalism is, however, itself regarded as a personality factor in the Omnibus Personality Inventory, and there are 11 religious items in the MMP1, only eight of which are scored in final scales. Eysenck's (1954) personality-based theory of social attitudes links religion with "neurotic introversion".

Deconchy (1985) has examined the epistemological problems behind the analyses of personality and general forms of belief. He concludes that the dominant position held by Christian beliefs and doctrines weakens the argument that locus of control or any other personality characteristic can be, even in theory, a good dependent measure of religiousness. He also argues that since personality assessments involve positively or negatively evaluated variables and traits, they return us directly to the distinction between approved and disapproved forms of religion. It is worth emphasizing that a link between belief and personality has most commonly been looked for with negative traits like low self-esteem, dependence, inadequacy, (low) intelligence, suggestibility, and conservatism.

Tyson (1982), who examined why some people believe that horoscopes give true descriptions of their personality, points out that the personality desciptions that are accepted as correct are couched in favourable terms and depend on an accepted authority. These effects are stronger among those with an external locus of control, while people who have found an astrologer and paid for advice are further predisposed to believe what they are told. Those effects do not offer a model for relationships between personality and religious beliefs nor do they imply a particular form of religious personality (cf. Sosis *et al.*, 1980; Mayo *et al.*, 1978).

Ward and Beaubrun (1981), in another context, assert that the "underlying mechanism, associated personality correlates and psychopathological aspects of spirit possession remains incomplete and unsynthesized after three decades of research". Their data from a community of Pentecostals in Trinidad suggest that those:

> socialized in communities pervaded by supernatural and animistic beliefs employ possession as a psychological defence to cope with frustration and conflict ... [and that it] ... does afford some advantages in terms of temporary escape from unpleasant reality, absolution of guilt and responsibility by attributing the reaction to supernatural causes, and evocation of sympathy and affection from family and friends.

Pierson (1967) noted the coexistence of spiritualism and Catholicism in Brazil, and Thouless (1954) had been impressed that Christianity and Buddhism coexisted in Ceylon. Others are surprised that Christianity should have continued in China after the Liberation in 1949, unless it proved impossible to suppress it. Such apparent contradictions in belief may only be a problem for those who expect consistency and do not have Chairman Mao's calmness about resolving "contradictions among the people" (1977). Many people are, however, disconcerted by the inconsistences they find between politics and religion or religion and science and within religious traditions themselves.

Styles of response

Religious systems of belief permeate European and other cultures in ways that will not go away, even when they are redefined sociologically, because the traditions continue and their doctrines are widely accepted. We have seen that appropriate items and subjects can expose differences between Catholics and Protestants, and between the major Protestant denominations, while large religious groups, like the Church of England, have parties and groupings that tend to hide such effects.

Religious doctrines are not simply believed or disbelieved. They also represent the "objects" or issues that social groups and religious parties rally around. Although doctrines of election and the real presence are good examples of the way disagreement and dissent have produced schismatic groups, they, like concepts of sin and grace, have been disregarded by psychologists of religion who have preferred to explore less divisive beliefs. Such doctrines may also have lost their ability to break up any Church, especially in the present climate which looks for unity. That people seem to prefer comparatively simple tenets in both religion *and* politics is reinforced by Bruner and Postman's (1948) finding that broad rather than narrow categories are more usual. So Butler and Stokes's (1969) data show that most voters do not know in detail the policies of the parties and candidates for which they have voted. Disapproval or prejudice against religious groups therefore focuses on the socially relevant features of their traditions more than on their specific doctrines.

The meanings found in religious beliefs implicitly assess their authenticity, and what is rejected is judged against abstracted criteria about what are the best or most appropriate ways to be religious. So Allen and Spilka (1967) found that an undifferentiated consensual orientation to religion aligns with political conservatism and a prejudiced stance. Similar findings have led to differences being identified between behavioural and ideational forms of religion or between acted and internalized religion (Roof, 1979), which extend beyond what is believed to the personal consequences of any beliefs.

The widely used set of orientations based on differences between an internal or personal and an external or context-based locus of control (Rotter, 1966; Lefcourt, 1982; Langer, 1983) may not be applicable to religion because God, as traditionally construed, can be both outside and beyond but also within people. Even those who believe that they have accepted their religion deliberately, carry vestiges of external control, if, for example, they believe that its truth can only be established eschatologically. Deconchy (1985, p. 89) notes that religious control can also be directly experienced as good "luck" or misfortune, as a gracious intervention or indirectly by the way the world has been planned. Luck can be invoked in social rituals or found in the signs or symbols of God's presence. Although this locus of control concept has been over-worked, internal control has been related to general religiosity (Rohrbaugh and Jessor, 1975) and to religious practice (Benson and Spilka, 1973). Lefcourt (1982) argues that since internal control is generally endorsed by our society, we prefer belief in our own control to chance, fate or luck. While we have rejected the notion of separate spheres of influence for Venus, Orpheus, or Mars, and the rest of the Greek pantheon, the actions of the Christian God are still unified and personally focussed. The contradictions of control appear there, since even an internally controlled person might resort to religious rituals to bring external forces under control. Deconchy (1985) therefore argues that religion lies somewhere between the inner and outer poles and that one function for institutional forms of religion is to make that distension credible and their interconnections possible, in cognitive and emotional as well as in social or historical terms. For a religious person to use representations of God appropriately requires balancing an internal-external polarity against dichotomies set up by personal and social, individual and institutional, or intrinsic and extrinsic orientations.

Beyond stable patterns of beliefs about, for example, the nature of God, are the beliefs separately elaborated by each believer or disbeliever around some received core. That cellular level has yet to be exploited because it is so complex, and there has been a preference for group comparisons among samples greater than one or two. While a person's professed beliefs may remain stable, the reasons and meanings that support them are not, and historical changes in traditions are assumed to be a result of secular pressures and the chiliastic or conciliatory roles that religious beliefs themselves play (Wadsworth and Freeman, 1983). Currie *et al.* (1978, p. 123), however, argue that "the effect on membership retention of a change in personal life circumstances is similar to that of historical and social changes which tend to disturb the settled life of the section of the population into which any given individual may have been born". That analysis of community change neglects the directly intellectual *or* "psychological" reasons that drive individuals towards or away from religious beliefs, independently of the social or educational functions of Church traditions and groups. It is almost impossible, however, to document those changes because they are so readily overridden by the demands placed on individuals to express age (and sex) appropriate behaviour, beliefs and values.

The 1946 British Birth Survey offers some information about generational differences in beliefs, from its continued enquiries among a large sample of parents, and their children who are now 41. Wadsworth and Freeman (1983) report data on answers to questions about being brought up in a faith or religious denomination in relation to the strength of their current religious beliefs. Although these were crude measures of "religious belief" they show interesting differences between males and females in denominational attachments and strength of belief. Overall, "67.4 per cent were believers at age 26 years as compared with 87.1 per cent of families of origin". Of those with no educational qualifications, 72 per cent of men and 77 per cent of women said they had not changed their beliefs, and the change away from belief was most strongly associated with an education beyond the G.C.E. Advanced level, which Wadsworth and Freeman link to the family disengagement and geographical mobility that results from education itself. Although they also stress the role of emotional experience in religious change, that conclusion rests on the finding that only the mother's recent death was associated with strong religious beliefs, although not significantly so. Furthermore, "Those who became believers for the first time were more often rated as having emotional disturbances that received hospital treatment when compared with those who lost or who did not change their beliefs''. While only 19.7 per cent had moved from their parent's religion, 43.3 per cent from a Tory background had changed their political affiliation.

Explicit defection from religion is comparatively rare and it is more common to "back-slide", and then find that one has moved too far to recover, or there is the realization that no longer are the received beliefs accepted. Since any claim on belief is a claim for its credence, religious beliefs are typically latent and only occasionally activated explicitly except by those who are strongly committed *or* professionally involved. Assertions about one's religious beliefs are therefore more often statements about their claimants than about their truth. Wittgenstein (1966, p. 90) went further, to assert that "the language-game of reporting can be given such a term that a report is not meant to inform the hearer about its subject matter but about the person making the report''. So Kotre (1971) found that to lapse from Catholicism is not to reject specific beliefs but the institutional structure and its particular approach, from which, of course, the beliefs derive.

Peter *et al.* (1982) examined the increasing defections among the Hutterites, who are currently undergoing significant transformations in their life-styles because of conversions to evangelical revivalistic Protestantism, and not because of the appeal of their open, consumer-oriented, host society or because of any internal disorganization of their colonies. This puts those who defect, and who are also mobile, into competition with their traditional collectivist ideology, which supports the closed groups. Those conflicts are settled in favour of the individualistic conceptions of salvation that are offered by outsiders.

The beliefs of individuals

Clayton and Gladden (1969), who argued for the dominance of an ideological dimension in religion over any others, found support in Faulkner and De Jonge's (1965) statement that "the ideological dimension was unmistakably of pervasive importance''. That dimension accounted for 78 per cent of the variance in Clayton and Gladden's first study and for 83 per cent in another. They selected their items from institutionally defined doctrines and an implicit phenomenology of religion. While it is unwarranted to assume that every individual's responses are so derived, that most people's responses are derived in that way shows the primacy of established structures over any personal or psychological principle that can organize belief.

In a repertory grid study of religious constructs among a set of Catholics, O'Connor (1983) elicited from each of them separately "the people, places and things known and thought about, believed in and valued'' (p. 131). The idiosyncratic nature of this material is shown by the loadings in Table 11 from Slater's *INGRID* analyses of the grids of five individuals, for God the Father, Jesus Christ and the Holy Spirit (and Mary or St. Paul when they were given).

Table 11 *INGRID factor loadings from a repertory grid study of Catholic Religious (from O'Connor, 1983)*

	Factors	Elements God the Father	Jesus Christ	Holy Spirit	
Person A	1	− 1.90	− 2.97	− 1.90	
	2	1.35	1.92	3.62	
	3	4.21	− 0.63	0.26	
					Mary Our Lady
Person B	1	− 4.17	− 4.67	− 2.10	− 3.55
	2	− 1.07	− 0.38	− 0.51	− 0.25
					St. Paul
Person C	1	− 4.24	5.76	5.76	5.52
	2	− 1.07	0.55	0.55	− 0.40
Person D	1	− 3.37	− 2.34	− 4.27	
	2	1.77	2.96	1.20	
	3	− 1.61	1.41	− 0.40	
					St. Paul
Person E	1	− 4.44	− 4.44	− 3.75	− 3.97
	2	2.68	2.68	3.35	2.29

It is apparent from these data that for person A there are separate factors for each Person in the Trinity. Each of the other four subjects has these Persons on a single dimension, although D also produced another factor for Jesus Christ, while E has two Trinitarian factors with opposite loadings, which include St. Paul.

Psychobiographies have constructed details of those like St. Augustine who emphasized God's redemptive functions, and Luther who stressed Christ as mediator. Augustine resolved the problems he had with authority by relying on the Church rather than scripture, which has been thought to fit with the description in his *Confessions* of the dominating place his mother held in his childhood, and his close, continuing relationships with her. Symbolic equivalence supports these interpretations, although the fantasies Augustine records about his relationship with his mother seem to mirror the theological doctrines he accepted, with their stress on pride and sensuality. The beliefs Augustine developed are, however, too easily understood as solutions to his conflicts.

Religious doctrines do not have the same implications for everyone. The reality of God's presence that is immediately apprehended and reasonable to one person can be frankly irrational, or illusory to another and a poetic construction for others. These boundaries between belief (or faith) and fact change, as Malinowski emphasized when he identified religion as primitive science. Although we accept heliocentric theories of the solar system, theories of evolution are still being disputed and rejected unequivocally by a few. So fundamentalism as an interpretive position seems more potent than any traditional doctrines themselves, which are too widely accepted to allow predictions of what any Congregationalist or Anglican might believe about miracles or the Virgin Birth, although they can be expected to recognize the Bible.

The Prayer Book's catechist who says, "Rehearse the Articles of thy Belief" wants the Apostles' Creed as the answer. The catechist then asks about the Ten Commandments, the Lord's Prayer and the nature of the sacraments. No explicit reservations or reformulations are allowed then or when Anglican clergy are asked to affirm that the doctrine of the Church of England, in the Book of Common Prayer and 39 Articles, is agreeable to the word of God, because they are giving formal assent to a position and not stating their own beliefs. The pressures for a public acceptance of traditional religious statements could account for the apparent primacy of a conservative fundamentalism that contrasts with those for whom religion is a fleeting, "hidden dimension", or who have tried to think through and enunciate their personal construction in public.

Responsible Christians from Luther to John A. T. Robinson and David Jenkins, Lloyd Geering in New Zealand and Ted Noffs in Australia have found how easy it was to get into trouble with the news media or ecclesiastical authorities when they have disclosed what they find (or do not find) in the traditional doctrines. Prophets have generally had a hard time, and as Thurstone (1931) noted, self-disclosures are not made easily because of the social controls over what can be said.

An established tradition in psychology has assumed that explicit social characteristics are less important for understanding behaviour than are subjective traits or experiences. But every group uses explicit rules and values to regulate or control its members, and to identify what is real. These rules organize the responses of individuals and impose pressures to orthodoxy (Deconchy, 1982). Precursors to this view are found in the use of authoritarianism (Adorno *et al.*, 1950), dogmatism (Rokeach, 1960) and conservatism (Wilson, 1973) to explain why beliefs are strongly held.

Any assumption that the primary reference for committed religious people is cast vertically (Bem, 1970, p. 7) neglects the horizontal and parataxic conceptions of God's involvement, and not only the deviants' attempts to realize their beliefs directly in the physical or social world. Although Kushner's (1967) patient enucleated an eye in response to a biblical injunction, others believe they arc possessed by a divine power, or will simply assert that it is God's will that they should work as missionaries. While social sanctions support the last but not the first of these instances, spirit possession is still ambiguous because religious beliefs correspond with an ordered, coherent and widely accepted theory of the world.

That view aligns religion with a code that individuals share in but cannot grasp in its entirety, with their participation constrained by what Sherif and Sherif (1965) called "a range of convenience", with the religious words or concepts that are used being constrained by the way they fit with other social pressures and knowledge.

From another perspective, religion implies a kind of "game" played by its insiders, which loses its credibility when the conventions or rules seem to break down because others won't agree. The sources of conflict between believers and the systems they subscribe to deserve to be investigated directly, since either separate beliefs or the whole system are inadequate to handle the demands imposed on them, especially when the rewards or punishments from a religion are not immediate, although immediate consolation and social support will be among the reasons that sustain continued religiousness.

The pressures to uniformity within religious groups and their resistance to *new* religious beliefs are hard to dispute. Recent arguments about Church union on the one hand, and the ordination of women on the other show that for proposals of change to be accepted they must be made consistent with the existing doctrines or beliefs. Some religious doctrines, like legal utterances, entail powerful actions, as when a person is granted absolution, baptized or ordained:

> At one end of the scale 'guilty' in the law court; at the other, '$2 \times 2 = 5$' because the courts say so. But in the middle 'monetary supply is the cause of inflation', 'Proust was a great moralist' (and Jesus was the Son of God) may have the force of legal truth and not be distinguished for certain speakers and hearers from the truth claims proper (Chilton, 1984 p. 137)

Chilton points out that this is the distinction George Orwell made between "letting the meaning choose the word" and "the invasion of one's mind by ready made phrases", which is a characteristic of much religious and other language or communication. A close analogy can be found with beliefs about politics and other social issues. Some people simply "hold" political beliefs while others work hard for them. Doing that strengthens their commitment to them.

It is not uncommon to find that religious ideas are reified, since as Philipp (1977) points out:

> religion in its widest sense fills a deep-seated need in every human being. Everybody tries to understand life and its meaning and then to interpret the basis of his feelings. One accepts the teaching of his kindred group, another revolts against it and adopts an opposite stance, others try to think completely afresh by themselves.

In that sense "belief" refers to a philosophy rather than to "basic attitudes", although as Roof and Roof (1984) emphasize, most surveys of religion focus on "the strength of belief commitment, but seldom on the content of belief itself". Their analysis of responses to 12 images of God in a national survey in the US found that "Creator" was dominant (82 per cent) and "spouse" the least popular (17 per cent) (although one wonders why it was accepted at all). Although feminine images of God were secondary to the traditional "father" image, females accepted them strongly more than males.

Unlike scientific beliefs, religious beliefs are also guides to life and morality. For that reason Needham (1972, p. 54) distinguished doctrinal from contingent or necessary beliefs, and from moral beliefs. Physical (and other) scientists can, however, still grant the existence of a "Divine Ground" (Huxley, 1941, p 13) that is beyond investigation but realized as an experience that is referred to a transcendental system or cosmology. Rituals emphasize the power of religion, and their apparent inconsistencies are easily resolved. While a dance or prayer may not bring rain its performance does not challenge the belief that it could do so. By giving accounts of such failures they can be maintained by a fear of what could happen if they were not performed (Langer, 1956).

J. B. Pratt (1920, p. 224) argued that a (positive) attitude to the "Determiner of Destiny" *is* religion, and that it "has always an essentially practical colouring". While religion involves belief, "belief is never a matter of pure theory, but bears a reference, more or less explicit, to the fate of the individual's values". These, he claims, necessarily involve "the question of the future in store for the individual believer", which can be understood as a concrete place or state. Pratt argues that belief in a future life is based on "primitive credulity, habit and authority (or teaching), on reason, on some form of feeling, or will" (p. 225), and relates closely to "the fact of death". Perhaps this is the area of belief that has changed more than any other, although Tertuilian argued that the human soul is not only religious by nature but naturally Christian. One consequence of that belief was the holy wars against the infidels, with their contemporary parallels in the Middle East and in Northern Ireland. The term "unbelief" itself suggests a deviation, although Kierkegaard's leap of faith suggests that non-belief might be the natural state, and Bonhoeffer's "religionless Christianity" showed that authentic Christianity must be detached from the corruptions of "religion". In a similar way no psychology of religious or other beliefs can be explicitly committed to the ideology that psychology is simply being used to understand; so that belief and unbelief, faith and doubt, religion and irreligion are related dialectically, like a black and white chess board. Such decentration requires both implicit and explicit assumptions, that in Western society are consonant with a Judeo-Christian perspective (although the growth of new religious movements points to the failure of conventional Western spirituality and of materialism).

Reductionistic explanations can account for supernatural beliefs as needs and satisfactions, fantasies and illusions, with reference to social traditions and processes, or in cognitive terms. These explanations are all hard to test directly. But even William James observed that when beliefs chime in with an emotional mood no more evidence is asked for, since "all propositions are believed through the very fact of being conceived". Kohlberg (1980) noted that in relation to values clarification, "all mental events have both cognitive and affective aspects" (p. 40).

Mature or decentred believers are expected to see through the specific content, claims, or metaphors of their belief system to some deep structure, even if they still believe that it can resolve problems, buffer dependency and solve their longing for security, or instil hope about the future. Although the direct evidence for those meta-psychological assertions is weak (cf. Argyle and Beit-Hallahmi, 1975) religious beliefs are still popularly interpreted in that way or as an innate disposition to respond to the numinous.

Although psychologists may have become more sophisticated about religion, the implicit beliefs about it have changed only slowly. McCloskey (1983) similarly noted that early scientific concepts about the physics of motion have persevered, and that many adults' explanations of the way objects move contradict Newton's laws and echo theories of motion that were popular in the Middle Ages. As children grow they get worse before they can become better at predicting the paths of moving objects (perhaps as a consequence of the way they are taught). Our intuitive and primitive beliefs might also make religious cosmologies and techniques, aesthetics and social structures more plausible than any particular theology. Under that view, the doctrines to be accepted are a mere formality.

While evidence can be used to fix belief states, habitual responses about goodness or badness involve evaluative judgements of the whole. That view evades questions about how information from the separate components of a belief proposition are integrated (Anderson, 1967), beyond the "search for meaning", or a simple commitment to *some* beliefs.

Any account of belief must recognize that some people seem incapable or unwilling to elaborate or question what they believe, which returns us to the argument in *The Authoritarian Personality* (Adorno *et al.*, 1950) that prejudice stems from the way beliefs are accepted, including an uneducated point of view, as Roger Brown (1965) argued, and not from any characteristics of the beliefs themselves. Allport (1950) therefore found that while "genuine" and conventional believers hold to similar doctrines, only the latter showed ethnic prejudice.

It is obvious that many people, but especially children, accept the doctrines they are offered before they can articulate or understand them, and that the naive or animistic philosophies about the natural world (Piaget, 1931) are stereotyped and lack the precision of either theological or scientific explanations. Because religious explanations are tested existentially rather than empirically (despite Galton's (1873) efforts to disprove the efficacy of prayer), support for them is found in logic, insight, and the ways they are traditionally supported. Confidence in religious beliefs must be built or found, and they usually appear ambiguous to an outsider. The process of diagnosing religious beliefs as delusional points that up, since some normative base or reference is required to identify any belief that is inconsistent with the believer's life or context, as being pathological.

An important defect of the conventional measures of belief is the closed-response categories they use and their disregard of where the support for them is to be found. That doctrines can be believed but not understood is shown by those whose responses are indiscriminately pro-religious, although William James (1902) had asserted that a person is unlikely "to say he believes something he does not imagine that he understands" (p. 327). James similarly argued for a distinction between the elements of a proposition and an attitude to the proposition as a whole (p. 325).

Strong beliefs about our own religious beliefs and those of other people depend on where one stands (Roiser, 1981) and on the boundaries that are set between beliefs, facts, and whatever evidence can be accepted. Frances Young (1975, p. 35) asked if her own religious myths would cease to be real if she found it "intellectually impossible to make the ontological equation: Jesus = God". Tension between symbolic and literal meanings is not easily resolved so that, "When the science becomes out-dated (and literal interpretations are in one sense scientific) the myth is endangered" (ibid., p. 36). Psychological investigation may have stayed too close to the literal interpretation of religious meanings for too long.

Summary

Belief and disbelief are processes by which individuals align themselves with traditionally defined doctrines on the one hand and with their experiences of reality on the other, in a way that spills over to attitudes, values and knowledge. That cognitive view of religious beliefs has competed against the alternative formulation which holds that styles of responding, typically in terms of dogmatism, authoritarianism or conservatism, are themselves facets of personality that are closely linked with religious belief.

9　Readiness for religion

It is true, as Pascal says, that "to believe, to doubt and to deny well are to the man what the race is to the horse", but only in that order. We must believe before we can doubt, and doubt before we can deny. And, with the exception of autistic children, we all do begin by believing what we are told.

Of course, Behaviourism "works". So does torture. Give me a no-nonsense, down-to-earth behaviourist, a few drugs, and simple electrical appliances, and in six months I will have him reciting the Athanasian Creed in public.

W. H. Auden, *A Certain World*, 1971, pp. 33–34.

Elkind (1971), who reviewed research on descriptions of critical changes in religious experience and the developmental studies that delineate the content or form of religious understanding and its successive changes, and the teaching of biblical material, within the developmental tradition that Piaget established, noted that "studies regarding the growth of religious understanding are not numerous by today's research standard" (p. 656). Central to that work has been a contrast between "spontaneous religion" and the need to teach religion deliberately. G. Stanley Hall (1904) saw religious development as a necessary recapitulation of the history of mankind moving from an animistic stage to myth-forming, then to a polytheistic stage, an ethical, and finally to a maturely spiritual stage. A simpler view distinguished prepersonal from personal religion, and identified the situations in which religion is invoked as either recurrent and habitual or acute, because of the effect of some unusual or unexpected event (Elkind and Elkind, 1962).

Regardless of whether religion is to be 'taught' or 'caught', some concept of developmental stages is intrinsic to both formal and common-sense theories about religious and other forms of psychological change, especially as children grow into adulthood. These theories are probably based more closely on the way children are expected to progress than on any independent assessments or measurements of how they do change. In that sense they are prescriptive rather than empirical generalizations, although we know that everyone crawls before they can walk. In the same sense, we expect development to be a continuous process, that any stages overlap and that we might

187

go backwards. The nature and status of every stage-based theory of development has drawn continuing controversy (cf. Brainerd, 1978).

Probably the most widely cited set of religious "stages of faith", as a "psychology of human development and the quest for meaning", are those described by Fowler (1981). His first stage involves a pre-conceptual and pre-linguistic trust that is characterized as an "intuitive-projective faith" which is fantasy-filled and not restrained by logical thought, and in which God is construed as magical and pre-anthropomorphic. The second stage, between seven and 11 years, involves a mythic-literal faith in which God is an anthropomorphic, kingly but fair law-giver who recognizes the intentionality of action. The third stage involves a symbolic-conventional faith that incorporates widening social experiences into a unifying identity or outlook. Although this stage develops during adolescence, it describes the religious attitude of a majority of adults, and is changed by a deepening self-awareness and a recognition of the relativity or decentredness of one's own experience. Fowler says that the fifth stage of "paradoxical-consolidative faith" does not develop until mid-life, with its anarchic voices of "deep-self" that construct a highly personal God, while the sixth and final stage of "a universalizing faith" is found in the lives of a few exceptional people. (My account of these stages is paraphrased from Webster, 1984.)

Fowler developed this sequence of stages over many years of counselling and with intellectual debts to the theories of cognitive, emotional and moral development that have been advanced by Piaget, Erikson and Kohlberg. The primary support for this system has been through semi-clinical interviews, which necessarily confuse what is being explained or described with the explanatory material itself. Independent evidence for these stages is needed which goes beyond their inherent plausibility. But as Webster argues, Fowler's scheme works "at the level of practical theology rather than scientific theory", and it identifies what we expect, or will allow at particular ages of those having a "religious" perspective. There are, however, other and more empirical perspectives on religious development.

The idea of God

The most formal approach to religious development has been through studies of the conceptions of God, some of which we have already examined (p. 81). Elkind notes, however, that these structured methods have found only slight age differences, whereas with unstructured methods quite definite stages have been identified.

Klingberg (1959), who asked 630 Swedish children aged nine to 13 to complete the statement, "Once when I thought about God ...", found that those compositions referred to formal worship, situations of distress, experiences in nature, and moral experiences.

In the very early works by Barnes (1892), Bose (1929), MacLean (1930) and Harms (1944), age-dependent changes were found. Harms's study of children's drawings of God, for example, identified a fairy tale stage, followed by a "realistic stage" and then an individualistic stage, while Deconchy (1967), who used a word association procedure to study the development of ideas about God and Christ held by 2,316 boys and 2,344 girls aged eight to 16 in Northern France, found 19 categories that were set along three dimensions. God's remoteness and attributes were most frequently mentioned by eight to ten year olds, with a personalization among 11 to 14 year olds and interiorization (or doubt and fear) among the 14 to 16 year olds. Mailhiot (1961), on the other hand, asked teachers to elicit drawings from their pupils and found that a third refused to draw God, although all of them were willing to draw Jesus. Mailhiot also collected their prayers and found that most of them involved a demand or direct request, or a reprisal.

Graebner's (1960) results from an "Ideas About God Inventory" led him to conclude that, "When the answers for most of the questions in the study were reviewed along a grade continuum, it was found that similarity of answers at all grade levels was the rule rather than the exception" (p. 75). In this same tradition Brown (1968) made a cross-cultural and cross-sectional study of beliefs about the efficacy and appropriateness of prayer from age 12 to 17. With direct questions about the use of prayer in defined situations, an age trend away from belief in the efficacy of prayer was found, although there was no such trend in the beliefs about its appropriateness. Those beliefs about the appropriateness and efficacy of petitionary prayer reflect teaching about what to pray for. Since there is little explicit teaching about the efficacy of prayer these beliefs must depend on age, whereas beliefs about the appropriateness of prayer in different situations are made quite explicit. That is consistent with the findings of Godin and Van Roey (1959) and Thouless and Brown (1964). Long *et al.*, (1967), using more conventionally Piagetian questions like, "Do cats and dogs pray?" and "Where do prayers go?", found stages that covered a vague and indistinct understanding of prayer through a concrete interpretation of its appropriateness, and then to prayer as a private conversation with God. When Elkind (1964) looked at religious identity he found a global and undifferentiated conception among five to seven year olds, followed by concretely differentiated conceptions from seven to nine, with an abstract and differentiated conception emerging around ages ten to 12, which is a classical Piagetian sequence.

Hutsebaut (1972) used conventional Likert scale studies of adolescents' conceptions of God as well as answers to open questions about their meaning, and found in them attitudes of dependence, confirmation of one's autonomy, revolt or guilt, identification with Christ as one's model, sociality, and God as an ethical norm. It is of some importance that the older subjects gave the most abstract descriptions of God, typically in terms of God as the "meaning of life".

The religious world of a pre-schooler is largely fixed by the child's family, and specifically by the parents. Piagetian approaches that have identified the thoughts of very young children as animistic, anthropomorphic and egocentric are tinged with Freudian ideas about immaturity and concepts of power. The most systematic work in this field has been under Godin's guidance and is published in *Lumen Vitae*. Throughout this material, however, there is a tension between the children's spontaneous questions and conclusions, and their responses to adult-imposed tasks which carry implicit but strong demands, especially when children are asked by adults to draw a picture of God, or when they are asked questions that they know adults already can answer.

Spontaneous religion

Lawrence (1965) solved the problem of direct questions with the help of a group of cooperative parents who recorded the questions their children asked spontaneously. A content analysis of the religious questions that were collected from 87 children aged between seven and 12 showed that 35.6 per cent concerned the nature of the deity, 28 per cent concerned suffering and death, 22 per cent were about the Church and 13 per cent asked about the supernatural. Lawrence used a concrete/abstract distinction to interpret his results:

> Between eight and eleven or twelve years of age the child has the capacity to classify, order, see cause or effect relationships, and use the basic tools of logic — but in a concrete setting. He does not yet appreciate the force of a concept which signifies a set of abstract relationships. The religious educator's problem therefore is identified as dealing with abstract concepts which the pupils cannot understand or give satisfying definitions of, so that material memorised is not understood, and so the teaching is ineffective.

It may be, however, that as children develop their understanding they reject what has been taught, which, as Lawrence notes, prematurely hardens their religious ideas and gives little understanding to them. With a fragile assent to doctrines or beliefs, the meaning of which remains obscure, it is hard to defend them when they are attacked.

Lawrence concluded that the majority of the questions children ask about religion are broadly doctrinal, and that none of them concerned the implications of religious belief for everyday life. It seems as if the forms of religion that children are offered puzzle them, especially when they accord, not with whatever religious ideas or beliefs they may already have, but with the ideas that adults expect their children to have. Francis (1979) has shown that children react against a great deal of explicit teaching of religion, especially when it is not supported by the parents' own religious involvement. He also noted that educational researchers have ignored "Christian development" and the factors that influence it, and that theologians have undervalued the contribution that educational research might make to religious education. He therefore stressed the importance of finding what children themselves want to know. Loukes (1961) explored that in a number of group discussions which he summarized with direct quotations and a listing of interests (p. 103) that the teaching of Christianity "must be seen to bear on" (p. 105).

Goldman (1964) used a method of picture and story interpretation to study religious development and scaled the answers with a Guttman procedure to identify age-related sequences in answers to questions about, for example, Moses and the Burning Bush, the crossing of the Red Sea and the temptations of Jesus. He concluded that these replies moved from concrete to abstract, and that teachers should not expect too much from young children. (Goldman's (1982) most recent work has been concerned with the development of children's thinking about sex.)

Although most studies have been interpreted in terms of the autonomous development or growth of a child's understanding, a more direct explanation is in terms of the child's socialization or training into a religious perspective. Despite the relative absence of investigations of children's spontaneous questioning in real situations, as opposed to the artificiality of most controlled investigations, experimentally controlled studies produce results that are inconsistent with children's obviously superior skills with "real" material. Houssiadas and Brown (1980) showed that while "egocentricity" can explain the failure of children to solve artificial problems which demand some decentration and a coordination of perspectives, they correctly use the natural language in ordinary conversation so that, for example, personal pronouns are not wrongly assigned, which would not be expected with a truly egocentric perspective.

The view has recently been advanced by Donaldson (1978) that children develop intellectually through their daily contact with the language and discourse in which they are embedded. If we are therefore to test whether a child behaves logically, we must first instruct them in the problem, before expecting them to solve it logically. When children (like adults) properly understand what they are being asked to do, they show none of the difficulties that have been thought typical of the separate or isolated developmental stages, or even of the faulty reasoning of adults. When Donaldson repeated Piaget's three mountains problem as a game of hide and seek she found that their "primitive matrix" of acquaintance with everyday activities helped to organize and structure the correct responses. As Shotter (1984, p. 122) puts it, "children, rather than acting 'out of' their own resources, act 'into' a maturationally structured situation".

This is not dissimilar to Wittgenstein's (1966, p. 63) "conversation" on religious belief, in which he said, "Take 'God created man'. Pictures of Michelangelo showing the creation of the world. In general, there is nothing which explains the meanings of words as well as a picture, and I take it that Michelangelo was as good as anyone can be and did his best, and here is a picture of the Deity creating Adam. If we ever saw this, we certainly wouldn't think this the Deity." Furthermore, we can conclude almost nothing about Michelangelo's understanding of God from that painting, or about Fechner's animistic thinking from the anthropomorphic statements he made about the nature of the world (cf. Brown and Thouless, 1965). Wittgenstein therefore goes on to say:

> It is quite clear that the role of pictures of Biblical subjects and the role of the picture of God creating Adam are totally different ones. You might ask this question: 'Did Michelangelo think that Noah in the ark looked like this, and that God creating Adam looked like this?' He wouldn't have said that God or Adam looked as they look in his picture. (ibid.)

Expressing doubt and uncertainty, and knowing what to say is an essential part of any religious development (cf. Brusselmans, 1980).

As Donaldson argues, our primary task is to grasp the meaning, or "the ability to 'make sense' of things, and above all to make sense of what people do, which of course includes what people say" (1978, p. 38). It is not possible to study that if artificial questions are asked, or if the problems to be solved are difficult or tricky and do not have sensible answers.

Religious education

The 1944 Education Act in Britain made important concessions to the interests of the Churches when it prescribed daily collective worship and made religious education the only compulsory component of the curriculum, leaving it to be controlled by the Churches, which have defined it in educational rather than confessional terms. Over the years the time that is available for religious education has been reduced.

Francis (1984), however, found that religious education in Gloucestershire is more traditional "than current educational theory or educational philosophy would wish to promote". He also notes the important role that head teachers have in fixing what their schools provide and the close link, which is age related, between this and their own church attendance. "While 79 per cent of the heads in their sixties attend church at least once a month, this proportion falls to 66 per cent of those in their forties and fifties, and to 55 per cent of those in their thirties." To identify the formal influences that impinge on religious development requires a multivariate analysis in which home, church (or church school), and age are included as factors. When Francis explored the relationships between parish structures and the numbers of six to nine year olds who are directly involved, he found that the population of the benefice, the number of its adult members, and a young clergyman had the most important effects.

Religious doubt

Conclusions about the religious beliefs of adolescents and young adults, which find that they *are* capable of "understanding", align with an interest in answers to real questions, as Havighurst and Keating (1971) emphasize in their summary of the evidence for an increased doubt and uncertainty, that presumably reflects an increasing independence from parents over the period from 12 to 18. Kuhlen and Arnold (1944) found, for example, that the percentages who believe that "Only good people go to heaven" declined from 72 per cent at 12 years to 45 per cent at 15 and 33 per cent at 18, whereas "There is heaven" drew support from 82 per cent at 12 through 78 per cent at 15 and 74 per cent at 18.

The doctrinal and consensual differences between those statements is clear, and Havighurst and Keating conclude from the studies they reviewed that the young *are* concerned about their religious beliefs, and that while their values reflect those of adults, their priorities are different from what adults expect, with their religious knowledge being consistently related to day-to-day experience and choices (1971, pp. 714–715).

Feldman (1969) has reviewed the changes in religious belief through college. While an accelerated rate of change is the norm, Feldman stresses the extent to which individual differences in the degree and direction of change does not match the mean changes, and that the results of studies among students have not been adequately compared with those from non-students. Academic institutions themselves, the field of study, residence, other activities, friends and social background have all been found to have some effect. Feldman also stressed that "most colleges and curricula are not designed to have specified effects on religious views" (1969), and that we need "to establish the social-psychological linkages between the student's background and social structure, on the one hand, and the change (or stability) of his religious attitudes, on the other".

That family training is the simplest explanation of how anyone develops a religious perspective is supported by numerous studies, with the recent work on lapsing from religion, or apostasy, showing that positive attitudes to religion which have been inculcated in the family are the most resistant to change (Kotre, 1971; Hunsberger and Brown, 1984). Francis (1984) developed a reliable 28 item scale to assess the attitudes to religion of young people at school, with items that include "I find it boring to listen to the Bible", "I know that Jesus helps me" and "God is very real to me". He found "a steady and persistent decline in attitude towards Christianity from the first year in the junior school to the fourth year in the secondary school". This linear trend showed an accelerated decline between the ages of 15 and 16 that is interpreted as ·a progressive "disenchantment with what they observe about Christianity". Thus the item, "I know that God helps me" was answered positively by 79 per cent of eight year olds and by 27 per cent of 16 year olds. A regression analysis showed strong links between a favourable attitude to Christianity and involvement in a Church, although as Francis says, "very few Churches seem able to maintain the active involvement and interest of their young members". This study, originally carried out in 1974, was replicated in 1978 and again in 1982. He found an accelerated decrease in the positive responses to religion then that was paralleled in attitudes to music, but not in attitudes to school in general or to games, history, maths or English. In a further study Francis compared the answers of people in local authority, Church of England and Roman Catholic schools, and found significantly more favourable attitudes to religion among those in Roman Catholic than in either of the other two kinds of school. Regression analyses showed that girls have more favourable attitudes than boys and that age and higher social class, which influences parental religious behaviour, are the best predictors of religious attitudes. While the Roman Catholic primary schools have a positive, and the Church of England schools have a negative effect on pupil attitudes, that effect was less in the 1978 than in the 1974 data. These results which are summarized in Figure 3, suggest that a child's religiousness, assessed by attitudes, beliefs, and behaviour (in terms of churchgoing, prayer and Sunday School) is most strongly influenced by the parents' behaviour and by the religious orientation of the school.

Religious change

Greeley (1976) reported a replication after 11 years of a 1963 study of value-oriented education in Roman Catholic schools in the United States (Greeley and Rossi, 1966), to document the effect of the Second Vatican Council and other changes, including the numbers of clergy who have resigned, and altered attitudes to sex (pp. 7–8). Beyond documenting the sociological base

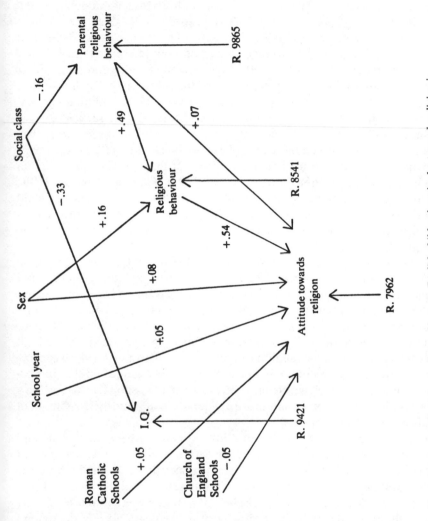

Fig. 3 *A fixed path diagram of the effects on English children's attitudes towards religion in 1978 (from Francis, 1984)*

of US Catholicism and attitudes to "sexual orthodoxy" the study shows a decrease in the direct effects of a Catholic schooling on doctrinal orthodoxy, although religious education was "more strongly related to Catholic activism" in 1973 than in 1963.

Greeley's analytic model of activism in adult life assumes that sex, age and the religiousness of parents is the first step, to which is added the spouse's educational achievement (p. 167). With religious activism as the dependent variable, 31 per cent of the variance could be accounted for in the 1963, and 38 per cent in the 1974 data (p. 168). Racial attitudes and economic achievement, as non-religious variables, show slight advantages for a Catholic education (pp. 182 ff.). But the over-riding effects of the childhood education and training on adult religion is again emphasized in these results.

There is still a conflict between what people "should" know and what they understand. That some beliefs cannot be questioned and that others are hard to explain, at least to some people, is also a problem, although Goldman (1964) stressed the lack of a "real awareness" of religious concepts until "the top end of the grammar schools". Negative attitudes to religion make a child unwilling to learn about or practise religion, and boys are consistently found to be less religious than girls and to have a less benevolent conception of God (Wright and Cox, 1967).

Wright and Cox (1971) showed from a 1963 survey that they repeated in 1970 that moral beliefs, especially about sexual behaviour, gambling and drunkenness, changed over that period. While the changes were independent of religious commitment and age, girls changed more than boys. This finding is important because of the widespread assumption that religion helps to maintain the standards and morals of society and that, "To lead a good life it is necessary to have some religious belief". (In a British ITA (1970) survey, those items were agreed to by 89 per cent and 69 per cent of adults, respectively.) In a further review, Wright (1971) stressed the support there is for a close relationship between church attendance, commitment to Christian beliefs and exacting moral beliefs.

Shoben (1963), having confirmed a low correlation between "virtue and religion", emphasized that moral values derive from the larger society and that even such maxims in the New Testament as "the weak shall inherit the earth" cannot be directly followed without setting oneself against other broadly social norms. Scholl and Beker (1964), however, found no difference in the expressed religious attitudes of delinquent and non-delinquent adolescent boys. Other approaches to these problems have involved direct behavioural measures of actually resisting temptation or performing good deeds (Batson *et al.*, 1985), with the general conclusion that private behaviour is independent of religious training, although moral beliefs are religiously influenced.

That a religious training or commitment generates conflict between religious ideas or practice and the norms of other social traditions can be explained with reference to group processes and alignments (cf. Turner and Giles, 1981). Yet secondary school pupils *are* attracted to the reality of God, and they readily adopt a search or questing orientation to what religious beliefs can do. This process of "wondering about" or seeking clarification, as opposed to doubting, was found by Kuhlen and Arnold (1944) to be a predominant distinction between the beliefs of 12 and 18 year olds.

The results are clear, but they suggest an intangibility in the material itself, because the questions children are asked are dominated by adults' lack of understanding of what childhood is like and their expectations of what children should be. Children have too often been presented with material that has forced responses that are as stereotyped as those the evangelists use for their challenges to those who are older. Argyle therefore concluded in 1958 that intellectual doubt about religious matters was expressed around a mental age of 12, and that the associated emotional stress was resolved by a conversion at about 16. Yet the Protestant assumption of conversion is not shared by the Catholic Church which expects infant baptism, first communion around age seven and a continuing Church involvement uninterrupted by crises, whether among adolescents or older people.

Kotre (1971), who interviewed 50 Catholics who were still in the Church and another 50 who said they had moved out, was convinced that "one's position of being in or out of the Church was not arrived at on the basis of what might be called empirical evidence, for the same evidence could be and was acknowledged by both Ins and Outs" (p. 52). They agreed about the unacceptable and irrelevant doctrines, racism among Catholics and the "formalism, pomp and circumstance of the hierarchy". Those who stayed in had, however, redefined these things "in a way compatible with their beliefs", and these constructions "seemed more a question of wanting than a question of seeing" (p. 53), the reasons for this being found in a web of interpersonal relationships in which these people were situated, in the past as well as the present. In detailed statistical comparisons of the answers from those two groups, beliefs about "God and the other world" (especially in the items "Christ rose from the dead" and "Christ is really present in the Eucharist") were the most important (p. 72). Those who were "Outs" strongly rejected "the instrumental links between membership and values" (p. 90), so that those who are "Out" delineate an institutional Church that centres on a powerful clerical hierarchy that is "rigid, conservative, dogmatic and orthodox" (p. 118) while the others stress God, with Church members having the power "to move the Church away from the hierarchy and toward the people". As Kotre says, membership "is, to a large extent, determined by a person's own criteria, although religious practice turns out to be more an empirical criterion for membership than some Ins realize" (p. 118). In general he found that females were more religious, less likely to leave and more orthodox in their beliefs, and that the Ins were more often from families in which both parents were practising Catholics and in which "no basic antipathy was created between parent and child" (p. 164).

The evidence, across the last 30 years at least, converges on recognizing the primary importance of the home and the parents' own religious attitudes and behaviour in setting up a person's religious beliefs. The effects of both age and sex on religious beliefs could simply reflect others' beliefs and norms about the new information that it is appropriate to acquire and the knowledge that it is possible to question, since religion is still inextricably tied into the cultural and social processes that sanction and carry it. The theoretical interpretations of this material have changed little during that time, and converge on the effects of cognitive development rather than on the information that is being taught (cf. Nye and Carlson, 1984).

Questions about the readiness for religion therefore involve the problems that must be confronted at particular ages. We still do not know what makes religious beliefs plausible, whether for parents or their children, except for the familiarity that comes from having been acquainted with them (Zajonc, 1968). So, beliefs about God, Christ and perhaps hope are unquestioned, because they are basic or "primitive" in Rokeach's sense. It is also likely that many parents still believe that not only does religion *give* an appropriate morality, but that religious beliefs are peculiarly suited to children, which could explain why the studies of apostasy show that rejecting religious beliefs entails rejecting the parents' beliefs and their stance (Hunsberger and Brown, 1984). While the trend in social psychological theorizing is away from an emphasis on individual traits and characteristics, and towards social or contextual influences, when the personality processes involved in religion have been explored, little evidence has been found that those processes directly influence religious functioning. We are therefore left with the view that arguments about the readiness for religion are theological or traditional (for example, about the best age to be baptized, confirmed, admitted to communion, or for making a "decision for Christ"), and attributional (in terms of when a person is expected to be able to make their own decisions and develop appropriate insight). People are inevitably trained into religion and the broad ideology that governs it, as they are trained in music or mathematics, which do not carry the same evaluative overtones. Because of that Godin and Van Roey (1959) argued that religious education delays children's development and understanding.

The age changes in religious identity that Elkind (1964) identified depend on the forms of question that are asked. But he says that, "It is not an easy task to get at the true meaning [sic] behind children's remarks". Elkind's

(1971) theory of religious development therefore stressed the extent to which religion provides ready-made solutions for the problems of adaptation that a child meets or is confronted with by adults.

Other religious concepts

Long *et al.* (1967) identified the stages in the development of prayer concepts as "a global conception in the sense that their comprehension of the term was both vague and fragmentary" (i.e. they didn't understand it), and from a "concrete differentiated conception of prayer" to an abstract conception that regarded prayer as an internal activity derived from personal conviction and belief. "Only at the third stage did prayer emerge as a true communication between the child and what he considered divine, between the I and the Thou". This formulation illustrates the prescriptive nature of such interpretations, which Long *et al.* aligned with a "parallel between the development of prayer in the child and in Western civilization".

Writing of prayer, Godin and Van Roey (1959) said that "what children as well as adults must be taught (in appropriate ways) is the ... nature of prayer", and that "what characterizes truly religious and adult souls" is "a laborious discovery". Godin and Marthe (1964) argued for a counterpoint between magical and sacramental mentalities in that thinking, which is not limited to children. Animistic and sacramental thinking are almost impossible to diagnose, the former being used commonly and quite deliberately (even by scientists) as a shorthand and an aid to problem solving.

Survey data show a curvilinear pattern of Church involvement by age, which, under the usual conditions, declines in the late teens and early 20's, increasing again after that. Moberg (1965) observed that, "Study after study in various parts of the nation and in different types of communities have found that the aged (like most younger people) are more apt to be church members than members of any other type of voluntary organization and, indeed, than of all other associations together." (St. Augustine said, "Lord save me, but not yet".)

Covalt (1958) rejected the assumption that people turn to religion as they grow older. As a doctor, he said that patients don't talk about religion with their physicians and that the religious attitudes of most old people are those they grew up with, and are likely to involve a simple and direct faith. Survey data which suggests that belief in a life-after-death increase with age are confounded by the fact that it is easier for many people growing up now to resist or reject such conventional religious beliefs. Moberg (1965), however, concluded from his analysis of the early literature that "a sense of serenity and decreased fear of death tend to accompany conservative religious beliefs. This does not necessarily prove, however, that religious faith removes the fear of death" which may involve social integration or other cultural attitudes to death that are associated with denial. It is not only those who are old who look on death as a "welcome guest" (as did Dido), or an acceptable transition. Moberg also thought that all religious indicators (except attendance, which is influenced by mobility) show that more Church involvement is associated with greater happiness and adjustment (cf. Bergin. 1983).

Vergote (1969, p. 21) identified "fear, hope of a future life, wonder in the face of the mystery of the world and existence, the immediate meaning of participation in the universe, guilt and still other factors" as psychological roots for "the content of lived religion". The religious life is therefore "made of theory-elements, cosmogonical and genealogical myths, ideograms and so on, which also make the sacred present" (p. 37). This broad sense of the sacred blends with and informs other domains, becoming "a harmony of contrasts" (p. 55). It is not clear whether that entails some "natural" or inevitable appeal for divine help or support and even what prepares one for it, although one must recognize that our culture gives us God-concepts that can be interpreted as a device to tame the cruelties of nature, which other aspects of civilization disregard. Since reality resists many of our desires, they are transferred to the control of some power that we expect to be able to influence.

Vergote (ibid.) outlines and criticizes that theory for its empirical weakness, and he says that G. Sholem, "a specialist in the history of the Jewish religion", believed it would not be mentioned now, had not Freud written about it. Yet it emphasizes the spontaneity with which those in distress turn to religion. This could rest on culturally specific metaphors, or involve a direct plea for help. Freud found his theory confirmed by the extent to which believers defend themselves against all that calls their faith into question, because they know unconsciously that it is an illusion, despite continued popular and scholarly arguments or disputes about the existence of God. Perhaps many religious believers have simply foreclosed on positive answers, with a deep understanding that by-passes the arguments they regard as intellectual exercises. Freud's second strand of evidence for his theory was in the retreat of religion from those domains in which there has been scientific and technical mastery over nature. Despite that, medicine has not replaced pilgrimages to healing shrines, at least for those suffering with chronic conditions, whose hope is maintained. "Divine providence" implies far more than a mere "nostalgia for the father".

Many people spontaneously turn towards God when they are in moral or material difficulty, and Vergote (1978, p. 16) reports a study of 50 Italian workers who reported 84 instances of spontaneously thinking of God, to find that 40 had recourse to prayer in "material misery" and 13 in moral difficulties. He also reports on 180 students aged from 11 to 18, where "15 per cent thought of God in material difficulties, 41 per cent in moral difficulties, 11 per cent in moments of unhappiness and 7 per cent with reference to the beauty of nature". Vergote interprets those finding in terms of the "religion of demand" that he also found in a study of prayer, in which the subjects were asked to imagine frustrating situations and describe their reactions to it and their tendency to prayer. Prayer was said to be used when human or material help fails, as in drowning, a fatal accident or in terminal illness when the struggle for life continues. As he said, "It is distress that is experienced with the highest intensity, where one's very life is threatened, which most often results in a spontaneous recourse to divine providence" and in which optimism prevails. Stouffer *et al.* (1949) similarly reported that 75 per cent of US soldiers affirmed that prayer had helped them more than anything else in perilous situations during the Second World War. That finding was independent of education or religious conviction. Among those who had been in combat, 29 per cent said they became more religious as a result of that, 30 per cent became less religious and 41 per cent had not changed, and while 79 per cent had increased their "faith in God", 19 per cent had less faith and two per cent had not changed.

Testimonies about ecstatic experiences are highly nuanced and forcefully articulated claims to a divine causality, that is supported by implicit beliefs about what can be seen or heard. Belief and experience are not necessarily independent, as psychologists have known at least since the "new look in perception" (Bruner and Postman, 1952), and visions or appearances are no more enigmatic than is any dream or inspired solution. To recognize them as paranoid delusions depends largely on the way they are used and responded to. Theresa of Avila (*Life*, Ch. 40) said, "Life became a kind of dream, when I see things, I nearly always seem to be dreaming". Mystical experience gives an immediate awareness as the answer to faith.

Most people know well how and when to distance themselves from the "realities" of demons or angels, although the resurgence of exorcism may have recreated an unfortunate reality for them. This counter-point between concrete and abstract realities, between debt and desire in responses to religion (Vergote, 1978), or between pure and impure thoughts or ideas, theological and psychological perspectives, or between natural and revealed forms is intrinsic to religion. It is a question of which pole rules, and how it can be interpreted. Wright (1983), who argues that "the origins of practical morality are quite independent of any kind of religious belief or practice", also notes that a religious perspective influences one's "theoretical morality" directly through understanding, and by contributing to the "philosophy of life within which morality is embedded". This breach between practice and explanation (or theory) is crucial and must be recognized, unless one is to hold religious beliefs that are closed to any new information and developing perspectives. But, as Wright concludes, "the religious educators' task is to stimulate the student into articulating and discussing his own world view, and in that process to draw upon all aspects of his experience and knowledge ... (but especially) to draw attention to the experience of the unknowable or the experience of being transcended. Such experiences can only be talked about in paradox, symbol and other enigmatic utterances. If they are formulated into beliefs held to be true, the essential nature of the experience dies."

Summary

We no longer need a concept of "religious readiness". In appropriate contexts most people are ready to question their beliefs, and can recognize them for what they are. Any discussion about the sacred involves some knowledge of how to find it and when to tell the children about that. That religious discourse is an under-explored domain for the psychology of religion emphasizes that we have not yet come to terms with what is believed, beyond simply assenting to the doctrines. As Wittgenstein (1966, p. 54) put it "if we have a belief, in certain cases we appeal again and again to certain grounds, and at the same time we risk pretty little (except perhaps our credibility) — if it came to risking our lives on the grounds of this belief. There are instances where you have a faith — where you say 'I believe' — and on the other hand this belief does not rest on the fact on which our ordinary everyday beliefs normally do rest."

While we must expect children to develop in their knowledge and understanding we cannot look for more or different information from the trick questions they have been asked about what they think, than we would accept from adults' answers to similar questions. We must not rely on children's answers to those puzzles as solutions to difficult questions about symbols, metaphors and the other meanings that change with increasing experience and sophistication, and which require many people to drop an established religious orientation while they look around at the alternatives.

There has been a great deal of moralizing about religious development and the appropriate methods that might facilitate it. Much of that has been highly principled, in terms of psychology, epistemology, and religion itself. While it can be adaptive to believe that a child's understanding develops in a regular sequence, the concept of age-appropriate norms or stages for such development has not been well supported since it is critically dependent on what children are offered and allowed to say. It could be partly because of this that developmental psychologists have discarded the study of religion. Rest (1983, p. 608), in Mussen's revision of *Carmichael's Manual*, makes the only reference to it in a one line remark that distinguishes religion from morality.

10 Conclusions

There is no historical task which so reveals a man's true self as the writing of a life of Jesus. (Albert Schweitzer, *The Psychiatric Study of Jesus*, 1913)
Being led astray by God is a sort of punishment for unbelief. Verily, those who do not believe in the signs of God, God will not guide and for them is in store a punishment painful. (*Qur'an*, 16, 106)
A Muslim knows what to do since it is prescribed in considerable detail in the *Qur'an*, but has he or she the strength of mind to do it? (R. Harré, *Personal Being*, 1983, p. 244)

My analysis of religious "belief" has emphasized that while *belief* may be a defining characteristic of a religious orientation, religious beliefs are not independent of the traditions that sustain them or of the experiences that realize them. They are conventionally identified by their content, or from the actions or conclusions that prime and support them. Prototypic results show that women, young people, the elderly and the less well-educated constitute the most "religious" groups and that religion is expressed in a way that most often aligns it with conservative social and political attitudes. Those findings have made religionism into a component of the social conservatism that supports prejudiced opinions and gives a respect for orthodoxy and traditional authorities. But religion is more than that since it has profound effects on those who need it, and for those who accept it as part of their life, not simply because it is God's will or because of what "the Bible says".

A general finding in Britain is that about 90 per cent of the population say they believe in God, while about 33 per cent claim some kind of religious experience and ten per cent go to church at least once a year. A similar wide and perhaps unthinking consensus about religious beliefs is supported by the results of many opinion surveys here and elsewhere, although detailed psychological study is not necessary to emphasize discrepancies among the beliefs that most people hold, or about the specific actions and their consequences that can be supported with reference to religious beliefs and experience. When Stark and Glock (1968) found that 75 per cent of a national sample said their three best friends were in the same religion (p. 141) he was emphasizing another facet of the support that religion gives.

Not only are religions widely distributed, they appear to serve purposes beyond guiding people's lives, including wish fulfilment, hope, fantasy, and focussing social relationships and interactions. Early psychologists were directly interested in it, and sociologists have found religion a good tool with which to explore social processes. While many critics have used psychological and social theories to discredit religion, its supporters have applied those perspectives in developing a contemporary theology (e.g. Paul Tillich and H. A. Williams). Too many of those interpretations of religion have, however, been based on informal and over-generalized observations, partly because of the problems of gathering systematic data but also because of prejudices among religious believers against the empirical study of religion.

The argument that religion involves specific modes of response is no longer tenable, and it is now recognized that responses to non-religious beliefs and social groups can function in ways that are similar to those that religions follow, even if religious categories and models have been used to track the character of those other forms. Nevertheless, religion offers unique dilemmas because of the meanings that lie between myth and reality, truth and illusion or life and death. Any orientations to religion can become a point of reference that accounts for the differing effects that are encapsulated in typologies and classifications of religion including true and false, or the intrinsic, extrinsic and questing forms that depend on the relative importance that is given to religion as objectively true or as a socially constructed experience.

Every classification goes beyond what is believed or thought to be credible, to a deeper structure. Runciman (1983, p. 24) advocated testing the primary understanding or plausibility of religious beliefs by asking people to identify the most irrational belief that anyone they know holds, and the most rational action they know of anyone doing. He says, "To me, the most irrational belief which I know of anyone's holding is the belief that there exists an omnipotent and at the same time benevolent God". Yet he recognizes that others sincerely subscribe to this belief, although he admits that discussion with them, "always ends, after a predictable detour through the so-called Free Will Defence, in an impasse where I am left with nothing more to say than that for God to permit the avoidable suffering which he does isn't my idea of benevolence ... [which] ... leads me to realize that I have not understood that belief in either the secondary or tertiary sense" (*ibid*). (To understand, in Runciman's secondary sense, is to explain, and in the tertiary sense it is to understand fully, as a participant can do.) To believe therefore requires presuppositions and the possibility of being misunderstood by those who cannot know how or what it is that one believes.

For that reason Rokeach (1960) distinguished primary from secondary beliefs, the former being laid down by our experiences of other people and of the world itself, and aligns with basic trust (or mistrust), in Erikson's sense. Rokeach's secondary beliefs are derived from an authority or tradition and carry assumptions about its basic goodness or trustworthiness, as well as the control that one has oneself as opposed to what others have (Rotter, 1966; Lefcourt, 1976), and beliefs about the essential justice of the world (Lerner, 1980).

When D. H. Lawrence (1928) examined insincerity he wrote that, "Sentimentalism is the working off on yourself of feelings you haven't really got. We all *want* to have certain feelings of love, of passionate sex, of kindliness and so forth. Very few people really feel love, or sex passion or kindliness, or anything else that goes at all deep. So the mass just take these feelings inside themselves" (p. 545). That statement captures the derived, extrinsic attitude to religion that is probably the typical response to it. Psychologists have been unable to specify the grounds on which authentic and intrinsic religious experiences are based, although biblical models suggest that some child-like trust might be required for that. Stories about the lives of legendary religious figures nevertheless testify to the existential validity that can be found in religion, which is more readily revealed by autobiography than in detached psychological studies. Some commitment and conviction can be readily claimed after talking oneself into (or out of) those experiences; to play the role of a believer at an evangelistic meeting (Johnson, 1971) or to find oneself successfully converted there depends on the credibility and the prestige of the appeal itself and the claims that can be made on it, as well as the emotional states it generates, which range from anxiety to commitment, depending on the support that is made available (cf. Argyle and Beit-Hallahmi, 1975, pp. 41–46).

Since the core of a religion can be found in its doctrines, its settings or situations, practices or rituals, and also in the people who carry it and make it "work", any model for the psychological analysis of religion's effects are set between three poles.

1.   There is the grounding in a tradition that is found or made available, and in the structures it provides which people are initiated or trained into.

2.   Then there are the psychological roots (Argyle, 1964) or "elements" (Thouless, 1923) which are put into a religiously prepared ground to make it real in cognitive, emotional or social terms.

3.   Finally, there are the "fruits", effects or consequences of such grounding for individuals, groups and societies. They include whether believers become opinionated, open or closed-minded, and whether their religion becomes practical (and explicit) or remains hidden and covert.

While particular religious metaphors need not be taken literally, we must recognize that they are theologically or doctrinally grounded in a tradition, and that psychological reactions relate to that tradition, and to the social support or institutional consequences of a particular nexus of theological and other psychological pressures. Despite our dependence on tradition, religious alignments have been directly interpreted as symptomatic of underlying psychological states or traits, as expedient alignments to achieve some social advantage, and less frequently as a response to the truth-value of these claims. They can also be seen as predominantly aesthetic or metaphysical judgements that are intellectually or emotionally based, depending on the climate within which they are offered. When religious questions are raised, the variability in the response to them is reduced to an unknown degree by the implicit effects of their institutional or doctrinal formulations and the control they exercise. For that reason religious institutions were identified by Pratt as a "secondary system". Individuals who accept or reject those systems identify religion as public and orthodox or as private and subjective.

Since people can take many separate paths to their religious commitment, simple explanations of those processes are inadequate, although the modal course, which gives a superficial conservatism, has invited an explanation in terms of rather constricted people searching for simple solutions. That is not, however, the Christian ideal. Not only is a stance that waits for others to identify the truth inadequate as the prototypic religious orientation, it fails to recognize the tension in Christianity between law and prophecy. Many explanations of religion are clearly ideological, in the sense that they rely directly on some other set of beliefs for its analysis. The ambiguity of religion itself means that it might be unreasonable to account for it in terms of any single psychological process, unless "religion" is simply to be identified with public actions, membership, and other obvious signs that can be easily recognized. In studying religion we are not, however, looking simply at a process that the believers have themselves thought up, but at their alignments with traditions which support particular meanings couched in both religious and psychological terms.

Margaret Mead argued that a good ethnography must be recognizable as such by those who have been described. Although Freeman (1983) concluded that she had misunderstood the Samoans, hers is a good maxim to follow. Most descriptions of religious behaviour, however, seem superficial to those for whom religion provides and resolves the meaning and purpose of life, not only because of the language that is used to carry and to describe religion and psychology. Burn (1964) notes that the attitude to God's will among educated and believing Christians in mid-nineteenth century England was in terms of "duty" and "lesson". "God 'taught' lessons and it was the duty of men to learn them; as it was the duty of schoolboys to learn what their masters sought to teach them. The colonial and garrison chaplain of Sierra Leone wrote in 1850 of the drowning of his predecessor and three other officials on an occasion when three intending passengers had been at the last minute prevented from joining the boat party. 'The over-ruling ways of Providence are wonderful and sometimes exemplified in so striking a manner that it is impossible not to see in them an intention to teach the living a lesson they are too apt to forget ... Such was the Will of Him whose mercies are inscrutable, yet merciful and just' " (p. 44). Many have looked for this will of God, which is now often found in some metaphorical sense, although we do not know with what passion *or* suspicion it was acknowledged in nineteenth-century England. "Was all the talk about 'duty' and 'prayers' and 'religion' hypocritical humbug?" asked Burn, and, "Was the whole age a hollow sham?" Runciman asserts that it was not, "or at any rate not for the country as a whole: and that which may appear to be bullshit to us needs to be understood in the tertiary sense by reference to the nature of the beliefs which the kind of people he (Burn) has in mind did actually hold" (Runciman, 1983 p. 262). We may be too close to the religions of our own time to venture such opinions about them.

Henry Miller (1961, p. 176) wrote of Grover that, "It is a pity that he had to use Christ for a crutch, but then what does it matter how one comes by the truth so long as one pounces upon it and lives by it". That, like any attitude, is hard to diagnose so clearly, since the style of language which makes religion possible for some is opaque and implausible to others. The same applies to the language that psychology uses for its theories, explanations and descriptions (Mandler and Kessen, 1959).

Psychological concepts have changed, as also has what a psychology of religion would explain, whether that is the experience of conversion (Hall, 1904), mysticism (Leuba, 1925), religious behaviour (Argyle, 1958), belief or unbelief (Pruyser, 1974). What can persuade has also changed, producing uncertainty about the evidence for religion and the meaning of words like "God", in which poetry, paradox, incoherence and silence have all been found. Yet psychology is sure that empirical measurements allow its theories to be tested. Crystal (1965, p. 84) notes that, "Literature, humour and religion are the three main areas that explore language's edges, and the fact of such explanation reflects a basic human need to express more than our ordinary, rule-governed behaviour allows, and to be opaque and inexact upon occasion". Psychologists have neglected religious language, and just as there are gaps between the language of art criticism and the psychology of art, or between biology and the study of sexuality, so there are gaps between theology and a psychological understanding of religion that could be based in learning, emotion, personality, experience or prejudice and not in theological terms like trust, hope, and guilt.

Few "facts" about religion can be explained independently of what is traditionally prescribed by them. Without knowing that "the fatherhood of God" is a traditional Christian formula, one could mistakenly expect a personal or idiosyncratic construction that aligns concepts of God with those of the natural father. Not only is the evidence for this hypothesis weak, the doctrine itself is so deeply prescribed socially that it may not be able to draw out any idiosyncratic meanings.

That there are many paths to religious insight is emphasized by the Gospel narratives of how the Disciples came to believe or recognize the Resurrection. The empty tomb only convinced John, and the others concluded that someone had removed the body. The women's stories were dismissed as exaggerated or idle talk. As further experiences brought conviction, Thomas still refused to believe "unless he saw in his hands the print of the nails". John's certainty could have involved wish-fulfilment, but there was evident surprise in finding what had been predicted. The most likely explanations had to be discarded by some of the others. It is still not clear what engenders religious confidence, and although wary scepticism may produce agnosticism, "hope" (as opposed to a wish) can suppress doubt. For that reason, Smith *et al.*, (1956) separated the sources of beliefs from their intensity and their content. It is easier to remain uncertain about the matters of fact that can be verified, than about matters of faith that must be accepted, rejected, or reinterpreted before they become credible. While the acquisition, and the maintenance or protection of beliefs involve separate processes, there seems to be no evidence for a general "need" for certainty among religious believers, despite the links that have been claimed between authoritarianism, dogmatism, and Machiavellianism, as personality traits, and religiousness. Batson (1976), however, showed that the consequences of religious beliefs for action may be directly mediated by the orientations or forms of commitment to them, which are in their turn most influenced by the religion of the family within which one has grown up.

There are also discrepancies between our psychological constructs and interpretive frameworks, and the ways individuals understand how their own beliefs and behaviour are related to action. In some circumstances the choices we make will be over-justified or distanced, depending on our commitment and the expected rewards that are offered (cf. Eiser, 1980, p. 128f.), and the religious demands made on us may be tailored to fit our assumed characteristics. These aspects of motivation, and the explanations for action that have been considered by attribution theorists, assume that the accounts and explanations of actors themselves differ from those given by observers. But the Australian novelist Patrick White (1981) complained in his autobiography that, "I am accused of not making myself explicit" and he wrote of the "face in the glass" that has spent a life-time searching for what is believed, but can never be proved to be the truth.

To generate a coherent set of beliefs or attitudes requires a socially acceptable, and even a detached perspective on the self that tries to resolve the pressures from other systems of belief or from a society that can enforce an apparently conservative religiousness. Religion can itself achieve that since it is an explanatory system with vivid models by which to challenge the taken-for-granted nature of secular and physical reality; and more than a third of all adults in England report that they have been influenced by a presence or power, whether referred to God or not, that is different from their everyday selves. Those experiences are reported more often by women than men, for whom they may be hard to acknowledge publicly, and can be interpreted as symptoms of illness or as a special "gift". Back and Bourque's (1970) suggestion that what some call a religious experience others identify as aesthetic deserves renewed attention.

Religion has more often been thought to compensate those who are weak than as a consequence of learning, indoctrination or social conformity, although it has also been aligned with sentiments or a personal identity, and as commitment, preference, interest, belonging, or membership. Yet religion is psychologically unified in the sense that whenever religious items are analysed against items referring to other social issues, it emerges as a single factor which does, however, break down, both within its own domain and among religious subjects affiliated with a denomination, particular Church, or social tradition.

To be accepted, any expression of religion must be appropriate to its context, and not to any specific personality characteristics. Donahue (1985) emphasized the limited range of personality variables that have been aligned with religion and which reflect our cultural expectations of such relationships anyway. But a complete analysis of the relationships that have been examined between the major personality and religious variables would be impossible. Dittes (1969, p. 636) therefore organized his review of the psychological basis of religion around "the general supposition that religion is associated with deficiencies of personality", a view that he said is "widely held". He concluded that religion *is* associated with a "weak or constricted ego". On the other hand, Argyle and Beit-Hallahmi (1975) identified the positive effects of religion on adjustment, health and coping (p. 201) as well as the greater authoritarianism, dogmatism, suggestibility, dependence, inadequacy and anxiety among those who are "religious" (p. 282). Those negative traits or effects may, however, be traced back to an orthodoxy which maintains that such responses are social sequelae of a conservative stance. Batson and Ventis (1982), who emphasized the methodological problems in establishing any of these links, nevertheless conclude that in general "the relationship between religious involvement and mental health is negative rather than positive" (p. 231) and that there are no relationships between religion, and personality unification and organization, or "appropriate social behaviour". Bergin's (1983) careful meta-analysis of the 458 product moment correlations he derived from 141 separate sources found only three of them·in clinical-counselling journals. He notes that "apparently there is relatively little interest in the relationship between religion and non-pathological personality measures among such researchers". He also emphasized the willingness of researchers to use their own measures and to neglect standard scales (a point that Gorsuch (1984) also makes). (Perhaps the psychology of religion moved away from its early position in the mainstream of psychology simply because of an unwillingness to rely on or develop an accepted or paradigmatic approach.) Bergin also notes the concern with relatively few religious links, such as with the fear of death, IQ and academic ability, sex behaviour (to find "a general negative relationship between religiousness and premarital intercourse"), marital satisfaction, and a "relationship between dogmatism and authoritarianism with measures of belief and fundamentalism". He also notes that "many belief measures are themselves fundamentalistically worded. ... Since such theologies are often characterized by dichotomous saved/damned approaches, it may be that these correlations are also auto-correlations". That would, however, apply only to those with a fundamentalist or extrinsic orientation. On the question of causality he notes that, "If dogmatic individuals seek out dogmatic religion, then only certain types of religious orientation would be expected to display high dogmatism scores." It is essential that the implications of different orientations to religion are recognized in any attempts to link it with personality, and Bergin concludes, the "data on the relationship between religion and personality are not particularly impressive" although what there is centres on sexual control, marital satisfaction and authoritarianism or orthodoxy.

With broad perspectives on religious orientations we might, however, find similar curvilinear relationships with psychological variables that Allport first noted between extrinsic and intrinsic perspectives and prejudice. Such relationships have been found for obedience in a Milgram paradigm (Bock and Warren, 1972), happiness, mental and physical health (Shaver *et al.*, 1980) and fear of death (Nelson and Cantrell, 1980). Gorsuch and Aleshire (1974) therefore argue that a person needs "a strong internalized value system and a willingness to deviate to be *either* a nuclear church member or to have no contact with the church", but also, for example, to reject "the widely accepted norm of racism." Thouless (1971) similarly noted that strong believers and strong disbelievers are equally confident about their religious beliefs, and therefore either accept or reject the generic religionism that is built into Western cultures. Such confidence is independent of an intrinsic commitment that defies immoral authorities yet accepts death, and also fosters good mental health, optimism and a confident open-mindedness.

Those who affirm a "non-religion" through their active commitment to science, Marxism or secular humanism may also show little fear and "oppose the milquetoast religion that most accept as a superstitious obstacle to progress, as an opiate that prevents liberation and as a hot bed of prejudice that does more harm than good" (Donahue, 1985). These controlling perspectives can be transformed, although to live that way could be similar to using religion as a means to achieve social or personal goals, which can make one narcissistically hedonistic and individualistic. Donahue (1985) therefore concludes that, "The items of the extrinsic scale call for agreement with the treating of religion as simply one of many influences on life or as a source of contact and social support. It is therefore not surprising to find it basically uncorrelated with other measures of both belief and commitment."

Intrinsic religiousness is positively correlated with internal locus of control and purpose in life, negatively with feminism and fear of death, and it is uncorrelated with prejudice, unless the measures are directly behavioural, in which case intrinsic people appear to be unprejudiced. While females score higher on intrinsicness than males, a generally "intrinsic religiousness tends to be positively correlated, and extrinsic religiousness is uncorrelated" with the variables "of interest to religion", while the "intrinsics and indiscriminate individuals are generally indistinguishable" on religious variables (Donahue, 1985). Such complex interactions can no longer be neglected by assuming consistent linear relationships. David Riesmann's concepts of inner, outer, and other-directedness that were displaced by Rotter's simple contrast of inner and outer control could usefully be applied to these findings. An other-directed philosophy of life characterizes those with a decentred but committed approach despite the similarity in the beliefs held by people at the poles of religiousness (cf. Wiebe and Fleck, 1980), and those who are indiscriminately pro or anti-religious might be expected to have similar personalities.

Nevertheless, Donahue (1985) shows that there are linear relationships between religion and marital stability, low premarital intercourse and drug abuse. An absence of relationships between religion and delinquency or altruism (Batson *et al.*, 1985) reflects the general requirements of society to which a religious stance adds nothing. Because all specifically religious responses are shaped by the ideologies behind religious doctrines, they are linked by them to social values or norms. The normative demands that are imposed on religious people and the real, as well as the promised consequences of religious beliefs, and the claims that encourage support for them deserve more attention than they have received. (So Jehovah's Witnesses now have difficulty avoiding essential blood transfusions.)

What, therefore, is the psychological nature of religion, and how can it be expressed "maturely"?

Allport understood mature religion as integrative and involved with a readiness to doubt, self-criticism and tentativeness (Batson and Ventis, 1982, p. 149). Batson assessed these aspects of "religious life" with items that asked about the importance of others in religious development (especially Church, clergy, and parents), the internal or personal needs for religion and an "interactional" or "quest" orientation among those "continually raising ultimate whys" (Batson, 1976, p. 32).

Batson's quest orientation might reflect uncertainty, agnosticism, or an unwillingness to allow oneself to become committed and bound to a point of view. It is a perspective characteristic of students, or among those who have an academic rather than a more practical orientation (cf. Dittes, 1971), who have formed a majority of the subjects used in psychological studies of religion. Contrasts between the quest for truth and holding a stable perspective that is recognized as true (on whatever ground) is a fundamental ambiguity for religion, as for other ideologies. Hood (1978) resolved that simply by recognizing the contrast between religion as a part of life (and so extrinsic) or as the meaning of life (and intrinsic). In that sense, those who are indiscriminately pro or anti-religious have not adopted either of those positions. To focus only on religious believers gives too limited a perspective for any psychological analysis, since Batson's quest orientation could lead one either to religion or irreligion and evades what the Old Testament prophets identified as "faithfulness" to God, which might itself require a convergent stance. It is unfortunate that Allport disregarded the inconsistently anti-religious group in his original work.

Allport (1950) adopted a strictly psychological perspective when he claimed that:

> Mature religion is less of a servant, and more of a master, in the economy of life. No longer guided and steered exclusively by impulse, fear, wish, it tends rather to control and to direct these motives toward a goal that is no longer determined by mere self-interest (p. 72). ... Though it has known intimately "the dark night of the soul," it has decided that theoretical skepticism is not incompatible with practical absolutism. While it knows all the grounds for skepticism, it serenely affirms its wager. In so doing, it finds that the successive acts of commitment, with their beneficent consequences, slowly strengthen the faith and cause the moments of doubt gradually to disappear (p. 83).

The extrinsic orientation to religion identifies the stance that has given religion a bad name, because of its instrumental character and its links to oppression, prejudice and dogmatism (Hoge and Carroll, 1973), trait anxiety (Baker and Gorsuch, 1982) and fear of death (Minton and Spilka, 1976). While we can assume that religion does make a difference to those who believe, and that there are different responses to it, our generic religiousness is referred to God as the common ground. Those who become committed cannot be identified simply by their belief or practice, because that is so widespread. We should therefore be more concerned with what people find on the screen of belief and practice, although for those with settled beliefs, religion no longer competes with other activities and sources of comfort or meaning, and it can be accepted naively by those from "religious" families who have not had to rebel against it.

This raises a meta-theoretical issue about the position from which any observations are made. Those with a liberal religious stance are easily criticized by conservatives, and others' beliefs can be dismissed because they do not follow the "true religion" that has been found by those who are fundamentalist or evangelical. Because of that, Rokeach (1960) found a clear scale for denominations in terms of the orthodoxy they prescribe, while Richardson (1985) concluded that the appeal of new religious movements lies in the collective solutions they offer and not in their individual problem-solving strategies. The truth of religion is a matter for philosophical or theological enquiry and for individual solutions, although when reductionistic psychological arguments challenge its credibility the motives, needs or reasons for believing or not believing, may, following Pascal's wager, be based on hope, a gamble, or in an illusion that is independent of any claims to objective validity because the expected consequences of religion can be self-fulfilling.

Religious believers seem, however, to be threatened by an analysis that leaves them unsure whether they believe because their beliefs are true, because they have been told to believe, or have been led to believe by psychological needs they are unaware of. Belief itself becomes the religious person's theory by which the world is understood, and the network through which information can be filtered to explain events or reduce threats to the ego (Rokeach, 1960). Religions therefore offer a reference point to those who are able to accept them.

Because it is impossible to verify religious beliefs themselves directly, there has been a constant tension between explaining or understanding them as errors or cognitive distortions *and* with reference to emotional or other processes (Kruglanski and Ajzen, 1983), or simply as prescribed solutions to life and the nature of the world. At a cultural level those beliefs form stereotyped (or archetypal) symbols that are embedded in religious language, and draw on, for example, family models because they are aligned with social life. While new meanings can be found for traditional statements, and old concepts are kept alive (in "creation science", for example); idiosyncratic constructions are disclosed in the contexts that can tolerate them. That religion offers solutions to our problems does not itself turn it into a psychologically important process.

But the psychological problems that Dittes identified in 1969 continue to dog current work. Is religion explicit and differentiated or subjective and diffused? How does religion link with personality, social attitudes and psychological development? Does religion involve a specific psychological process? What is the nature of religious experience, the meaning and understanding of religious doctrines, and the explicit effects of religious beliefs? While it has proved difficult to find a convincing amalgam of the internal, personality-based and the external or social and communal processes that religion involves, orientations, religious attributions and the situationally specific effects of religion are displacing the older explanations that were in terms of traits or needs.

The recognition that experimental studies of religion *are* possible has allowed us to capture and control some of the intangibility and the concreteness of religion. Many religious people, however, resolve their surprise about what is unexpected by a routine and committed certainty in which they *appear* to use their religion. Those taken-for-granted solutions are not, however, to be directly interpreted without question.

An effective psychology of religion must recognize its different forms and the many ways it can be fitted into the lives of those who carry it. Like sport, art, politics and leisure, religion bores some people, saves some from boredom and sustains or fulfils others. Those kinds of response are not evenly distributed, and claims to the truth or falsity of religion are themselves data for further psychological analyses of the external system that provides the texts, and the inner responsiveness that enables their acceptance and integration. The tension between the inner and outer aspects of religion must be resolved for constructive solutions to be possible, although differences between religious individuals may simply involve their training, preferences or values: authoritarian and dependent styles of religion do not suit everybody and the polls show that religious belief and practice has not declined as much as has been assumed.

Because there is now less interest in explaining religion, or explaining it away, than in understanding the effects it appears to have, there is a search for new theoretical models. With religious experience in particular less vulnerable to potential criticism, religious groups are less polarized than they were, and the positive effects of religion are being recognized.

Answers to the question, "What has changed in the psychology of religion in recent years?", must therefore be, "a great deal". Not only has the amount of work published increased, but a consensus is developing about how to proceed in measurement (Gorsuch, 1984) and in experimental designs (Deconchy, 1985). Despite its vicissitudes and the early taboos against it, the psychology of religion had an important place in the development of modern psychology, with the first book entitled the *"Psychology of Religion"* published in 1899 by Starbuck. It may be re-establishing itself and the Churches themselves, in their emphasis on personal development, clinical and pastoral counselling and values clarification have adopted psychological perspectives, and use counselling skills to advise, console, and treat those who present to them as alienated or demoralized.

A basic question is, however, "Why do individuals accept religion?" Dogmatism and authoritarianism may be an answer at one level and an epistemological individualism (Wallis, 1984) has been suggested at another, since the Churches depend on their members. Given the identification with some religious tradition that a majority of the population claim (although those claiming "no religion" have increased in Australia to about 17 per cent) and that about one quarter of our population claim to be involved with religious membership or practice, how are we to account for the discrepancies between those religious indicators? One simple explanation is in terms of the functional irrelevance of religion for many people, except when they are in crisis. Those who go to church are more involved with a religious identity that is set within a membership and not simply a reference group. An active religious membership appears to be most important for those who are young and for those beyond middle-age, especially when it includes a recognition of their ethnicity.

Religious beliefs are so widely accepted that they have assumed the status of primitive or primary beliefs, and are unquestioned. Those believing in that way do not think that their religion is being *used*, but that it is to be enjoyed or lived (perhaps like art or sport), and that it is true. Apparent inconsistencies are then forgotten, and conviction carries the beliefs beyond their own explanations into solutions to what is puzzling, or as metaphors to live by (Lakoff and Johnson, 1980). Those who can do without a "religious consciousness" find other explanations, like paranormal beliefs, humanism, rationalism, communism, gardening, CND, ecology, folk music, and so on. Many religious people carry these interests or beliefs too, and resort to religious explanations only occasionally. There is nothing special about that. When our basic needs for survival or consistency are met, we want to be creative, enjoy ambiguities, and things that are ephemeral or transitory. Doing that still requires conformity to a normative structure with its supporting social context.

The sacred canopy is not just a security blanket. It holds social structures together within the forms of religion found in Churches or sects, in alignments with the world or withdrawn from it, maintaining existing patterns or rebelling against them, offering a set path or making one's own. All this emphasizes the ambiguity of religious attachments and reduces the distinction between the rational and what is judged irrational (Dodds, 1951). The cloister or sanctuary, with its mysteries, is not the only place where meaning can be found to humanize the environment.

So what is religion? Those making prescriptive or proscriptive definitions usually refer to the content of beliefs and doctrines, and not to a "mental state" that is beyond any specific beliefs, or even to attributes like soul or spirit. Definitions that refer to the transcendent necessarily invoke belief or experience. Although no psychological method is epistemologically neutral, once philosophical psychology was given back to the philosophers, our methods could directly tap into what is self-evidently "religious" — and to its formal manifestations. Recent investigators have kept close to common-sense, and while it is only occasionally that the findings are counter-intuitive and based on experimentally controlled studies, they have shown that prior experience or knowledge of a religious tradition overwhelms most of the other effects on the data. In one sense each person seems to create their own religion and in another they react to what is made available to them.

References

Abelson, R. P. (1959). Models of resolution of belief dilemmas. *Journal of Conflict Resolution, 3*, 343–352.

Abelson, R. P. (1973). The structure of belief systems, In K. Colby and R. Schank (eds), *Computer Simulation of Thought and Language*. San Francisco: Freeman.

Abelson, R. P. and Rosenberg M. J. (1958). Symbolic psycho-logic: A model of attitudinal cognition. *Behavioural Science, 3*, 1–13.

Abrams, M., Gerard, D. and Timms, N. (1985). *Values and Social Change in Britain*. London: Macmillan.

Abric, J. C. (1984). A theoretical and experimental approach to the study of social representations in a situation of interaction. *In* R. M. Farr and S. Moscovici (eds), *Social Representations*. Cambridge: Cambridge University Press, pp. 169–284.

Adorno, T. W., Frenkel-Brunswik, E., Levinson, D. J. and Sanford, R. N. (1950). *The Authoritarian Personality*. New York: Harper.

Allen, R. O. and Spilka, B. (1967). Committed and consensual religion: A specification of religion-prejudice relationships. *Journal for the Scientific Study of Religion, 6*, 191–206.

Alliott, R. (1855). *Psychology and Theology: Or Psychology Applied to the Investigation of Questions Relating to Religion, Natural Theology, and Revelation*. London: Jackson and Walford.

Allport, F. H. (1934). The J-curve hypothesis of conforming behaviour. *Journal of Social Psychology, 5*, 141–183.

Allport, G. W. (1935). Attitudes, *In* C. Murchison (ed.), *Handbook of Social Psychology*. Worcester, Mass.: Clark University Press, pp. 798–884.

Allport, G. W. (1950). *The Individual and His Religion, A Psychological Interpretation*. New York: Macmillan.

Allport, G. W. (1954). *The Nature of Prejudice*. Cambridge, Mass.: Addison-Wesley.

Allport, G. W. (1960). *Religion and Prejudice in Personality and Social Encounter*. Boston: Beacon Press, Ch. 16.

Allport, G. W. (1966). The religious context of prejudice. *Journal for the Scientific Study of Religion, 5*(3), 448–451.

Allport, G. W. (1968). Historical background of modern social psychology. *In* G. Lindzey and E. Aronson (eds), *Handbook of Social Psychology*. Vol. 1, Reading, Mass.: Addison-Wesley, pp. 1–80.

Allport, G. W., Gillespie, J. M. and Young, J. (1948). The religion of the post-war college student. *The Journal of Psychology, 25*, 3–33.

Allport, G. W. and Ross, J. M. (1967). Personal religious orientation and prejudice. *Journal of Personality and Social Psychology, 5*(4), 432–443.

Allport, G. W., Vernon, P. E. and Lindzey, G. (1960). *Study of Values*. Boston: Houghton-Mifflin, Third Edition.

220 *The psychology of religious belief*

Alvarez, A. (1984). *Life After Marriage: Scenes from Divorce*. London: Fontana.
American Psychiatric Association (1980). *DSM III: Diagnostic and Statistical Manual of Mental Disorders*, Third Edition.
Ames, E. S. (1910). *The Psychology of Religious Experience*. New York: Houghton-Mifflin.
Anderson, N. H. (1967). Averaging model analysis of set size effect in impression formation. *Journal of Experimental Psychology, 75,* 158–165.
Argyle, M. (1958). *Religious Behaviour*. London: Routledge and Kegan Paul.
Argyle, M. (1964). Seven psychological roots of religion. *Theology, 67*(530), 1–7.
Argyle, M. and Beit-Hallahmi, B. (1975). *The Social Psychology of Religion*. London: Routledge and Kegan Paul.
Argyle, M., Furnham, A. and Graham, J. A.(1981). *Social Situations*. Cambridge: Cambridge University Press.
Asch, S. E. (1946). Forming impressions of personality. *Journal of Abnormal and Social Psychology, 41,* 258–290.
Asch, S. E. (1952). *Social Psychology*. New York: Prentice Hall.
Ashbrook, J. B. (1966). The relationship of Church members to Church organisations. *Journal for the Scientific Study of Religion, 5,* 397–419.
Augustin, J. W., Miller, A. L. and Kirschen, D. S. (1979). Factors affecting generalised suppression of overt behaviour during resistance to temptation: the priest effect. *Psychological Reports, 45*(1), 259–262.
Austin, J. L. (1962), *How To Do Things With Words*. Oxford: Oxford University Press.
Back, C. W. and Bourque, L. B. (1970). Can feelings be enumerated? *Behavioral Science, 15,* 487–496.
Bagley, C. *et al.* (1979). *Personality, Self-esteem and Prejudice*. Farnborough: Saxon House.
Bakan, D. (1974). Paternity in the Judeo-Christian tradition. *In* A. W. Eister (ed.), *Changing Perspectives in the Scientific Study of Religion*. New York: John Wiley and Sons, pp. 203–216.
Baker, M. and Gorsuch, R. (1982). Trait anxiety and intrinsic-extrinsic religiousness. *Journal for the Scientific Study of Religion, 21,* 119–122.
Bandura, A. (1977). *Social Learning Theory*. Englewood Cliffs: Prentice Hall.
Barbour, I. G. (1974). *Myths, Models and Paradigms: The Nature of Scientific and Religious Language*. London: SCM Press.
Barnes, E. (1892). Theological life of a California child. *Pedagogical Seminary, 2,* 442–448.
Barth, K. (1957). *The Word of God and the Word of Man*. New York: Harper.
Bassett, R. L. *et al.* (1981). The shepherd scale: separating the sheep from the goats. *Journal of Psychology and Theology, 9*(4), 335–351.
Batson, C. D. (1976). Religion as prosocial: agent or double agent. *Journal for the Scientific Study of Religion, 15*(2), 29–45.
Batson, C. D. (1977). Experimentation in the psychology of religion: an impossible dream. *Journal for the Scientific Study of Religion, 16*(4), 413–418.
Batson, C. D., Schoenrade, P. A. and Pych, V. (1985). Brotherly love or self-concern? Behavioural consequences of religion. *In* L. B. Brown (ed.), *Advances in the Psychology of Religion*. Oxford: Pergamon Press, pp. 185–208.
Batson, C. D. and Ventis, W. L. (1982). *The Religious Experience; A Social-psychological Perspective*. New York: Oxford University Press.
Beit-Hallahmi, B. (1974). Psychology of religion, 1880–1930: the rise and fall of a psychological movement. *Journal of the History of the Behavioural Sciences, 10,* 84–90.
Beit-Hallahmi, B. (1977). Curiosity, doubt and deviation: the beliefs of psychologists and the psychology of religion. *In* H. N. Malony (ed.), *Current Perspectives in the Psychology of Religion*. Grand Rapids: Eerdman, pp. 381–391.

Beit-Hallahmi, B. (1985). Religiously based differences in approach to the psychology of religion: Freud, Fromm, Allport and Zilboorg. *In* L. B. Brown (ed.), *Advances in the Psychology of Religion*. Oxford: Pergamon Press, pp. 18–33.

Bellah, R. N. (1967). Civil religion in America. *Daedalus, 96*(Winter). 1–21.

Bem, D. J. (1970). *Beliefs, Attitudes and Human Affairs*. Belmont, California: Brooks Cole.

Bender, I. E. (1958). Changes in religious interest: a retest after fifteen years. *Journal of Abnormal and Social Psychology, 57*, 41–46.

Benson, J. M. (1981). The polls: a rebirth of religion. *Public Opinion Quarterly, 45*, 576–585.

Benson, P. and Spilka, B. (1973). God image as a function of self-esteem and locus of control. *Journal for the Scientific Study of Religion, 12*(8), 297–310.

Berelson, B. (ed.) (1966). *Family Planning and Population Programmes*. Chicago: Chicago University Press.

Berger, P. L. (1967). *The Sacred Canopy: Elements of a Sociological Theory of Religion*. Garden City, New York: Doubleday.

Berger, P. L. (1971). *A Rumour of Angels: Modern Society and the Rediscovery of the Supernatural*. Harmondsworth: Penguin Books.

Berger, P. L. (1973). *Invitation to Sociology: A Humanistic Perspective*. Woodstock, New York: The Overlook Press.

Berger, P. L. and Luckmann, T. (1972). *The Social Construction of Reality: A Treatise in the Sociology of Knowledge*. Harmondsworth: Penguin Books.

Bergin, A. E. (1983). Religiosity and mental health: a critical re-evaluation and meta-analysis. *Professional Psychology: Research and Practice, 14*(2), 170–184.

Bhaskar, R. (1978). *A Realist Theory of Science*. Second Edition. Atlantic Highlands, New Jersey: Humanities Press.

Billig, M. (1978). *Fascists: A Social Psychological View of the National Front*. London: Academic Press.

Black, A. W. (1983). Organised irreligion: the New South Wales Humanist Society. *In* A. W. Black and P. E. Glasner (eds), *Practice and Belief*: Studies in the Sociology of Australian Religion. Sydney: Allen and Unwin, pp. 154–166.

Blaikie, N. W. H. (1983). Styles of ministry: some aspects of the relationship between 'the Church' and 'the world'. *In* A. W. Black and P. E. Glasner (eds.), *Practice and Belief*: Studies in the Sociology of Australian Religion. Sydney: Allen and Unwin, pp. 43–61.

Bock, D. C. and Warren, N. C. (1972). Religious belief as a factor in obedience to destructive commands. *Review or Religious Research, 13*, 185–191.

Bogardus, E. S. (1927). Race, friendliness and social distance. *Journal of Applied Sociology, 11*, 272–287.

Boisen, A. T. (1936). *The Exploration of the Inner World: A Study of Mental Disorder and Religious Experience*. Chicago, New York: Willett, Clark and Co.

Bonhoeffer, D. (1953). *Letters and Papers from Prison*. Edited by Eberhard Bethge. Translated by Reginald H. Fuller. London: SCM Press.

Boring, E. (1929). *A History of Experimental Psychology*. London: The Century Co.

Bose, R. G. (1929). Religious concepts of children. *Religious Education, 24*, 831–837.

Bouma, G. D. (1983). Australian religiosity: some trends since 1966. *In* A. W. Black and P. E. Glasner (eds), *Practice and Belief: Studies in the Sociology of Australian Religion*. Sydney: Allen and Unwin, pp. 15–24.

Bourque, L. B. and Back, K. W. (1971). Language, society and subjective experience. *Sociometry, 34*(1), 1–21.

Bowers, M. (1968). *Conflicts of the Clergy: A Psychodynamic Study with Case Histories*. New York: Thomas Nelson.

Bowker, J. (1973). *The sense of God: Sociological, Anthropological and Psychological*

Approaches to the Origin of the Sense of God. Oxford: Clarendon Press.

Boyd, K. M. (1980). *Scottish Church Attitudes to Sex, Marriage and the Family, 1850–1914.* Edinburgh: John Donald.

Bragan, K. (1977). The psychological gains and losses of religious conversion. *British Journal of Medical Psychology, 50,* 177–180.

Brainerd, C. J. (1978). The stage question in cognitive developmental theory. *The Behavioural and Brain Sciences, 1*(2), 173–182, 207–213.

Brink, T. L. (1978). Inconsistency. *Review of Religious Research, 28*(1), 82–85.

Brock, T. C. (1962). Implications of conversion and magnitude of cognitive dissonance. *Journal for the Scientific Study of Religion, 1*(2), 199–203.

Broen, W. E. (1957). A factor analytic study of religious attitudes. *Journal of Abnormal and Social Psychology, 54,* 176–179.

Brothers, J. (1964) *Church and School: A Study of the Impact of Education on Religion.* Liverpool: Liverpool University Press.

Brown, D. and Lowe, W. (1951). Religious beliefs and personality characteristics of college students. *Journal of Social Psychology, 33,* 103–129.

Brown, L. B. (1962). A study of religious belief. *British Journal of Psychology, 53*(3), 259–272.

Brown, L. B. (1964). Classifications of religious orientation. *Journal for the Scientific Study of Religion, 4*(1), 91–99.

Brown, L. B. (1965). Religious belief and judgment of brief duration. *Perceptual and Motor Skills, 20*(1), 33–34.

Brown, L. B. (1968). Some attitudes underlying petitionary prayer. *In* A. Godin (ed.), *From Cry to Word.* Brussels: Lumen Vitae Press, pp. 65–84.

Brown, L. B. (1969). Confirmation and religious belief. *Victoria University of Wellington Publications in Psychology,* No. 22, 1–53.

Brown, L. B. (1977). Psychology and privacy. *University of New South Wales Occasional Papers,* No. 2, 5–8.

Brown, L. B. (1981a). Another test of Yinger's measure of nondoctrinal religion. *Journal of Psychology, 107,* 3–5.

Brown, L. B. (1981b). The religionism factor after 25 years. *Journal of Social Psychology, 107*(1), 7–10.

Brown, L. B. and Forgas, J. P. (1980). The structure of religion: A multi-dimensional scaling of informal elements. *Journal for the Scientific Study of Religion, 19*(4), 423–431.

Brown, L. B. and Pallant, D. J. (1962). Religious belief and social pressure. *Psychological Reports, 10,* 813–814.

Brown, L. B. and Thouless, R. H. (1965). Animistic thought in civilised adults. *Journal of Genetic Psychology, 107*(1), 33–42.

Brown, R. (1965). *Social Psychology.* New York: Free Press.

Bruner, J. S. and Goodman, C. C. (1947). Value and need as organizing factors in perception. *Journal of Abnormal and Social Psychology, 43,* 33–44.

Bruner, J. S. and Postman, L. (1948). Symbolic values as an organizing factor in perception. *Journal of Social Psychology, 27,* 203–208.

Brusselmans, C. (ed.) (1979). *Toward Moral and Religious Maturity.* New Jersey: Silver Burdett.

Bultmann, R. K. (1953). *Kerygma and Myth: A Theological Debate.* London: SPCK.

Burn, W. L. (1964). *The Age of Equipoise: A Study of the Mid-Victorian Generation.* New York: Norton.

Butler, D. E. and Stokes, D. (1969). *Political Change in Britain: Forces Shaping Electoral Choice.* London: Macmillian.

Caird, D. and Law, H. G. (1982). Non-conventional beliefs: their structure and measurement.

Journal for the Scientific Study of Religion, 21(2), 152-163.

Campbell, D. T. and Fiske, D. W. (1959). Convergent and discriminant validation by the multi-trait multi-method matrix. *Psychological Bulletin, 56*, 81-105.

Campbell, J. (1960). *The Masks of God: Primitive Mythology*. London: Secker and Warburg.

Capps, D. (1974). Contemporary psychology of religion. *Social Research, 41*(2), 362-383.

Capps, D. (1980). Research models and pedagogical paradigms in the psychology of religion. *Review of Religious Research, 21*(2), 218-227

Capps, D., Rambo, L. and Ransohoff, P. (1976a). *Psychology of Religion: A Guide to Information Sources*. Detroit: Gale Research Company.

Capps, D., Ransohoff, P. and Rambo, L. (1976b). Publication trends in the psychology of religion to 1974. *Journal for the Scientific Study of Religion, 15*, 15-28.

Carey, R. G. (1971). Influence of peers in shaping religious behaviour. *Journal for the Scientific Study of Religion, 10*(2), 157-159.

Carroll, J. D. and Chang, J. J. (1970). Analyses of individual differences in multi-dimensional scaling via an N-way generalisation of Eckert-Young decomposition. *Psychometrika, 35*, 283-319.

Chapman, A. J. and Jones, D. M. (1980). *Models of Man*. Leicester: British Psychological Society.

Chave, E. J. (1939). *Measure Religion: Fifty-two Experimental Forms*. Chicago: Distributed by the University of Chicago Bookstore.

Chiffister, J. and Marty, M. E. (1983). *Faith and Ferment: An Interdisciplinary Study of Christian Beliefs and Practices*. Minneapolis: Augsburg.

Chilton, P. (1984). Orwell, language and linguistics. *Language and Communication, 4*(2), 129-146.

Christie, R. and Geis, F. (eds.) (1968). *Studies in Machiavellianism*. New York: Academic Press.

Christie, R. and Jahoda, M. (eds.) (1954). *Studies in the Scope and Method of 'The Authoritarian Personality'*. New York: Free Press.

C. I. O. (Church Information Office) (1970). *Report of the Archbishop's Commission, Church and State*. Westminster: C. I. O.

Clark, E. T. (1929). *The Psychology of Religious Awakening*. New York: Macmillan.

Clark, W. H. (1958a). How do social scientists define religion? *Journal of Social Psychology, 47*, 143-147.

Clark, W. H. (1958b). *The Psychology of Religion: An Introduction to Religious Experience and Behaviour*. New York: Macmillan.

Clark, W. H. (1963). Religion as a response to the search for meaning: its relation to scepticism and creativity. *Journal of Social Psychology, 60*(1), 127-137.

Clayton, R. R. (1971). 5-D or 1? *Journal for the Scientific Study of Religion, 10*(1), 37-40.

Clayton, R. R. and Gladden, J. W. (1969). The five dimensions of religiosity: toward demythologizing a sacred artifact. *Journal for the Scientific Study of Religion, 13*, 135-143.

Cline, V. B. and Richards, J. M. (1965). A factor-analytic study of religious belief and behaviour. *Journal of Personality and Social Psychology, 1*(6), 569-578.

Coan, R. W. (1974). *The Optimal Personality*. London: Routledge and Kegan Paul.

Coe, G. A. (1900). *The Spiritual Life: Studies in the Science of Religion*. New York: Eaton and Mains.

Coe, G. A. (1909). Psychological aspects of religious education. *Psychological Bulletin, 6*(6), 185-187.

Coe, G. A. (1915). Recent publications on mysticism. *Psychological Bulletin, 12*, 459-462.

Cohn, N. (1975). *Europe's Inner Demons: An Enquiry Inspired by the Great Witch-hunt*. Brighton: Sussex University Press.

Cook, S. W. and Selltiz, S. (1964). A multiple-indicator approach to attitude measurement. *Psychological Bulletin, 62*, 36–55.

Cooper, L. A. and Shepard, R. N. (1973). Chronometric studies of the rotation of mental images. *In* W. G. Chase (ed.), *Visual Information Processing*. New York: Academic Press.

Covalt, N. K. (1958). The meaning of religion to older people — the medical perspective. *In* D. L. Scudder (ed.), *Organised Religion and the Older Person* Gainsville: University of Florida Press.

Cox, H. G. (1965). *The Secular City: Secularization and Urbanization in Theological Perspective*. New York: Macmillan.

Cronbach, A. (1928). The psychology of religion: a bibliographical survey. *Psychological Bulletin, 25*(12), 701–717.

Cronbach, A. (1933). The psychology of religion. *Psychological Bulletin, 30*, 327–361.

Crystal, D. (1965). *Linguistics, Language and Religion*. Leicester: Burns and Oates.

Crystal, D, (1980). *A First Dictionary of Linguistics and Phonetics*. London: Andre Deutsch

Curran, C. A. (1963). Some psychological aspects of Vatican Council II. *Journal for the Scientific Study of Religion, 2*, 190–194.

Currie, R., Gilbert, A. and Horsley, L. (1977). *Churches and Churchgoers: Patterns of Church Growth in the British Isles Since 1700*. Oxford: Clarendon Press.

Daly, R. J. and Cochrane, C. M. (1968). Affective disorder taxonomies in middle-aged females. *British Journal of Psychiatry, 114*, 1295–7.

Daniel, M. P. (1978). Etudes experimentales de l'effet de lay croyance religieuse sur les comportements d'assistance. *Archives de Sciences Sociales des Religions, 46*, 161–164.

Davidson, J. D. (1972a). Religious belief as an independent variable. *Journal for the Scientific Study of Religion, 11*, 65–75.

Davidson, J. D. (1972b). Religious belief as a dependent variable. *Sociological Analysis, 33*, 81–94.

Deconchy, J-P. (1967). *Structure Genetique de L'idee de Dieu Chez les Catholiques Francais: Garçon et Filles 8 a 16 Ans*. Brussels: Lumen Vitae Press.

Deconchy, J-P. (1980). *Orthodoxie Religieuse et Science Humaines Suivi de? (Religious Orthodoxy, Rationality and Scientific Knowledge)*. Paris: Mouton.

Deconchy, J-P. (1981). Laboratory experimentation and social field experimentation: an ambiguous distinction. *European Journal of Social Psychology, 11*(4), 323–347.

Deconchy, J-P. (1982). Ideological commitment and scientific knowledge: a preliminary experimental study. Paper read to the Second Symposium for Psychologists of Religion, Nijmegen.

Deconchy, J-P. (1985). Non-experimental and experimental methods in the psychology of religion. *In* L. B. Brown (ed.), *Advances in the Psychology of Religion*. Oxford: Pergamon Press, pp. 76–112.

Demerath, N. J. and Levinson, R. M. (1971). Baiting the dissident hook: some effects on measuring religious belief. *Sociometry, 34*(3), 346–359.

Department of Statistics Bulletin. (1966). *New Zealand Census of Population and Dwellings*, Vol. 3. Wellington: N.Z. Government Printer.

Deutscher, I. (1984). Chasing ancestors: some consequences of the selection from intellectual traditions. *In* R. M. Farr and S. Moscovici (eds). *Social Representations*. Cambridge: Cambridge University Press, pp. 71–100.

Dittes, J. E. (1961). Impulsive closure on a reaction to failure-induced threat. *Journal of Abnormal and Social Psychology, 63*(3), 562–569.

Dittes, J. E. (1969). Psychology of religion. *In* G. Lindzey and E. Aronson (eds.), *The Handbook of Social Psychology*, Vol. 5. Reading Mass.: Addison Wesley, pp. 602–659. Second Edition.

Dittes, J. E. (1971a). Typing the typologies: some parallels in the career of church-sect and extrinsic-intrinsic. *Journal for the Scientific Study of Religion, 10*, 375–383.

Dittes, J. E. (1971b). Two issues in measuring religion. *In* M. P. Strommen (ed.), *Research on Religious Development; A Comprehensive Handbook. A Project of the Religious Education Association.* New York: Hawthorn Books, pp. 78–108.

Dittes, J. E. (1971c). Religion, prejudice and personality. *In* M. P. Strommen (ed.), *Research on Religious Development; A Comprehensive Handbook. A Project of the Religious Education Association.* New York: Hawthorn Books, pp. 355–390.

Dittes, J. E. (1973). Beyond William James. *In* C. Y. Glock and P. E. Hammond (eds.), *Beyond the Classics.* New York: Harper and Row, pp. 291–354.

Dittes, J. E. (1977). Investigator as an instrument of investigation: some exploratory observations on the complete researcher. *In* D. Capps, W. H. Capps and M. G. Bradford (eds.), *Encounter with Erikson: Historical Interpretation and Religious Biography.* Santa Barbara: Scholars Press.

Dix, Dom Gregory (1960). *The Shape of the Liturgy.* London: Black. Second Edition.

Dodds, E. R. (1951). *The Greeks and the Irrational.* Berkeley: University of California Press.

Doise, W. (1978). *Groups and Individuals: Explanations in Social Psychology.* Cambridge: Cambridge University Press.

Donahue, M. J. (1985). Intrinsic and extrinsic religiousness: review and meta-analysis. *Journal of Personality and Social Psychology, 48*(2), 400–419.

Donaldson, M. (1978). *Children's Minds.* London: Croom Helm.

Douglas, M. (1978). *Purity and Danger: An Analysis of Concepts of Pollution and Taboos.* London: Routledge and Kegan Paul.

Douglas, W. (1963). Religion. *In* N. L. Farberow (ed.), *Taboo Topics.* New York: Atherton, pp. 80–91.

Dreger, R. M. (1952). Some personality correlates of religious attitudes as determined by projective techniques. *Psychological Monographs, 66*(3).

Ducasse, C. J. (1953). *A Philosophical Scrutiny of Religion.* New York: Ronald Press Co.

Dunlap, K. (1946). *Religion, Its Functions in Human Life; A Study of Religion from the Point of view of Psychology.* New York: McGraw-Hill.

Dynes, R. R. (1955). Church-sect typology and socio-ecnomic status. *American Social Development, 20*, 555–560.

Edwards, A. L. (1970). *The Measurement of Personality Traits by Scales and Inventories.* New York: Holt, Rinehart and Winston.

Edwards, A. L. and Kenney, K. C. (1946). A comparison of the Thurstone and Likert techniques of attitude scale construction. *Journal of Applied Psychology, 30*, 72–83.

Eisenman, R., Bernard, J. L. and Hannon, J. E. (1966). Benevolence, potency, and God: A semantic differential study of the Rorschach. *Perceptual and Motor Skills, 22*, 75–78.

Eiser, J. R. (1980). *Cognitive Social Psychology: A Guide Book to Theory and Research.* London: McGraw Hill.

Eiser, J. R. and Osman, B. E. (1978). Judgmental perspectives and the value connotations of response scale labels. *Journal of Personality and Social Psychology, 36*, 491–497.

Elkind, D. (1964). Piaget's semi-clinical interview and the study of spontaneous religion. *Journal for the Scientific Study of Religion, 4*, 40–47.

Elkind, D. (1970). The origins of religion in the child. *Review of Religious Research, 12*(1), 32–45.

Elkind, D. (1971). The development of religious understanding in children and adolescents. *In* M. P. Strommen (ed.), *Research on Religious Development; A Comprehensive Handbook. A Project of the Religious Education Association.* New York: Hawthorn Books.

Elkind, D. and Elkind S. (1962). Varieties of religious experience in young adolescents. *Journal for the Scientific Study of Religion, 2,* 102–112.

Embree, R. A. (1970). The religious association scales as an abilities measure of the religious factor in personality. *Journal for the Scientific Study of Religion, 9,* 299–302.

Embree, R. A. (1973). The religious association scales: a follow-up study. *Journal for the Scientific Study of Religion, 12,* 223–226.

Emmons, C. F. and Sobal, J. (1980). Paranormal beliefs — functional alternatives to mainstream religion. *Review of Religious Research, 22*(4), 301–312.

English, H. B. and English, A. C. (1958). *A Comprehensive Dictionary of Psychological and Psychoanalytical Terms.* London: Longmans, Green.

Erikson, E. (1958). *Young Man Luther; A Study in Psychoanalysis and History.* New York: Norton. First Edition.

Evans-Pritchard, E. E. (1965). *Theories of Primitive Religion.* Oxford: Clarendon Press.

Everett, C. C. (1902). *The Psychological Elements of Religious Faith.* New York: Macmillan.

Eysenck, H. J. (1954). *The Psychology of Politics.* London: Routledge and Kegan Paul.

Eysenck, H. J. (1981). *A Model for Personality.* Berlin: Springer-Verlag.

Faber, H. (1969). Importance of the three phases of Freud for the understanding of religion. *Zygon, 4,* 356–372.

Fairchild, R. W. (1971). Delayed gratification: a psychological and religious analysis. *In* M. P. Strommen (ed.), *Research on Religious Development; A Comprehensive Handbook. A Project of the Religious Education Association.* New York: Hawthorn Books.

Farberow, N. L. (1963). *Taboo Topics.* New York: Atherton.

Faris, E. (1914). Psychology of religion (practical). *Psychological Bulletin, 11,* 463–466.

Farr, C. B. and Howe, R. L. (1932). The influence of religious ideas on etiology, symptomatology and prognosis of the psychoses, with special reference to social factors. *American Journal of Psychiatry, 11,* 845–865.

Faulkner, J. E. and De Jong, G. F. (1965). Religiosity in 5-D: an empirical analysis. *In* J. P. Robinson and P. R. Shaver (eds.), (1973) *Measures of Social Psychological Attitudes.* Ann Arbor: University of Michigan Survey Research Center, pp. 650–655.

Feather, N. F. (1984). Protestant ethic, conservatism, and values. *Journal of Personality and Social Psychology, 46*(5), 1132–1141.

Feldman, K. A. (1969). Change and stability of religious orientations during college. Part 1. Freshman-senior comparisons. *Review of Religious Research, 11*(1), 40–60. Part 2, 11(2), 103–128.

Feldman, K. A. and Newcomb, T. M. (1969). *The Impact of College on Students.* Vols 1 and 2. San Francisco: Jossey-Bass.

Ferguson, L. W. (1939). Primary social attitudes. *Journal of Psychology, 8,* 217–223.

Ferre, F. (1968). *Language, Logic and God.* New York: Harper and Row.

Festinger, L. (1950). Experiments in group belonging. *In* J. Miller (ed.), *Experiments in Social Process.* New York: McGraw Hill, pp. 36–45.

Festinger, L. (1957). *A Theory of Cognitive Dissonance.* Evanston: Row, Peterson.

Fichter, J. H. (1954). *Social Relations in the Urban Parish.* Chicago; University of Chicago Press.

Finney, C. G. (1835). *Lectures on Revivals of Religion.* New York: Leavitt, Lord and Company.

Fischer, E. G. and Falke, N. E. (1984). B-endorphin modulates immune functions. *Psychotherapy and Psychosomatics, 42,* 195–284.

Fishbein, M. (1967). A behavioural theory approach to the relations between beliefs about an object and the attitude toward the object. *In* M. Fishbein (ed.), *Readings in Attitude Theory and Measurement.* New York: John Wiley and Sons, pp. 477–492.

Fishbein, M. and Ajzen, I. (1975). *Belief, Attitude, Intention and Behaviour: An Introduction to Theory and Research*. Reading, Mass.: Addison-Wesley.

Fishbein, M. and Raven, B. H. (1962). The AB scales: an operational definition of belief and attitude. *Human Relations, 15*, 35–44.

Flakoll, D. A. (1977). A history of method in the psychology of religion (1900–1906). *In* H. N. Malony (ed.), *Current Perspectives in the Psychology of Religion*. Grand Rapids: Eerdmans.

Fleck, J. R. and Carter, J. D. (1981). *Psychology and Christianity: Integrative Readings*. Nashville: Abingdon.

Flower, J. C. (1927). *An Approach to the Psychology of Religion*. New York: Harcourt, Brace and Co.

Fowler, J. W. (1981). *Stages of Faith*. San Francisco: Harper and Row.

Francis, L. J. (1978). Attitude and longitude: a study in measurement. *Character Potential, 8*, 119–130.

Francis, L. J. (1979). The priest as test administrator in attitude research. *Journal for the Scientific Study of Religion, 18*(1), 78–81.

Francis, L. J. (1979). School influence and pupil attitude towards religion. *British Journal of Educational Psychology, 49*, 107–123.

Francis, L. J. (1984). *Monitoring the Christian Development of the Child*. Abingdon: Culham College Institute.

Francis, L. J. (1985). Personality and religion: theory and measurement. *In* L. B. Brown (ed.), *Advances in the Psychology of Religion*. Oxford: Pergamon Press, pp. 171–184.

Francis, L. J., Pearson, P. R. and Kay, W. K. (1982). Eysenck's personality quadrants and religiosity. *British Journal of Social Psychology, 21*, 262–264.

Fransella, F. and Bannister, D. (1977). *A Manual for Repertory Grid Techniques*. London: Academic Press.

Freeman, D. (1983). *Margaret Mead, and Samoa: The Making and Unmaking of an Anthropological Myth*. Canberra: ANU Press.

Freud, S. (1907). Obsessive acts and religious practices. *Collected Papers*. 1907/1924. London: Hogarth Press.

Freud, S. (1928a). *The Future of an Illusion*. Translated by W. D. Robson-Scott. New York: Liveright Publishing Corp.

Freud, S. (1928b). *Totem and Taboo: Resemblances between the Psychic Lives of Savages and Neurotics*. New York: Dodd.

Freud, S. (1939). *Moses and Monotheism*. London: The Hogarth Press and The Institute of Psychoanalysis.

Fromm, E. (1950). *Psychoanalysis and Religion*. New Haven: Yale University Press.

Frye, N. (1982). *The Great Code: The Bible and Literature*. London: Routledge and Kegan Paul.

Fuller, P. (1984). Eastern promise. *New Society* (April-June), 102–103.

Fullerton, J. T. and Hunsberger, B. (1982). A unidimensional measure of Christian orthodoxy. *Journal for the Scientific Study of Religion, 21*(4), 317–326.

Furnham, A. (1982). The Protestant work ethic and attitudes towards unemployment. *Journal of Occupational Psychology, 55*, 277–286.

Furnham, A. and Lewis, A. (1985). *The Economic Mind: The Social Psychology of Beliefs and Behaviour*. Sussex: Wheatsheaf.

Gaede, S. (1976). A causal model of belief orthodoxy. *Sociological Analysis, 37*(3), 205–217.

Galanter, M., Rabkin, R., Rabkin, J. and Deutsch, A. (1979). The 'Moonies' — a psychological study of conversion and membership in a contemporary religious sect. *American Journal of Psychiatry, 136*(2), 165–170.

Galanter, M. and Buckley, P. (1978). Evangelical religions and meditation: psychological effects. *Journal of Nervous and Mental Diseases, 166*(10), 685–691.

Galton, F. (1873). *Inquiries into Human Faculty, and Development*. New York: Macmillan.

Galton, F. (1884). *Hereditary Genius; An Inquiry into Its Laws and Consequences*. New York: D. Appleton and Co.

Gay, J. D. (1971). *The Geography of England*. London: Duckworth.

Geering, L. (1968). *God in the New World*. London: Hodder and Stoughton.

Gellner, E. (1981). *Muslim Society*. Cambridge: Cambridge University Press.

Giles, H., Jones, S., Horton, M. and Lay, J. (1975). Toward a more dynamic social psychology of religion. *Bulletin of the British Psychological Association, 28*, 47–50.

Glock, C. Y. (1959). The sociology of religion, *In* R. Merton, L. Bloom and L. Cottrell (eds.), *Sociology Today*, pp. 153–177.

Glock, C. Y. (1973). Religious experience questionnaire. *Psychology Today, 7*(7), 114.

Glock, C. Y. (1974). Shifting forms of faith survey report: God in the Gut. *Psychology Today, 8*(6), 131–136.

Glock, C. Y. and Hammond, P. E. (1973). *Beyond the Classics: Essays in the Scientific Study of Religion*. New York: Harper and Row.

Glock, C. Y. and Stark, R. (1965). *Religion and Society in Tension*. Chicago: Rand McNally.

Godin, A. (1962). Importance and difficulty of scientific research in religious education: The problem of "criterion". *Religious Education*, (May–June), 163–172.

Godin, A. (1964a). *From Religious Experience to a Religious Attitude*. Brussels: Lumen Vitae Press.

Godin, A. (1964b). Belonging to a church: what does it mean psychologically? *Journal for the Scientific Study of Religion, 3*(2), 204–215.

Godin, A. (1967). The psychology of religion. *Quarterly Review of Religion and Mental Health, 5*(4), 1–6.

Godin, A. (ed.) (1968). *From Cry to Word*. Brussels: Lumen Vitae Press.

Godin, A. (1971). Some developmental tasks in Christian education. *In* M. P. Strommen (ed.), *Research on Religious Development: A Comprehensive Handbook. A Project of the Religious Education Association*. New York: Hawthorn Books.

Godin, A. (1972). Orthodoxie religieuse et psychologie sociale. *Nouvelle Revue Theologique, 104*(6), 620–637.

Godin, A. and Coupez, A. (1957). Religious projective pictures: a technique of assessment of religious psychism. *Lumen Vitae, 12*(2), 260–274.

Godin, A. and Hallez, M. (1964). Parental images and divine paternity. *Lumen Vitae, 19*, 253–284.

Godin, A. and Sister Marthe (1960). Magical mentality and sacramental life, *Lumen Vitae 15*(2), 277–296.

Godin, A. and Van Roey, B. (1959). Immanent justice and divine protection. *Lumen Vitae, 14*, 129–148.

Goldman, R. (1964). *Religious Thinking from Childhood to Adolescence*. London: Routledge and Kegan Paul.

Goldsen, R. K. *et al.* (1960). *What College Students Think*. Princeton, New Jersey: Van Nostrand.

Gorlow, L. and Schroeder, H. E. (1968). Motives for participating in religious experience. *Journal for the Scientific Study of Religion, 7*(2), 241–251.

Gorsuch, R. L. (1968). The conceptualization of God as seen in adjective ratings. *Journal for the Scientific Study of Religion, 7*, 56–64.

Gorsuch, R. L. (1984). Measurement: the boon and the bane of investigating religions. *American Psychologist, 39*(3), 228–236.

Gorsuch, R. L. and Aleshire, D. (1974). Christian faith and ethnic prejudice: a review and interpretation of research. *Journal for the Scientific Study of Religion, 13,* 281–307.

Gorsuch, R. L. McFarland, S. G. (1972). Single versus multiple item scales for measuring religious values. *Journal for the Scientific Study of Religion, 11*(1), 53–64.

Gorsuch, R. L. and Venable, G. D. (1983). Development of an 'age universal' I-E scale. *Journal for the Scientific Study of Religion, 22,* 181–187.

Goulder, M. D. (1974). *Midrash and Lection in Matthew; The Speaker's Lectures in Biblical Studies, 1969–1975.* London: SPCK.

Graebner, O. E. (1960). *Child Concepts of God.* Chicago: Lutheran Education Association.

Grassby, A. (1984). *Discrimination and Religious Conviction.* NSW, Australia: Anti-Discrimination Board.

Gray, D. B. (1964). *Factors related to a conception of the Church held by Presbyterian laymen.* University of Pittsburgh Ph.D. thesis.

Greeley, A. M. (1972). *The Denominational Society: A Sociological Approach to Religion in America.* Glenview: Scott, Foresman.

Greeley, A. M. (1974). *Ecstasy: A Way Of Knowing.* Englewood Cliffs: Prentice Hall.

Greeley, A. M. (1976). *Catholic Schools in a Declining Church.* Kansas: Sheed and Ward.

Greeley, A. M. (1982). *Religion: A Secular Theory.* New York: Free Press.

Greeley, A. M. and Rossi, P. H. (1966). *The Education of Catholic Americans.* Chicago: Aldine.

Green, B. F. (1954). Attitude measurement. *In* G. Lindzey (ed), *Handbook of Social Psychology.* Vol 1. pp. 335–369. Reading, Mass.: Addison-Wesley.

Grensted, L. W. (1930). *Psychology and God: A Study of the Implications of Recent Psychology for Religious Belief and Practice.* London: Longmans, Green.

Gross, M. L. (1978). *The Psychological Society.* New York: Simon and Schuster.

Gustafsson, B. (1972). The cemetery as a place for meditation. *Lumen Vitae, 27,* 85–138.

Guttman, L. (1950). The basis for scalogram analysis. *In* S. A. Stouffer *et al.* (eds.), *Measurement and Prediction.* Princeton: Princeton University Press.

Hall, G. S. (1904–1905). The Jesus of history and the Passion versus the Jesus of the Resurrection. *American Journal of Religious Psychology and Education, 1,* 30–64.

Hall, G. S. (1904). *Adolescence: Its Psychology and Its Relations to Physiology, Anthropology, Sociology, Sex, Crime, Religion and Education.* New York: D. Appleton and Company.

Hall, G. S. (1917). *Jesus, the Christ, in the Light of Psychology.* Garden City, New York: Doubleday, Page and Company.

Hampshire, S. (1959). *Thought and Action.* London: Chatto and Windus.

Hampshire, S. (1965). *Freedom of the Individual.* London: Chatto and Windus.

Hannay, D. R. (1980). Religion and health. *Social Science and Medicine, 14*(A), 683–685.

Harding, S. D. and Phillips, D. (1985). *Values in Europe: A Cross-National Survey.* London: Macmillan.

Hardy, A. C. (1966). *The Divine Flame.* London: Collins.

Hardy, A. C. (1975). *The Biology of God.* London: Jonathan Cape.

Hargrove, B. W. (1973). Organizational man on the frontier. *Journal for the Scientific Study of Religion, 12*(4), 461–466.

Hargrove, B. W., Dynes, R. R. and Newman, W. M. (1973). Reivew symposium on the sociology of Charles Y. Glock, *Journal for the Scientific Study of Religion, 12,* 459–473.

Harms, E. (1944). The development of religious experience in children. *American Journal of Sociology, 50*(2), 112–122.

Harré, R. (1983). *Personal Being.* Oxford: Basil Blackwell.

Harré, R. and Lamb, R. (1983). *The Encyclopedic Dictionary of Psychology.* Oxford: Blackwell Reference.

Harris, D. (1982). Counting Christians, *In* D. Harris, D. Hynd and D. Milliken (eds.), *The Shape of Belief: Christianity in Australia Today*. Homebush: Lancer, pp. 229–293.

Hartshorne, H. and May, M. A. (1982). *Studies in Deceit*. New York: Macmillan.

Hass, L. L. (1974). Personal construct systems and theological conservatism. University of Nebraska PhD thesis.

Hassall, D. (1981). Religious education in the multi-racial school. *In* J. Lynch (ed.), *Teaching in the Multi-Cultural School*. London. Ward-Lock Educational, pp. 40–47.

Havighurst, R. J. and Keating, B. (1971). The religion of youth. *In* M. P. Strommen (ed.), *Research on Religious Development; A Comprehensive Handbook. A Project of the Religious Educational Association*. New York: Hawthorn Books.

Hay, D. (1982). *Exploring Inner Space: Scientists and Religious Experience*. Harmondsworth: Penguin Books.

Heelas, P. (1985). Social anthropology and the psychology of religion. *In* L. B. Brown (ed.), *Advances in the Psychology of Religion*. Oxford: Pergamon, pp. 34–51.

Heider, F. (1946). Attitude and cognitive organization. *Journal of Psychology, 21*, 107–112.

Heintzelman, M. E. and Fehr, L. A. (1976). Relationship between religious orthodoxy and three personality variables. *Psychological Reports, 38*, 756–758.

Henderson, J. M. (1972). *Ratana: The man, the Church, the Political Movement*. Polynesian Society Memoirs, Vol. 36.

Hertel, B. R. (1980). Inconsistency of beliefs. *Review of Religious Research, 21*(2), 171–183.

Hick, J. (1977). *The Myth of God Incarnate*. London: SCM Press.

Hill, M. (1973). *A Sociology of Religion*. London: Heinemann Educational.

Hiltner, S. (1943). *Religion and Health*. New York: Macmillan.

Hilty, D. M. and Morgan, R. (1985). Construct validation for the religious involvement inventory: replication. *Journal for the Scientific Study of Religion, 24*(1), 75–86.

Hilty, D. M., Morgan, R. L. and Burns, J. E. (1984). King and Hunt revisited: dimensions of religious involvement. *Journal for the Scientific Study of Religion, 23*, 252–266.

Hjelle, L. A. and Lomastro, J. (1971). Personality differences between high and low dogmatism group of seminarians and religious sisters. *Journal for the the Scientific Study of Religion, 10*, 49–50.

Hoffman, M. L. (1971). Development of internal moral standards in children. *In* M. P. Strommen (ed.), *Research on Religious Development: A Comprehensive Handbook. A Project of the Religious Education Association*. New York: Hawthorn Books, pp. 211–263.

Hofstede, G. H. (1984). *Culture's Consequences, International Differences in Work-Related Values*. Beverley Hill: Sage.

Hogan, M. (1979). Australian secularists: the disavowal of denominational allegiance. *Journal for the Scientific Study of Religion, 18*(4), 390–404.

Hoge, D. R. and Carroll, J. W. (1973). Religiosity and prejudice in Northern and Southern Churches. *Journal for the Scientific Study of Religion, 12*, 181–197.

Homans, P. (1967). Towards a psychology of religion: by way of Freud and Tillich. *Zygon, 2*, 97–119.

Homans, P. (1970). *Theology after Freud: An Integrative Enquiry*. Indianapolis: Bobbs Merrill.

Homans, P. (1979). *Jung in Context: Modernity and the Making of a Psychology*. Chicago: University of Chicago Press.

Hood, R. W. (1975). The construction and preliminary validation of a measure of reported mystical experience. *Journal for the Scientific Study of Religion, 14*(1), 29–41.

Hood, R. W. (1978). Religious orientation and the experience of transcendence. *Journal for the Scientific Study of Religion, 12*, 441–448.

Hood, R. W. (1983). Social psychology and religious fundamentalism. *In* A. W. Childs and

G. B. Melton (eds.), *Rural Psychology*. New York: Plenum Press, pp. 168–198.

Houssiadas, L. and Brown, L. B. (1980). Ego-centrism in language and space perception. *Genetic Psychology Monographs, 101*, 183–214.

Huizinga, J. (1949). *Homo Ludens*, London: Routledge and Kegan Paul.

Hume, D. (1757). *The Natural History of Religion*. London: A. Millar.

Hunsberger, B. E. (1979). Sources of psychology of religion journal articles, 1950–1974. *Journal for the Scientific Study of Religion, 18*(1), 82–85.

Hunsberger, B. E. (1980). A re-examination of the antecedents of apostacy. *Review of Religious Research, 21*, 158–170.

Hunsberger, B. E. (1984). Apostacy: a social learning perspective. *Review of Religious Research, 25*, 21–38.

Hunsberger, B. E. and Brown, L. B. (1984). Religious socialization, apostacy and the impact of family background. *Journal for the Scientific Study of Religion, 23*(3), 239–251.

Hunsberger, B. E. and Ennis, J. (1982). Experimental effects in studies of religious attitudes. *Journal for the Scientific Study of Religion, 21*(2), 131–137.

Hunt, R. A. (1972) Mythological, symbolic, religious commitment — the LAM scales. *Journal for the Scientific Study of Religion, 11*, 42–52.

Hunt, R. A. and King, M. B. (1971). The intrinsic-extrinsic concept; a review and evaluation. *Journal for the Scientific Study of Religion, 10*, 339–356.

Hutsebaut, D. (1972/3). The representation of God: two complementary approaches. *Social Compass, 19*, 389–406.

Huxley, A. L. (1941). *Grey Eminence: A Study in Religion and Politics*. New York and London: Harper and Brothers.

Hynd, D. (1982). Christianity in Australia: a Bibliography. *In* D. Harris, D. Hynd and D. Milliken, *The Shape of Belief: Christianity in Australia Today*. Homebush: Lancer, pp. 201–228.

Inglis, K. S. (1960). Patterns of religious worship in 1851. *Journal of Ecclesiastical History, 11–12*, 74–86.

Isichei, E. (1970). *Victorian Quakers*. Oxford University Press.

ITA (Independent Television Authority) (1970). *Religion in Britain and Northern Ireland: A Survey of Popular Attitudes*. London: ITA.

James, W. (1889). The psychology of belief. *Mind, 14*(55), 321–352.

James, W. (1890). *The Principles of Psychology*. New York: H. Holt and Co.

James, W. (1902). *The Varieties of Religious Experience*. New York: Collier, and (1985) Vol. 15 in *The Works of William James*. Cambridge, Mass: Harvard University Press.

James, W. (1912). *The Will to Believe, and Other Essays in Popular Philosophy. New Impression*. New York: Longmans, Green and Co.

James, W. (1926). *The Letters of William James*. (edited by Henry James). New York: Longman, pp. 212–215.

Jaynes, J. (1976). *The Origin of Consciousness in the Breakdown of the Bi-Cameral Mind*. Boston: Houghton Mifflin, and (1982) Harmondsworth: Penguin Books.

Jeeves, M. A. (1957). Contribution on prejudice and religion. *Proceeding of the 15th International Congress of Psychology*. Brussels.

Jeeves, M. A. (1976). *Psychology and Christianity: The View Both Ways*. Downers Grove, Ill: Inter Varsity Press.

Jevons, F. B. (1896). *An Introduction to the History of Religion*. London: Methuen and Co.

Johnson, J. H., Null, C., Butcher, J. N. and Johnson, K. N. (1984). Replicated item level factor analysis of the full MMPI. *Journal of Personality and Social Psychology, 47*(1), 105–114.

Johnson, P. E. (1957). *Personality and Religion*. New York: Abingdon Press.

Johnson, R. A. (ed.) (1983). *Views from the Pews: Christian Beliefs and Attitudes.* Philadelphia: Fortress Press.

Johnson, W. I. (1971). The religious crusade; a revival or ritual? *American Journal of Sociology, 76,* 873–890.

Johnson-Laird, P. N. (1983). *Mental Models, Towards a Cognitive Science of Language, Inference, and Consciousness.* Cambridge: Cambridge University Press.

Jones, E. (1926). The psychology of religion. *British Journal of Medical Psychology, 6,* 264–269.

Jones, E. E. and Nisbett, R. E. (1971). The actor and the observer: divergent perceptions of the causes of behaviour. *In* E. E. Jones *et al.* (eds.), *Attribution: Perceiving the Causes of Behaviour.* Morristown: General Learning Press, pp. 79–94.

Jung, C. G. (1958). *Psychology and Religion: West and East.* London: Routledge and Kegan Paul.

Kallen, H. M. and Pemberton, P. L. (1961). An introductory word. *Journal for the Scientific Study of Religion, 1*(1), 3–4.

Katz, D. (1971). The functional approach to the study of attitudes. *Public Opinion Quarterly, 16,* 273–282.

Keene, J. J. (1967a). Religious behaviour and neuroticism, spontaneity, and world-mindedness. *Sociometry, 30,* 137–157.

Keene, J. J. (1967b). Baha'i world faith: redefinition of religion. *Journal for the Scientific Study of Religion, 6,* 221–235.

Kelley, D. M. (1972). *Why Conservative Churches Are Growing.* New York: Harper and Row.

Kelley, D. M. (1979). Commentary: Is religion a dependent variable? *In* H. R. Hage and A. A. Roozen (eds), *Understanding Church Growth and Decline, 1950–1978.* New York: Pilgrim Press, pp. 334–343.

Kelley, H. H. (1955). Salience of membership and resistance to change of group-anchored attitudes. *Human Relations, 8,* 275–290.

Kelly, G. A. (1955). *The Psychology of Personal Constructs.* Vols. 1 and 2. New York: Norton.

Keniston, K. (1968). *Young Radicals.* New York: Harcourt Brace and World.

Kenny, A. (1985). *A Path from Rome, An Autobiography.* London: Sidgwick and Jackson.

Kidder, L. H. (1981). *Selltiz, Wrightsman and Cook's Research Methods in Social Relations.* New York: Holt, Rinehart and Winston. Fourth Edition.

Kilbourne, B. and Richardson, J. T. (1984). Psychotherapy and new religions in a pluralistic society. *American Psychologist, 39*(3), 237–251.

Kilpatrick, D. G., Sutker, L. W. and Sutker, P. B. (1970). Dogmatism, religion and religiosity: a review and re-evaluation. *Psychological Reports, 26*(1), 15–22.

Kim, M. P. and Rosenberg, S. (1980). Comparison of two structural models of implicit personality theory. *Journal of Personality and Social Psychology, 38,* 375–389.

King, M. (1967). Measuring the religious variable: nine proposed dimensions. *Journal for the Scientific Study of Religion, 6,* 173–190.

King, M. B. and Hunt, R. A. (1975). Measuring the religious variable: national replication. *Journal for the Scientific Study of Religion, 14,* 13–22.

King, S. H. and Funkenstein, D. H. (1957). Religious practice and cardiovascular reaction during stress. *Journal of Abnormal and Social Psychology, 55,* 135–137.

Kirkpatrick, C. (1949). Religion and humanitarianism: a study of institutional implications. *Psychological Monographs,* Vol. 63. Whole number 304, pp. 1–23.

Klausner, S. Z. (1964). Methods of data collection in studies of religion. *Journal for the Scientific Study of Religion, 3*(2), 193–203.

Klausner, S. Z. (1970). Scientific and humanistic study of religion. *Journal for the Scientific Study of Religion, 9,* 100–106.

Klingberg, G. (1959). A study of religious experience in children from 9 to 13 years of age. *Religious Education, 54*, 211–216.

Knapp. R. H. and Goodrich, H. B. (1951). The origins of American scientists. *Science, 113*, 543–545.

Knox, R. A. (1950). *Enthusiasm: A Chapter in the History of Religion with Special Reference to the XVII and XVIII Centuries*. Oxford: Clarendon Press.

Koestler, A. and Crossman, R. H. S. (eds.) (1950). *The God that Failed, Six Studies in Communism*. London: Hamilton.

Kohlberg, L. (1980). Stages of moral development as a basis for moral education. *In* B. Munsey (ed.), *Moral Development, Moral Education and Kohlberg*. Birmingham, Alabama: Religious Education Press, pp. 45–98.

Kotre, J. N. (1971). *The View from the Border*. Dublin: Gill and Macmillan Ltd.

Kruglanski, A. W. and Ajzen, I. (1983). Bias and error in human judgment. *European Journal of Social Psychology, 13*(1), 1–44.

Kuhlen, R. G. and Arnold, M. (1944). Age differences in religious beliefs and problems during adolescence. *Journal of Genetic Psychology, 65*, 291–300.

Kuhn, M. S. and McPartland T. S. (1954). An empirical investigation of self attitudes. *American Sociological Review, 19*, 68–76.

Kunkel, F. (1943). *In Search of Maturity: An Inquiry into Psychology, Religion and Self-Education*. New York: Scribners.

Kupky, O. (1928). *The Religious Development of Adolescence*. New York: Macmillan.

Kushner, A. W. (1967). Two cases of auto-castration due to religious delusions. *British Journal of Medical Psychology, 40*, 293–298.

Lakoff, G. and Johnson, M. (1980). *Metaphors We Live By*. Chicago: University of Chicago Press.

Lalljee, M., Brown, L. B. and Ginsburg, G. P. (1984). Attitudes: disposition, behaviour or evaluation? *British Journal of Social Psychology, 23*, 233–244.

Langer, E. J. (1983). *The Psychology of Control*. Beverley Hills: Sage.

Langer, S. (1956). *Philosophy in a New Key: A Study of the Symbolism of Reason, Rite and Art*. New York: New American Library.

Lanternari, V. (1963). *The religion of the Oppressed: A Study of Modern Messianic Cults*. London: MacGibbon and Kee.

La Piere, R. T. (1934). Attitudes versus actions. *Social Forces, 13*, 230–237.

Larsen, L. and Knapp, R. H. (1969). Sex differences in symbolic conceptions of the deity. *Journal of Projective Techniques, 28*, 303–306.

Lawrence, D. H. (1928). *John Galsworthy*. London: Wishart.

Lawrence, P. J. (1965). Children's thinking about religion: a study of concrete operational thinking. *Religious Education, 60*, 111–116.

Lee, R. S. (1948). *Freud and Christianity*. London: James Clark.

Lefcourt, H. M. (1982). *Locus of Control*. Hillsdale, New Jersey: L. Erbaum. (Second Edition).

Lemon, N. (1973). *Attitudes and their Measurement*. London: Batsford.

Lenski, G. (1961). *The Religious Factor: A Sociological Study of Religion's Impact on Politics, Economics and Family Life*. Garden City, New York: Doubleday.

Lerner, M. J. (1980). *The Beliefs in a Just World: A Fundamental Delusion*. New York: Plenum Press.

Le Selle, S. (1975). *Speaking in Parables: A Study in Metaphor and Theology*. London: SCM Press.

Lester, D. (1967). Experimental and correlational studies of the fear of death. *Psychological Bulletin, 67*(1), 27–36.

Leuba, J. H. (1896). *Studies in the Psychology of Religious Phenomena: The Religious Motive, Conversion, Facts and Doctrines*. Worcester, Mass.: J. M. Orpha.

Leuba, J. H. (1912). *A Psychological Study of Religion: Its Origin, Function and Future*. New York: Macmillan.

Leuba, J. H. (1915). Religious psychology. *Psychological Bulletin, 12*, 456–458.

Leuba, J. H. (1915). The task and the method of psychology in theology. *Psychological Bulletin, 12*, 462–470.

Leuba, J. H. (1925). *The Psychology of Religious Mysticism*. London: Kegan Paul.

Levy-Bruhl, L. (1931). *La Mentalité Primitive*. Oxford: The Clarendon Press.

Likert, R. (1932). A technique for the measurement of attitudes. *Archives of Psychology*, Whole Number 140.

Lofland, J. and Stark, R. (1966). *Doomsday Cult: A Study of Conversion, Proselytization and Maintenance of Faith*. Englewood Cliffs: Prentice Hall.

Long, D., Elkind, D. and Spilka, B. (1967). The child's conception of prayer. *Journal for the Scientific Study of Religion, 6*, 101–109.

Long, L. and Long, T. J. (1976). Influence of religious states and religious attire on interviews. *Psychological Reports, 39*(1), 25–27.

Longino, C. F. (1973). To conservatives with love from 475. *Journal for the Scientific Study of Religion, 12*(4), 478–484.

Loukes, H. (1961). *Teenage Religion*. London: SCM Press.

Lowe, W. L. (1955). Religious beliefs and religious delusions. *American Journal of Psychotherapy, 9*, 54–61.

Luckmann, T. (1967). *The Invisible Religion*. New York: Macmillan.

McClain, E. W. (1978). Personality differences between intrinsically religious and non religious students: a factor analytic study. *Journal of Personality Assessment, 42*, 156–166.

McClelland, D. C. (1955). Religious and other sources of parental attitudes towards independence training. *In* D. C. McClelland (ed.), *Studies in Motivation*. New York: Appleton-Century Crofts.

McClelland, D. C. *et al.* (1961). *The Achieving Society*. New York: Van Nostrand.

McClelland, D. C. and Atkinson, J. W. (1953). *The Achievement Motive*. New York: Appleton-Century Crofts, pp. 389–397.

McCloskey, M. (1983). Intuitive Physics. *Scientific American, 248*(4), 114–122.

MacDonald, J. B. (1980). A look at the Kohlberg curriculum framework for moral education. *In* B. Munsey (ed.), *Moral Development. Moral Education and Kohlberg*. Birmingham, Alabama: Religious Education Press, pp. 381–400.

MacIntyre, A. (1957). The logical status of religious belief. *In* S. D. Toulmin (ed.), *Metaphysical Beliefs*, London: SCM Press.

MacLean, A. H. (1930). *The Idea of God in Protestant Religious Education*. New York: Columbia University Press.

McLoughlin, W. G. (1959). *Modern Revivalism: Charles Grandison Finney to Billy Graham*. New York: Ronald Press.

MacNamara, P. M. (1974). A theoretical review: the Sociology of Andrew M. Greeley. *Journal for the Scientific Study of Religion, 13*(1), 79–86.

Magni, K. G. (1970). Reactions to death stimuli among theology students. *Journal for the Scientific Study of Religion, 9*, 247–8.

Magni. K. G. (1972). The fear of death, *In* A. Godin (ed.), *Death and Presence: The Psychology of Death and the After Life*. Brussels: Lumen Vitae Press.

Mailhiot, P. (1961). And God became a Child. *Lumen Vitae, 16*, 503–507.

Malinowski, B. (1925). Magic, science and religion, *In* J. Needham (ed.), *Science, Religion and Reality*. New York: Macmillan, pp. 18–94.

Malony, H. N. (1976). New methods in the psychology of religion. *Journal of Psychology and Theology, 4*, 141–151.

Malony, H. N. (1977). *Current Perspectives in the Psychology of Religion*. Grand Rapids: Eerdman.

Malony, H. N. (1978). *Psychology and Faith: The Christian Experience of Eighteen Psychologists*. Washington, D. C.: University Press of America.

Malony, H. N. (1981). Religious experience: a phenomenological analysis of a behavioural event. *Journal of Psychology and Theology, 9*(4), 326–334.

Malony, H. N. (1985). An S — O — R model of religious experience. *In* L. B. Brown (eds.), *Advances in the Psychology of Religion*. Oxford: Pergamon Press, 113–126.

Malony, H. N. and Lovekin, A. (1985). *Glossolalia: Speaking in Tongues*. New York: Oxford University Press.

Mancias, P. T. and Secord, P. E. (1983). Implications for psychology of the new philosophy of science. *American Psychologist, 38*, 399–413.

Mandler, G. and Kessen, W. (1964). *The Language of Psychology*. New York: Wiley Science Editions.

Mao Tse-tung. (1977).*On Contradiction: Five Essays on Philosophy*. Peking: Foreign Languages Press.

Maranell, G. M. (1974). *Responses to Religion: Studies in the Social Psychology of Religious Belief*. Lawrence, Kansas: University of Kansas Press.

Marino, C. (1971). Cross-national comparisons of Catholic—Protestant creativity differences. *British Journal of Social and Clinical Psychology, 10*, 132–137.

Marks, D. and Kammann, R. (1980). *The Psychology of the Psychic*. Buffalo: Prometheus.

Martin, D. and Mullen, P. (eds), (1984). *Strange Gifts: A Guide to Charismatic Renewal*. Oxford: Basil Blackwell.

Martin, J. and Westie, F. (1959). The tolerant personality. *American Sociological Review, 24*, 521–528.

Marty, M., Rosenberg, S. E. and Greeley, A. M. (1968). *What Do We Believe? The Stance of Religion in America*. New York: Meredith Press, First Edition.

Martin, R. D., McDonald, C. and Shepel, L. F. (1976). Locus of control and 2 measures of irrational belief. *Psychological Reports, 39*, 307–310.

Maslow, A. H. (1956/1971). *The Farther Reaches of Human Nature*. New York: Viking.

Masson, J. M. (1984). *The Assault on Truth*. Harmondsworth: Penguin Books.

Mayo, J., White, O. and Eysenck, H. J. (1978). An empirical study of the relation between astrological factors and personality. *Journal of Social Psychology, 105*, 229–236.

Milgram, S. (1974). *Obedience and Authority*. London: Tavistock.

Miller, H. (1961). *Tropic of Cancer*. New York: Grove Press.

Minton, B. and Spilka, B. (1976) Perspectives on death in relation to powerlessness and form of personal religion. *Omega, 7*, 261–267.

Mischel, W. (1984). Convergences and challenges in the search for consistency. *American Psychologist, 39*, (4), 351–364.

Misiak, H. and Staudt, V. M. (1954). *Catholics in Psychology: A Historical Survey*. New York: McGraw Hill.

Mitchell, B. (1981). I believe: we believe. In *Believing in the Church: The Corporate Nature of Faith. A report of the Doctrine Commission of the Church of England*. London: SPCK, pp. 9–24.

Moberg, D. O. (1965). Religiosity in old age. *Gerontologist 5*, 78–87.

Mol, J. (1971). *Religion in Australia*. Melbourne: Nelson.

Mol, J. (1985). *The Faith of Australians*. Sydney: Allen and Unwin.

Monaghan, R. (1967). The three faces of the true believer: Motivation for attending a fundamentalist church. *Journal for the Scientific Study of Religion, 6,* 236–245.

Morris, C. (1956). *Varieties of Human Value.* Chicago: University of Chicago Press.

Moscovici, S. (1961). *Le Psychonanalyse: Son Image et Son Public.* Paris: Presses Universitaires de France.

Moscovici, S. (1980). Toward a theory of conversion behaviour. *In* L. Berkowitz (ed.), *Advances in Experimental Social Psychology,* Vol. 13.

Mulfuid, M. A. and Salisbury, W. W. (1964). Self-conceptions in a general population. *Sociological Quarterly, 5,* 35–46.

Murdock, G. P. (1961). *Outline of Cultural Materials.* New Haven: Human Relations Area Files Inc. Fourth Edition.

Murphy, G. and Murphy, L. (1968). *Asian Psychology.* New York: Basic Books.

Murray, H. A. (1938). *Explorations in Personality.* New York: Oxford University Press.

Muthen, B., Petterson, T., Olsson, V. and Stahlberg, G. (1977). Measuring religious attitudes using the semantic differential technique: an application of three-mode factor analysis. *Journal for the Scientific Study of Religion, 16,* 275–285.

Needham, R. (1972). *Belief, Language and Experience.* Oxford: Basil Blackwell.

Nelsen, H. M., Everett, R. F., Mader, P. D. and Hamby, W. C. (1976). A test of Yinger's measure of non-doctrinal religion: implication for invisible religion as a belief system. *Journal for the Scientific Study of Religion, 15,* 263–267.

Nelsen, H. M. and Kroliczak, N. (1984). Parental use of the threat "God will punish": replication and extension. *Journal for the Scientific Study of Religion, 23,* 267–277.

Nelson, L. D. and Cantrell, C. H. (1980). Religiosity and death anxiety: a multi-dimensional analysis. *Review of Religious Research, 21,* 148–157.

Nelson, M. O. (1971). The concept of God and feelings toward parents. *Journal of Individual Psychology, 27,* 46–49.

Ness, R. (1980). The impact of indigenous healing activity: an empirical study of two fundamentalist churches. *Social Science and Medicine, 14*(3), 167–180.

Newman, W. M. (1973). Glock as policy researcher. *Journal for the Scientific Study of Religion.* 12(4), 469–473.

Niebuhr, R. (1964). Introduction. *In*: Marx, K. and Engels, F. *Religion.* New York: Schocken Books.

Nye, W. C. and Carlson, J. S. (1984). The development of the concept of God in children. *Journal of Genetic Psychology, 145,* 136–142.

Oates, W. E. (1958). *What Psychology Says about Religion.* New York: Association Press.

Oates, W. E. (1973). *The Psychology of Religion.* Waco, Texas: Ward Books.

O'Connor, K. V. (1983). *The structure of religion: a repertory grid approach.* University of New South Wales Ph.D. thesis.

O'Dea, T. F. (1961). Five dilemmas of institutionalization of religion. *Journal for the Scientific Study of Religion, 1,* 30–39.

Orlowski, C. D. (1979). Linguistic dimension of religious measurement. *Journal for the Scientific Study of Religion, 18,* 306–311.

Orne, M. T. (1969). Demand characteristics and the concept of quasi controls. *In* B. Rosenthal and R. L. Rosnow (eds), *Artifact in Behavioural Research.* New York: Academic Press.

Osarchuck, M. and Tatz, S. J. (1973). Effect of induced fear of death on belief in after life. *Journal of Personality and Social Psychology, 27*(4), 256–260.

Osgood, C. E. (1952). The nature and measurement of meaning. *Psychological Bulletin, 49,* 197–237.

Osgood, C. E., Suci, G. J. and Tannenbaum, P. H. (1957). *The Measurement of Meaning.* University of Illinois Press.

Osgood, C. E. and Tannenbaum, P. H. (1955). The principle of congruity in the prediction of attitude change. *Psychological Review, 62*, 42–55.

Ostow, M. (1959). The nature of religious controls. *American Psychologist, 14*, 687–693.

Ostrom, T. M. (1969). The relationship between the affective, behavioural and cognitive components of attitude. *Journal of Experimental and Social Psychology, 5*, 12–30.

Otto, R. (1923). *The Idea of the Holy: An Inquiry into the Non-rational Factor in the Idea of the Divine and Its Relation to the Rational.* (translated by J. W. Harvey). Oxford: Oxford University Press.

Pahnke, W. N. (1966). Drugs and mysticism. *International Journal of Parapsychology, 52*(2), 295–324.

Pallone, N. J. (1964). Explanations in religious authority and social perception. *Acta Psychologica, 32*, 321–327.

Pallone, N. J. (1966). Religious authority and social perception. *Journal of Social Psychology, 68*, 229–241.

Palma, R. J. (1978). The prospects for a normative psychology of religion: G. W. Allport as a paradigm. *Journal of Psychology and Theology, 6*, 110–122.

Parker, G. B. and Brown, L. B. (1979). Repertories of response to potential precipitants of depression. *Australian and New Zealand Journal of Psychiatry, 13*, 327–333.

Parker, G. B., Tupling, H. and Brown, L. B. (1979). A parental bonding instrument. *British Journal of Medical Psychology, 52*, 1–10.

Pascal, B. (1960). *Pensées.* London: J. M. Dent.

Pearson, P. R. (1977). Psychiatry and religion: problems at the interface. *Bulletin of the British Psychological Society, 30*, 47–48.

Pearson, P. R. and Sheffield, B. F. (1976). Is personality related to social attitudes? An attempt at a replication. *Social Behaviour and Personality, 4*, 109–111.

Peter, K., Boltdt, E. D., Whitaker, I. and Roberts, L. W. (1982). The dynamics of religious defection among Hutterites. *Journal for the Scientific Study of Religion, 21*(4). 327–337.

Peterson, C. and Scott, W. A. (1983). Toward fundamental measurement of dimensionality, *British Journal of Social Psychology, 22*, 197–202.

Pfister, O. R. (1948). *Christianity and Fear: A Study in History and in the Psychology and Hygiene of Religion.* London: Allen and Unwin.

Philip, E. (1977). Belief: an essential factor in modern therapy. *New Zealand Medical Journal, 85*, 192–194.

Piaget, J. (1931). Children's philosophies. *In* C. A. Murchison (ed). *A Handbook of Child Psychology.* Oxford: Oxford University Press.

Pickering, W. S. F. (1967). The 1851 religious census — a useless experiment? *British Journal of Sociology, 18*, 382–407.

Pierson, D. (1967). *Negroes in Brazil.* Southern University Press.

Ploch, D. R. (1974). Religion as an independent variable: a critique of some major research. *In* A. W. Eister (ed.), *Changing Perspectives in the Scientific Study of Religion.* New York: John Wiley and Sons, pp. 275–294.

Poppleton, P. and Pilkington, G. (1963). The measurement of religious attitudes in a University population. *British Journal of Social and Clinical Psychology, 2*, 20–36.

Powell, G. E. and Stewart, R. A. (1978). The relationship of age, sex and personality to social attitudes in children aged 8–15 years. *British Journal of Social and Clinical Psychology, 17*(4), 307–317.

Poythress, N. G. (1975). Literal, antiliteral, and mythological religious orientations. *Journal for the Scientific Study of Religion, 14*(3), 271–284.

Pratt, J. B. (1906–1907). Types of religious beliefs. *American Journal of Religious Psychology and Education, 2*, 76–94.

Price, C. (1981). Religions and the Census. *St. Mark's Review*, pp. 2–7.

Prince, M. (1906). The psychology of sudden religious conversion. *Journal of Abnormal Psychology, 1*(1), 42–54.

Princeton Religion Research Center (1982). *Religion in America*. Princeton: Gallup Organisation.

Prothro, E. T. and Jensen, J. A. (1950). Interrelations of religious and ethnic attitudes in selected Southern populations. *Journal of Social Psychology, 32*, 45–9.

Proudfoot, W. and Shaver, P. (1975). Attribution theory and the psychology of religion. *Journal for the Scientific Study of Religion, 14*, 317–330.

Pruyser, P. W. (1968). *A Dynamic Psychology of Religion*. New York: Harper and Row.

Pruyser, P. W. (1974). *Between Belief and Unbelief*. London: Sheldon Press.

Putney, S. and Middleton, R. (1961). Dimensions and correlates of religious ideologies. *Social Forces, 39*, 285–290.

Ragan, C., Malony, H. N. and Beit-Hallahmi, B. (1980). Psychologists and religion: professional factors and personal beliefs. *Review of Religious Research, 21*, 208–217.

Ranck, J. G. (1961). Religious conservatism-liberalism and mental health. *Pastoral Psychology, 12*, 34–40.

Rauff, E. A. (1979). *Why people join the Church*. Pilgrim Press.

Ray, J. J. (1982). The Protestant Ethic in Australia. *Journal of Social Psychology, 116*(1), 127–138.

Reed, J. (1959). Back of Billy Sunday. *Metropolitan Magazine*.

Rest, J. R. (1983). Morality. *In* P. H. Mussen (ed.), *Cognitive Development*. (Vol. 3 of *Handbook of Child Psychology*, volume eds. J. H. Flavell and E. M. Markman.) New York: John Wiley and Sons.

Reynolds, V. and Tanner, R. E. (1983). *The Biology of Religion*. London: Longmans.

Richardson, J. T. (ed.) (1978). *Conversion Careers: In and Out of the New Religions*. Beverley Hills: Sage.

Richardson, J. T. (1980). People's Temple: a comparison and corrective critique. *Journal for the Scientific Study of Religion, 19*(3), 239–255.

Richardson, J. T. (1985). Psychological and psychiatric studies of new religions. *In* L. B. Brown (ed.), *Advances in the Psychology of Religion*. Oxford: Pergamon Press, pp. 209–224.

Ricoeur, P. (1967). *The Symbolism of Evil*. New York: Harper and Row.

Rieff, P. (1966). *The Triumph of the Therapeutic: The Uses of Faith after Freud*. New York: Harper and Row.

Robinson, J. A. T. (1964). *Honest to God*. London: SCM.

Robinson, J. P. and Shaver, P. R. (1973). *Measures of Social Psychological Attitudes*. Ann Arbor: University of Michigan Survey Research Center.

Rohrbaugh, J. W. and Jessor, R. (1975). Religiosity in youth: a personal control against deviant behaviour? *Journal of Personality, 43*(1), 136–155.

Roiser, M. (1981). A psychological approach to the explanation of displacement effects in the judgement of attitude statements. *British Journal of Social Psychology, 20*, 37–40.

Rokeach, M. (1960). *The Open and Closed Mind: Investigations into the Nature of Belief and Personality Systems*. New York: Basic Books.

Rokeach, M. (1968). *Beliefs, Attitudes, and Values: A Theory of Organization and Change*. San Francisco: Jossey-Bass.

Roof, W. C. (1972). Local cosmopolitan orientation and traditional religious commitment. *Sociological Analysis, 33*(1), 1–15.

Roof, W. C. (1979). Concepts and indications of religious commitment: a critical review. *In* R. Wuthnow, *The Religious Dimension*. New York: Academic Press, pp. 17–45.

Roof, W. C. (1980). The ambiguities of "religious preference" in survey research — a methodological note. *Public Opinion Quarterly, 44*, 403–407.

Roof, W. C. and Roof, J. L. (1984). Review of the Polls: images of God among Americans. *Journal for the Scientific Study of Religion, 23*(2), 201–205.

Roof, W. C., Hadaway, C. K., Hewitt, M. L., McCaw, D. and Morse, R. (1977). Yinger's measure of non-doctrinal religion: A Northeastern test. *Journal for the Scientific Study of Religion, 16*, 403–408.

Roof, W. C. and Hadaway, C. K. (1979). Denominational switching in the seventies: going beyond Stark and Glock. *Journal for the Scientific Study of Religion, 18*(4), 363–377.

Rorschach, H. (1921). *Psychodiagnostik*. Bern: Huber.

Rosch, E. and Lloyd, B. (1978). *Cognition and Categorization*. Hillsdale, New Jersey: Erlbaum Associates.

Rosegrant, J. (1976). The impact of set and setting on religious experience in nature. *Journal for the Scientific Study of Religion, 15*(4), 301–310.

Rosenthal, R. (1964). The effect of the experimenter on the results of psychological research. *In* B. A. Maher (ed.), *Progress in Experimental Personality Research*, Vol. 1, pp. 79–114.

Rotter, J. B. (1966). Generalised expectancies for internal versus external control of reinforcement. *Psychological Monographs, 80* (whole number 609).

Rottschaefer, W. A. (1978). Cognitive characteristics of belief systems. *American Psychologist, 33*, 89–92.

Royce, J. R. (1964). *The Encapsulated Man: An Interdisciplinary Essay in the Search for Meaning*. New York: Van Nostrand and Reinhold.

Ruether, R. R. (1983). *Sexism and God-Talk: Toward a Feminist Theology*. Boston: Beacon Press.

Rumke, H. C. (1952). *The Psychology of Unbelief*. London: Rockliff.

Runciman, W. G. (1983). *A Treatise on Social Theory*. Vol I, *The Methodology of Social Theory*. Cambridge: Cambridge University Press.

Sadler, W. A. (1970). *Personality and Religion: The Role of Religion in Personality Development*. New York: Harper and Row.

Saliba, J. A. (1974). The new ethnography and the study of religion. *Journal for the Scientific Study of Religion, 13*(2), 145–159.

Samarin, W. J. (1972). *Tongues of Men and Angels*. New York: Macmillan.

Sanai, M. (1952). An empirical study of political, religious and social attitudes. *British Journal of Psychology, 5*, 81–92.

Sanua, J. D. (1969). Religion, mental health, and personality: a review of empirical studies. *American Journal of Psychiatry, 125*(9), 1203–1213.

Sarason, S. B. (1981). An asocial psychology and a misdirected clinical psychology. *American Psychologist, 36*(8), 827–836.

Sargant, W. (1961). *Battle for the Mind: A Psychology of Conversion and Brain-Washing*. Baltimore: Penguin Books.

Sato, K. (1972). *The Zen Life*. (Photos by Sosei Kuzunishi.) New York: Wetherhill.

Schaub, E. L. (1926). The psychology of religion. *Psychological Bulletin, 23*, 681–700.

Schneider, L. and Dornbusch, S. M. (1958). *Popular Religion: Inspirational Books in America*. Chicago: University of Chicago Press.

Schneiderman, L. (1981). *The Psychology of Myth, Folklore and Religion*. Chicago: Nelson Hall.

Scholl, M. E. and Beker, J. (1964). A comparison of the religious beliefs of delinquent and non-delinquent Protestant adolescent boys. *Religious Education, 59*, 250–253.

Schweitzer, A. (1948). *The Quest of the Historical Jesus: A Critical Study of Its Progress from Reimarus to Wrede*. New York: Macmillan.

Scott, M. B. and Lyman, S. M. (1970). Accounts, deviance and the social order. *In* J. D.

Douglas (ed.), *Deviance and Respectability in the Social Construction of Word Meanings.* New York: Basic Books, pp. 89–119.

Scott, W. A. (1965). *Values and Organizations: A Study of Fraternities and Sororities.* Chicago: Rand McNally.

Scott, W. A. (1968). Attitude measurement. *In* G. Lindsey and E. Aronson (eds). *The Handbook of Social Psychology,* Vol 2, *Research Methods,* Reading, Mass.; Addison Wesley, pp. 204–273. Second Edition.

Scott, W. A. (1969). The structure of natural cognitions. *Journal of Abnormal and Social Psychology, 12,* 261–278.

Seigel, J. P. (1969). The enlightment and the evolution of a language of signs in France and England. *Journal for the History of Ideas, 30,* 96–115.

Shand, J. D. (1953). *A factor analytic study of Chicago Protestant Ministers' conceptions of what it means to be 'religious'.* University of Chicago Ph.D. thesis.

Shaver, P., Lenaver, M. and Sadd, S. (1980). Religiousness, conversion, and subjective well being. *American Journal of Psychiatry, 137,* 1563–1568.

Shaw, D. W. (1970). Religion and conceptual models of behaviour. *British Journal of Social and Clinical Psychology, 9*(40), 320–7.

Shaw, M. E. and Wright, J. M. (1967). *Scales for the Measurement of Attitudes.* New York: McGraw Hill.

Shepard, R. N. (1971). Mental rotation of 3-D objects. *Science, 171*(3972, Feb), 701–703.

Sherif, M. and Sherif, C. W. (1965). *Attitude and Attitude Change: The Social Judgement — Involvement Approach.* Philadelphia: Saunders.

Shoben, E. J. (1963). Moral behaviour and word learning. *Religious Education, 58,* 137–145.

Sholl, D. (1971). The contribution of Lawrence Kohlberg to religious and moral education. *Religious Education, 66,* 364–372.

Shotter, J. (1984). *Social Accountability and Selfhood.* Oxford: Basil Blackwell.

Siegman, A. W. (1963). A cross-cultural investigation of the relationships between introversion of social attitudes and social behaviour. *British Journal of Social Psychology, 2,* 196–208.

Simon, S. B., Howe, L. W. and Kirschenbaum, H. (1972). *Values Clarification: A Handbook of Practical Strategies to Teachers for Students.* New York: Hart.

Skinner, B. F. (1953). *Science and Human Behaviour.* New York: Macmillan.

Smart, N. (1969). *The Religious Experience of Mankind.* New York: Scribners.

Smart, N. (1971). *The Religious Experience of Mankind.* London: Collins (Fontana).

Smart, N. (1983). *Worldviews: Crosscultural Explorations of Human Beliefs.* New York: Scribners.

Smith, M. B., Bruner, J. S. and White, R. W. (1956). *Opinions and Personality.* New York: John Wiley and Sons.

Synder, C. R., Higgins, R. L. and Stucky, R. L. (1983). *Excuses: Masquerades in Search of Grace.* New York: John Wiley and Sons.

Snyder, J. G. and Osgood, C. E. (1969). *Semantic Differential Technique.* Chicago: Aldine.

Soderstrom, D. and Wright, E. W. (1977). Religious orientation and meaning in life. *Journal of Clinical Psychology, 33*(1), 65–68.

Sosis, R. H., Strickland, B. R. and Haley, W. E. (1980). Perceived locus of control and beliefs about astrology. *Journal of Social Psychology, 110,* 65–71.

Spilka, B. (1970). Images of man and dimensions of personal religion: values for an empirical psychology of religion. *Review of Religious Research, 11,* 171–182.

Spilka, B. (1976). The complete person: some theoretical views and research findings for a theological-psychology of religion. *Journal of Psychology and Theology, 4,* 15–24.

Spilka, B., Addison, J. and Rosensohn, M. (1975). Parents, self and God: a test of competing theories of individual-religion relationships. *Review of Religious Research, 46,* 154–165.

Spilka, B., Armatas, P. and Nussbaum, J. (1984). The concept of God: a factor analytic approach. *Review of Religious Research, 6*, 28–36.

Spilka, B. and Werme, P. (1971). Religion and mental disorder: a critical review and theoretical perspective. *In* M. P. Strommen (ed.), *Research on Religious Development: A Comprehensive Handbook. A Project of the Religious Education Association.* New York: Hawthorn Books, pp. 461–504.

Spilka, B., Comp, G. and Goldsmith, W. M. (1981). Faith and behaviour: Religion in introductory psychology texts of the 1950s and 1970s. *Teaching of Psychology, 8*(3), 158–160.

Spilka, B., Hood, R. W. and Gorsuch, R. L. (1985). *The Psychology of Religion: An Empirical Approach.* Englewood Cliffs: Prentice Hall.

Spilka, B., Shaver, P. and Kirkpatrick, L. A. (1985). A general attribution theory for the psychology of religion. *Journal for the Scientific Study of Religion, 24*(1), 1–20.

Spiro, M. E. and D'Andrade, R. G. (1958). A cross-cultural study of some supernatural beliefs. *American Anthropologist, 60*, 456–466.

Spranger, E. (1928). *Types of Men.* Holle: Maxe Niemeyer Verlag.

Stanley, G. S. (1964). Personality and attitude correlates of religious conversion. *Journal for the Scientific Study of Religion, 4*, 60–63.

Starbuck, E. D. (1897). Psychology of religion. *American Journal of Psychology, 9*, 70–124.

Starbuck, E. D. (1897). *Some Aspects of Religious Growth.* Worcester, Mass.:

Starbuck, E. D. (1899). *The Psychology of Religion; An Empirical Study of The Growth of Religious Consciousness* (with a preface by William James) London: W. Scott.

Stark, R. (1963). On the incompatibility of religion and science: a survey of graduate students. *Journal for the Scientific Study of Religion, 3*, 3–21.

Stark, R. and Bainbridge, W. S. (1980). Toward a theory of religion: religious commitment. *Journal for the Scientific Study of Religion, 19*(2), 114–128.

Stark, R. and Glock, C. Y. (1968). *American piety: The Nature of Religious Commitment.* University of California Press.

Stephenson, W. (1953). *The Study of Behaviour: Q-Technique and Its Methodology.* Chicago: University of Chicago Press.

Stewart, C. W. (1967). *Adolescent Religion.* New York: Abingdon.

Stich, S. P. (1984). *From Folk Psychology to Cognitive Science.* Cambridge, Mass.: MIT Press.

Stolz, K. R. (1937). *The Psychology of Religious Living.* Nashville: Cokesbury Press.

Stouffer, S. A. *et al.* (1949). *The American Soldier Vol 2; Combat and Its Aftermath.* Princeton: Princeton University Press.

Stratton, G. M. (1911). *Psychology of the Religious Life.* London: Allen and Unwin.

Stringer, M. and Cairns, E. (1983). Catholic and Protestant young people's ratings of stereotyped Protestant and Catholic faces. *British Journal of Social Psychology, 22*, 241–246.

Strommen, M. P. (1971). *Research on Religious Development: A Comprehensive Handbook. A Project of the Religious Education Association.* New York: Hawthorn Books.

Strommen, M. P. *et al.* (1972). *A Study of Generations.* Minneapolis: Augsburg.

Strunk, O. (1957). Present status of the psychology of religion. *Journal of Bible and Religion, 25*, 287–292.

Strunk, O. J. (1959). Perceived relationships between parental and deity concepts. *Psychological Newsletter, 10*, 222–226.

Strunk, O. (1962). *Religion: A Psychological Interpretation.* New York: Abingdon Press.

Strunk, O. (1966). Timed cross-examination: a methodological innovation in the study of religious beliefs and attitudes. *Review of Religious Research, 7*, 121–23.

Strunk, O. (1970). Humanistic religious psychology: a new chapter in the psychology of religion. *Journal of Pastoral Care, 24*, 90–97.

Strunk, O. (1971). *The Psychology of Religion, Historical and Interpretative Readings.*

Nashville: Abingdon Press.

Sullivan, J. J. (1962). Two psychologies and the study of religion. *Journal for the Scientific Study of Religion, 1*, 155–164.

Sullivan, P. A. and Adelson, J. (1954). Ethnocentrism and misanthropy. *Journal of Abnormal and Social Psychology, 49*, 246–250.

Sutcliffe, M. (ed.) (1984). *The Dictionary of Religious Education.* London: SCM Press.

Swanson, G. E. (1960). *The Birth of the Gods: The Origin of Primitive Beliefs.* Ann Arbor: University of Michigan Press.

Szasz, T. S. (1978). *The Myth of Psychotherapy: Mental Healing as Religion, Rhetoric, and Repression.* Garden City, New York: Anchor Press/Doubleday.

Tajfel, H. (ed.) (1982). *Social Identity and Intergroup Relations.* Cambridge: Cambridge University Press.

Tapp, R. B. (1971). Dimensions of religiosity in a post-traditional group. *Journal for the Scientific Study of Religion, 10*, 41–49.

Terman, L. M. and Miles, C. C. (1936). *Sex and Personality: Studies in Masculinity and Femininity.* New York: McGraw-Hill.

Thompson, A. D. (1974). Open-mindedness and indiscriminate anti-religious orientation. *Journal for the Scientific Study of Religion, 13*(4), 471–478.

Thouless, R. H. (1923). *The Psychology of Religion.* Cambridge: Cambridge University Press.

Thouless, R. H. (1935). The tendency to certainty in religious belief. *British Journal of Psychology, 26*, 16–31.

Thouless, R. H. (1954). *Authority and Freedom: Some Psychological Problems of Religious Belief.* Greenwich, Conn: Seabury Press.

Thouless, R. H. (1971). *An Introduction to the Psychology of Religion.* Cambridge: Cambridge University Press.

Thouless, R. H. and Brown, L. B. (1964). Petitionary prayer: belief in its appropriateness and causal efficacy among adolescent girls. *Lumen Vitae, 3*, 123–136.

Thurstone, L. L. (1931). The measurement of social attitudes. *Journal of Abnormal and Social Psychology, 26*, 249–269.

Thurstone, L. L. (1934). *The Theory of Multiple Factors.* Ann Arbor, Mich.: Edwards Brothers.

Thurstone, L. L. (1954). The measurement of values. *Psychological Review, 61*, 47–58.

Thurstone, L. L. and Chave, E. J. (1929). *The Measurement of Attitude.* Chicago: University of Chicago Press.

Tillich, P. (1952). *The Courage to Be.* New Haven: Yale University Press.

Tisdale, J. S. (1966). Selected correlates of extrinsic religious values. *Review of Religious Research, 7*, 78–84.

Todd, N. (1977). *Religious belief and personal construct theory.* Unpublished PhD thesis. University of Nottingham.

Tonner, A. E. (1906). Children's religious ideas. *Pedagogical Seminary, 13*, 511–513.

Torgerson, W. W. S. and Edwards, A. L. (1958). *Theory and Methods of Scaling.* New York: John Wiley and Sons.

Toulmin, S. (1977). *Metaphysical Beliefs.* London: SCM Press.

Triandis, H. C. (1971). *Attitudes and Attitude Change.* New York: John Wiley and Sons.

Triandis, H. C. and Fishbein, M. (1963). Cognitive interaction in person perception. *Journal of Abnormal and Social Psychology, 67*, 446–453.

Triandis, H. C. and Triandis, L. M. (1960). Race, social class, religion and nationality as determinants of social distance. *Journal of Abnormal and Social Psychology, 61*, 110–118.

Troeltsch, E. (1931). *The Social Teaching of the Christian Churches.* New York: Macmillan.

Turner, J. and Giles, H. (1981). *Intergroup Behaviour.* Oxford: Basil Blackwell.

Tversky, A. and Kahneman, D. (1974). Judgement under uncertainty: heuristics and biases. *Science, 185*, 1124–1131. (Reprinted in Kahneman, D. *et al*. (1982) *Judgement Under Uncertainty: Heuristics and Biases*. Cambridge: Cambridge University Press, pp. 3–20.)

Tylor, Sir, E. B. (1873). *Primitive Culture: Researches into the Development of Mythology, Philosophy, Religion, Language, Art, and Custom*. New York: H. Holt and Co. Second Edition.

Tyson, G. A. (1982). Why people perceive horoscopes as being true: A review. *Bulletin of the British Psychological Society, 35*, 186–8.

Ungar, S. (1980). Attitude inferences from behaviour performed under public and private conditions. *Social Psychology Quarterly, 43*(1), 81–89.

Valentine, C. W. (1962). *The Experimental Psychology of Beauty*. London: Methuen.

Vergote, A. (1969). *The Religious Man*. Dublin: Gill and Macmillan.

Vergote, A. (1978). *Dette et Désir: Deux Axes Chrétiens et La Dérive Pathologique*. Paris: Edition de Seuil.

Vergote, A. and Tamayo, A. (1980). *The Parental Figures and the Representation of God*. The Hague: Mouton.

Vernon, G. M. (1962). Measuring religion: five methods compared. *Review of Religious Research, 3*, 159–165.

Vernon, G. M. (1968). The religious 'nones': a neglected category. *Journal for the Scientific Study of Religion, 7*, 219–229.

Vernon, G. M. (1968). Marital characteristics of religious independents. *Review of Religious Research, 9*, 162–170.

Vine, I. (1978). Facts and values in the psychology of religion. *Bulletin of the British Psychological Society, 31*, 414–417.

Vitz, P. C. (1977). *Psychology as Religion: The Cult of Self-Worship*. Grand Rapids: Eerdmans.

Wach, J. (1944). *Sociology of Religion*. Chicago: University of Chicago Press.

Wadsworth, M. E. J. and Freeman, S. R. (1983). Generation differences in beliefs: a cohort study of stability and change in religious beliefs. *The British Journal of Sociology, 34*(3), 416–437.

Wallace, R. K. and Benson, M. (1972). The psychology of meditation. *Scientific American, 226*, 84–90.

Wallis, R. (1984). *The Elementary Forms of the New Religious Life*. London: Routledge and Kegan Paul.

Ward, C. and Beaubrun, M. H. (1981). Spirit possession and neuroticism in a West Indian pentecostal community. *British Journal of Clinical Psychology, 20*, 295–296.

Warren, N. (1977). Empirical studies in the psychology of religion. An assessment of the period 1960–1970. *In* H. N. Malony (ed.). *Current Perspectives in the Psychology of Religion*. Grand Rapids: Eerdman, pp. 93–100.

Watson, J. B. (1925). *Behaviorism*. New York: W. W. Norton and Company, Inc.

Wearing, A. J. and Brown, L. B. (1972). The dimensionality of religion. *British Journal of Social and Clinical Psychology, 11*, 143–148.

Weatherhead, L. D. (1935). *Psychology and Life*. New York: Abingdon Press.

Webb. E. J. *et al*. (1966). *Unobtrusive Measures: Non-Reactive Research in the Social Sciences*. Chicago: Rand McNally.

Webb, N. and Wybrow, R. (1982). *The Gallup Report*. London: Sphere Books.

Weber, M. (1930). *The Protestant Ethic and the Spirit of Capitalism*. London: George Allen and Unwin.

Webster, A. M. (1937). *Webster's New Dictionary of the English Language*. London: Bell and Sons.

Webster, D. H. (1984). James Fowler's theory of faith development. *British Journal of Religious Education, 14*, 14–15.

Weidman, J. (ed.), (1981). *Women Ministers: How Women are Redefining Traditional Roles.* San Francisco: Harper and Row.

Weima, J. (1965). Authoritarianism, religious conservatism and sociocentric attitudes in Roman Catholic groups. *Human Relations, 18*, 231–239.

Weisberger, D. A. (1958) *They Gathered at the River: The Story of the Great Revivalists and Their Impact upon Religion in America.* Boston: Little, Brown. First Edition.

Welford, A. T. (1946). An attempt at an experimental approach to the psychology of religion. *British Journal of Psychology, 46*, 55–73.

Welford, A. T. (1948). The use of archaic language in religious expression: an example of "canalised response". *British Journal of Psychology, 38*, 209–218.

White, P. (1981). *Flaws in the Glass: A Self Portrait.* London: Jonathan Cape.

Wicker, A. W. (1971). An examination of the "other variables" explanation of attitude behaviour inconsistency. *Journal of Abnormal and Social Psychology, 19*, 18–30.

Wiebe, K. F. and Fleck, J. R. (1980). Personality correlates of intrinsic, extrinsic and non-religious orientations. *Journal of Psychology, 105*, 181–187.

Wiggins, J. S. (1973). *Personality and Prediction: Principles of Personality Assessment.* Reading, Mass.: Addison-Wesley.

Wiles, M. (1976). *What is Theology?* Oxford: Oxford University Press.

Wills, T. A. (1984). Supportive functions of interpersonal relationships. *In* S. Cohen and L. Syme (eds.), *Social Support and Health.* New York: Academic Press.

Wilson, B. (1983). *Can God Survive in Australia?* Sutherland, NSW: Albatross.

Wilson, G. D. (1973). *The Psychology of Conservatism.* London: Academic Press.

Wilson, G. D. and Brazendale, A. H. (1973). Social correlates of Eysenck's personality dimensions. *Social Behaviour and Personality, 1*, 115–118.

Wilson, G. D. and Patterson, J. R. (1970). *Manual for the Conservatism Scale.* Windsor: NFER.

Wilson, W. and Miller, H. L. (1968). Fear, anxiety and religiousness. *Journal for the Scientific Study of Religion, 7*, 111.

Wing, J. K. (1974). *Measurement and Classification of Psychiatric Symptoms: An Instruction Manual for the PSE and Catego Program.* Cambridge: Cambridge University Press.

Wittgenstein, C. (1966). *Lectures and Conversations on Aesthetics, Psychology and Religious Belief.* Oxford: Basil Blackwell.

Wittgenstein, L. (1969). *On Certainty.* Oxford: Basil Blackwell.

Woodworth, R. S. (1940). *Contemporary Schools of Psychology.* New York: The Ronald Press Company.

Woodworth, R. S. (1958). *Dynamics of Behaviour.* New York: Holt.

Worsfold, J. E. (1974). *A History of the Charismatic Movements in New Zealand.* Julian Literature Trust.

Wright, D. (1971). *The Psychology of Moral Behaviour.* Harmondsworth: Penguin Books.

Wright, D. (1972). Psychology and meditation. *Question* (Jan), No. 5, 3–12.

Wright, D. (1983). Religious education from the perspective of moral education. *Journal of Moral Education, 12*(2), 111–115.

Wright, D. S. (1976). *Moral Development: A Cognitive Approach.* Milton Keynes: Open University Press.

Wright, D. S. and Cox, E. (1971). Changes in moral belief among sixth form boys and girls over a seven year period in relation to religious belief, age and sex differences. *British Journal of Social and Clinical Psychology, 10*, 332–341.

Wright, D. S. and Cox, E. (1976). Religious belief and co-education in a sample of sixth-form boys and girls. *British Journal of Social and Clinical Psychology, 6*(1), 23–31.

Wright, S. A. and D'Antonio, W. V. (1981). The substructure of religion: a further study. *Journal for the Scientific Study of Religion, 19*, 292–298.

Wundt, W. M. (1916). *Elements of Folk Psychology: Outlines of a Psychological History of the Development of Mankind.* (Authorized translation by Edward Leroy Schaub.) London: G. Allen and Unwin.

Wuthnow, R. (1979). *The Religious Dimension: New Directions in Quantitative Research.* New York: Academic Press.

Yeatts, J. R. and Asher, W. (1979). Can we afford not to do true experiments in psychology of religion? *Journal for the Scientific Study of Religion, 10*(1), 86–89.

Yinger, J. M. (1967). Pluralism, religion and secularism. *Journal for the the Scientific Study of Religion, 6*, 17–28.

Yinger, J. M. (1970). *The Scientific Study of Religion.* New York: Macmillan.

Yinger, J. M. (1977). A comparative study of the substructures of religion. *Journal for the Scientific Study of Religion, 16*, 67–86.

Young, F. M. (1975). *Sacrifice and the Death of Christ.* London: SPCK.

Zajonc, R. J. (1968). Attitudinal effects of mere exposure. *Journal of·Personality and Social Psychology,* Monograph Supplement, *9,* (2,2), 1–27.

Zanna, M. P., Olson, J. M. and Fazio, R. H. (1980). Attitude behaviour consistency: an individual difference perspective. *Journal of Personality and Social Psychology, 30*(3), 432–440.

Zilboorg, G. (1967). *Psychoanalysis and Religion.* London: Allen and Unwin.

Zingle, H. W. (1965). *A rational therapy approach to counselling underachievers.* PhD, University of Alberta.

Author Index

Subject Index